# THE REFORM OF THE REFORM?

Thomas M. Kocik

# THE REFORM OF THE REFORM?

*A Liturgical Debate:*
*Reform or Return*

IGNATIUS PRESS     SAN FRANCISCO

Cover design by Roxanne Mei Lum

© 2003 Ignatius Press, San Francisco
All rights reserved
ISBN 0–89870–946–6
Library of Congress Control Number 2002112869
Printed in the United States of America ∞

*I wish to dedicate this book to Donald and Nancy Pitcher,*
*my former parishioners at St. Francis Xavier*
*in Hyannis, Massachusetts.*
*Their love for the Church, for her sacred liturgy,*
*and for her priests continually edifies me.*

*If words could adequately express my gratitude for the*
*seemingly limitless support and generosity these dear friends*
*have shown me over the past four years,*
*I would have to write volumes.*

# CONTENTS

Acknowledgments                                          9

Abbreviations                                           11

Introduction                                            13

I    The Traditionalist Position in Brief              19

II   The Reformist Position in Brief                   23

III  Return to the Old Rite, or Fix the New?          25

     Renewal or Rupture?                               26
        Guiding Principles of the Reform               30
        The 1962 and 1970 Missals Compared             38
           — The Ordinary of the Mass                  40
           — Ritual Actions                            47
           — Prayers                                   49
        Commentary                                     50
        Distinguishing between the Rite and Its
           Common Usage                                76
        Other Considerations                           82
     What Place Ought the Pre-conciliar Roman
           Liturgy to Have?                            87
        Is There a Right to the Old Rite?              87
        Other Considerations                           91

Conclusion                                            101

Epilogue, by the Reverend Peter M.J.
     Stravinskas                                      105

Appendix I: Order of Mass, 1962 Missal     113

Appendix II: Order of Mass, 1970 Missal     135

Appendix III: The Postconciliar Eucharistic
Liturgy: Planning a "Reform of the
Reform", by Brian W. Harrison, O.S.     151

Appendix IV: Salutary Dissatisfaction:
An English View of "Reforming
the Reform", by Aidan Nichols, O.P.     195

Appendix V: A Reform of the Reform?,
by the Reverend J. P. Parsons     211

Appendix VI: A Question of Ceremonial,
by Monsignor Peter J. Elliott     257

# ACKNOWLEDGMENTS

I am sincerely grateful to two of my brother priests for their assistance in preparing this book. The Reverend Peter Stravinskas, S.T.D., of the Newman House Oratory in Mount Pocono, Pennsylvania, read the initial draft and reassured me that it merited publication. A diocesan confrere, the Reverend Timothy Driscoll, scrutinized the entire manuscript and offered helpful suggestions. It is a comfort to me to know that these two friends deem my work a useful contribution to the escalating (and often passionate) discourse about the reform of the sacred liturgy following the Second Vatican Council.

Also deserving recognition is the Reverend Monsignor Paul Langsfeld, S.T.D., Professor of Systematic Theology at Mount Saint Mary Seminary in Emmitsburg, Maryland. Though he was neither directly nor knowingly involved in the making of this book, his courses on sacramental theology greatly enriched my understanding of the inexhaustible depths of tradition and brought me to appreciate the authentic liturgical movement that began long before the 1960s. It is a testimony both to his enthusiasm for the subject and to his pedagogical aptitude that, nearly a decade later, I remain unwilling to dispose of my class notes.

# ABBREVIATIONS

CCC      *Catechism of the Catholic Church*

MRR     Joseph A. Jungmann, S.J., *The Mass of the Roman Rite: Its Origin and Development* (Missarum Sollemnia), trans. Francis A. Brunner, C.SS.R., 2 vols. (New York: Benziger Brothers, 1951 and 1955)

SC       Vatican II, Constitution on the Sacred Liturgy, *Sacrosanctum Concilium* (December 4, 1963).

# INTRODUCTION

The reform of the sacred liturgy has been one of the most debated and divisive issues in the Roman Catholic Church since the Second Vatican Council (1962–65). Traditionally minded critics of the revised liturgy generally fall into two groups: those who are attached to the pre-Vatican II liturgy and those who call for a "reform of the liturgical reform". For the sake of convenience, we shall call the former group "traditionalists" and the latter "reformists".[1]

---

[1] These labels, like most, are simplistic: neither group can lay exclusive claim to either term. The "reformists" are traditional, in that they seek to restore a manifestly God-centered and genuinely Catholic *ethos* to the liturgy and to bring the reform back into continuity with the liturgical tradition of the Latin Church. At the same time, "traditionalist" apologists admit that the Roman liturgy has undergone development and refinement over the centuries and in theory do not oppose authentic reform.

It should be noted that traditionalists are a diverse lot. Many belong to communities that, if not formally schismatic, exhibit a schismatic or sectarian mind-set. At the extreme are those who deny the validity of the revised sacramental rites and sedevacantists who believe that there is presently no legitimate pope occupying the See of Peter.

The most well-known traditionalist associations are: the Society of St. Pius X (S.S.P.X), established in 1970 by French Archbishop Marcel Lefebvre; the Priestly Fraternity of St. Peter, formed by S.S.P.X priests following Lefebvre's illicit consecration of bishops in 1988; the International Una Voce Federation, a lay movement founded in 1967, with affiliated associations in several countries (Una Voce America was founded in 1996); and the Centre International d'Études Liturgiques (C.I.E.L.), an international forum of scholars created in 1994 for the intellectual defense of the preconciliar Roman liturgy.

Reformist associations in the United States are (among others): Adoremus Society for the Renewal of the Sacred Liturgy, established in 1995 by Joseph Fessio, S.J. (Ignatius Press), Helen Hull Hitchcock (Women for Faith and Family), and Fr. Jerry Pokorski (CREDO); the Society for Catholic Liturgy, founded in 1995 by Msgr. M. Francis Mannion (presently director of the Mundelein Liturgical Institute in Chicago); and the Society of St. John Cantius (Chicago),

Neither group is pleased with the contemporary liturgical situation in the Western Church. Massive ignorance about the fundamental nature of the Mass; the precipitous decline in the rate of Mass attendance everywhere since 1965; loss of belief in the Real Presence of Christ in the Blessed Sacrament; the removal of tabernacles and the destruction of communion rails; the replacement of the altar with a table; doctrinally ambiguous and offensively banal prayers; the manipulation of the liturgy for every conceivable personal, ideological, and political agenda (feminism, fuzzy ecumenism, and so on); an archaizing and sometimes neo-gnostic tendency toward arcane rites and equally abstruse language to accompany them ("scrutinies", "mystagogy", "catechumenate");[2] the diminution of the priest's role in the face of new lay "ministries" (extraordinary ministers of the Eucharist, among others) and the (allegedly) consequent dearth of priestly vocations; the wholesale abandonment, almost overnight, of a centuries-old sacred language and musical patrimony; the glorification of the profane ("folk" Masses, "rock" Masses, liturgical dance)—

---

a religious community founded in 1998 by C. Frank Phillips, C.R., celebrating both the pre- and postconciliar rites.

The vast majority of practicing Catholics do not see themselves as part of any camp or movement. A lot of them are uneasy, if not disgusted, with what passes for divine worship in their parishes but cannot articulate their feelings for want of formal theological training and knowledge of liturgical norms. Some hunt for parishes where the liturgy is celebrated in a "conservative" manner; others seek refuge in Eastern-rite Catholic Churches (Byzantine, Maronite, and so on); while others join schismatic or canonically irregular Latin Mass communities. Many just carry on, praying that things will work out right.

[2] Cf. Andrew M. Greeley, "Against R.C.I.A.", *America* 161 (October 14, 1989): 231–34 [RCIA = Rite of Christian Initiation of Adults].

these are the fruits of a sweeping revolution that occurred in the wake of Vatican II. Joseph Cardinal Ratzinger, a *peritus* at the Council and now the prefect of the Sacred Congregation for the Doctrine of the Faith, is candid in his appraisal of the contemporary liturgical scene: "We have seen the sacred liturgy degenerate into a sort of show, in which an attempt is made to make religion look interesting by using fashionable follies and shallow clichés, which, for the liturgical innovators, produces a fleeting success, but only serves to repel more and more those who are looking for God rather than a spiritual show-master in the liturgy." [3]

Traditionalists and reformists alike seek to restore a pronounced sense of the sacred and transcendent dimensions of worship and to halt the seemingly endless array of banalities, abuses, and innovations that mark the modern liturgical landscape. Precisely how to go about this, however, is a point of contention. For traditionalists, the remedy

---

[3] From the preface to Msgr. Klaus Gamber, *La Réforme liturgique en question*, French trans. (Le Barroux, 1992). Extracts appear in the English translation of this book: *The Reform of the Roman Liturgy: Its Problems and Background* (San Juan Capistrano, Calif.: Una Voce Press, and Harrison, N.Y.: Foundation for Catholic Reform, 1993). Cardinal Ratzinger described Msgr. Gamber (in the preface to Gamber's book) as "the one scholar who, among the army of pseudo-liturgists, truly represents the liturgical thinking of the center of the Church".

Especially helpful to understanding the underlying reasons for the depredation of the Roman liturgy are: Gamber, *Reform*, chap. 2 ("The Root Causes of the Debacle of Modern Liturgy"), and Aidan Nichols, O.P., *Looking at the Liturgy: A Critical View of Its Contemporary Form* (San Francisco: Ignatius Press, 1996), chap. 1 ("A Historical Inquest"). Our study will not attempt to take on those members of the liturgical establishment—and their name is Legion—who blithely deride anyone critical of the status quo, regardless of that critic's academic or ecclesiastical standing. (It is futile to engage the willfully superficial.)

for our liturgical malaise is a return to the "old Latin Mass", the rite of Mass celebrated just prior to the Vatican II reforms. Reformists, on the other hand, call for an implementation of what they perceive to be the true intentions of the Council. Each side deems the other's agenda inherently flawed and ultimately unsatisfying. The reformed liturgy itself is problematic, say traditionalists, based as it is on questionable liturgical theory and ambiguous theology; hence, "reforming the reform" is like rearranging the deck chairs on the Titanic. Reformists counter that liturgical abuses happened before the Council, too (though these were often of a different kind), that Vatican II did in fact order a revision of the traditional Roman rite, and that not all changes have been for the worse; better, then, to reform the reform than to cling stubbornly to obsolete liturgical books.

Which movement, the "traditionalist" or the "reformist", is the more feasible one? Which better serves the Church? And must one side prevail?

Thus far, what these two camps of liturgical conservatives have been saying about each other has been unflattering, if not vilifying, despite the fact that there is more that unites than divides them.[4] And there has been virtually no direct interaction between them. This book aims

---

[4] A leading traditionalist periodical was highly critical, if not scornful, of the proponents of a new liturgical reform. "The only relevant battle today is between the modernists and the traditionalists", opined one writer, dismissing the reformists as "the tiny group that is neither hot nor cold", whose "pride in their own liturgical expertise blinds them to the futility of their cause" (Jeffrey Tucker, "Reforming the Unreformable?", review of *Beyond the Prosaic: Renewing the Liturgical Movement*, ed. Stratford Caldecott, in *The Latin Mass*, fall 1998, p. 22).

to redress that problem, even if in a contrived way, by bringing traditionalists and reformists into dialogue. I am convinced that both sides have legitimate arguments and concerns that neither side can afford to ignore. Also, I believe that their heretofore mutual antagonism is counterproductive and that a traditionalist-reformist engagement can go a long way toward achieving the liturgical stability and suitability so desperately needed in Roman-rite Catholicism.

# CHAPTER I

# THE TRADITIONALIST POSITION
# IN BRIEF

"The traditional Mass", "the ancient Mass", "the Mass of the ages", "the immemorial Latin Mass"—these terms refer to the Roman rite of Mass as it was celebrated up to Vatican II. In 1969, four years after the Council ended, Pope Paul VI introduced a rite of Mass wholly divorced from the long, uninterrupted tradition of the Roman rite—a tradition codified by the Council of Trent (1545–63); hence also the terms "Tridentine Mass" and "Mass of Saint Pius V". Despite all protestations to the contrary,[1] there is no seamless continuity or substantial identity between the pre- and postconciliar rites. The *Missale Romanum* of 1962 (the last of the preconciliar editions of the Roman Missal) constitutes the last codification of the Mass of the Roman rite. Save for its use by traditionalist

---

[1] For example, Pope Paul VI's address to the General Audience on November 19, 1969: "Nothing has been changed of the substance of our traditional Mass.... So do not let us talk about 'the new Mass'. Let us rather speak of the 'new epoch' in the Church's life." Also J. D. Crichton, *Liturgical Changes: The Background* (Catholic Truth Society pamphlet): "In spite of everything, the New Order of Mass is *not* new except in one or two minor details"; quoted in Michael Davies, *The Roman Rite Destroyed* (Kansas City, Mo.: Angelus Press, 1992), p. 14.

communities (whether in communion with Rome or not), the Roman Catholic Mass would be virtually extinct.[2]

Intoxicated with the strange brew of progressivism, primitivism, rationalism, and ecumenism, the architects of the reform purposely downplayed the allegedly out-moded Catholic dogmas of transubstantiation and sacrifice. Not only is the new rite doctrinally anemic, it is also heavily laden with rationalist philosophy and consequently lacks the mystical spiritual quality of the ancient Mass.[3] Because the disparity between the traditional rite

---

[2] To give just a few bold and provocative citations supporting this thesis: "[W]e now contemplate at our feet the ruins, not of the Tridentine Mass, but of the ancient Roman rite" (Msgr. Klaus Gamber, *The Reform of the Roman Liturgy: Its Problems and Background* [San Juan Capistrano, Calif.: Una Voce Press, and Harrison, N.Y.: Foundation for Catholic Reform, 1993] p. 26); "[I]n the place of liturgy as the fruit of development came fabricated liturgy. We abandoned the organic, living process of growth and development over the centuries, and replaced it—as in a manufacturing process—with a fabrication, a banal on-the-spot product" (Joseph Cardinal Ratzinger, preface to Gamber, *Reform*); "We must make it clear to all and sundry that we are attached to nothing less than the Roman rite, of which the last major historical epoch, the four hundred years since the Council of Trent, can be called the Tridentine period. The Missal of 1962 is not its previous codification but its current one" (John W. Mole, O.M.I., "Problema Idem Perduret: A Look at the Roman Rite and Its Future", *The Latin Mass*, spring 2001, p. 17).

[3] For philosophical critiques of the liturgical reform (positing Enlightenment, or rationalist, influences on the new rite), see Fr. Chad Ripperger, F.S.S.P., Ph.D., "Modern Philosophy and the Liturgical Development", *Christian Order* 41 (August/September 2000): 416–23; also, Aidan Nichols, O.P., *Looking at the Liturgy: A Critical View of Its Contemporary Form* (San Francisco: Ignatius Press, 1996) (e.g., p. 96: "It must be borne in mind... that the roots of the pressure for *versus populum* [facing the people] celebration in the modern liturgical movement lie in the soil of the eighteenth-century Enlightenment, where they are hard to disentangle from a conscious effort to divert attention away from the Eucharist as sacrifice—a term as opaque to rationalistically inclined Catholics then as to many of our contemporaries now—and toward the much more comprehensible notions of the Eucharist as assembly and as meal"). Opposing

and the new rite is best expressed by the term "rupture", the so-called "reform of the reform" is a pipedream. Even in its official form, the *Novus Ordo Missae*[4] is not the traditional Mass of the Roman rite. It is, on the contrary, an "artificially concocted and ecumenically tainted" rite,[5] a Frankensteinian hodgepodge of occidental and oriental, traditional and contrived, Catholic and Protestant elements.

The traditional Mass, on the other hand, robustly and unambiguously expresses the unchanging truths of the Catholic faith, especially the sacrificial nature of the Mass, the Real Presence of Christ in the Blessed Sacrament, and the unique and indispensable role of the ordained priest. It is the fruit of 1500 years of natural development. It speaks to the heart as well as the head, and it does not easily lend itself to manipulation or doctrinal deviation. Tried, tested, and true, the old Mass should be available to all Catholics (leaving aside the question of what to do with the new rite), especially since (a) Vatican II

---

the thesis of rationalism's impact on the reform is Archimandrite Boniface Luykx, "The Liturgical Movement and the Enlightenment?", *Antiphon* 3, no. 1 (1998): 23–25. (Luykx was a *peritus* at Vatican II and a member of the drafting committee for *Sacrosanctum Concilium*.)

[4] *Novus Ordo Missae* ("New Order of the Mass"), or simply *Novus Ordo*, refers to the rite of Mass authorized by Pope Paul VI in 1969 and laid out in the Roman Missal of 1970 (and subsequent editions). Traditionalists use the term *Novus Ordo* pejoratively (and loosely) in reference to the contemporary liturgical situation, on the premise that the Pauline Missal itself is the cause of (or at least fosters) the current debacle. No official Church document uses the term, however.

[5] Michael Davies, *Liturgical Shipwreck: 25 Years of the New Mass* (Rockford, Ill.: TAN Books, 1995), p. 35.

never abrogated the Missal revised by Saint Pius V, and (b) the Catholic Church has always tolerated a multiplicity of rites, even in the West.[6]

---

[6] Until about the eighth century most of Western Europe, outside Rome, used variants of the Gallican rite as used in Gaul. Two remnants of the Gallican rite remain, namely, the Ambrosian rite (still used at Milan) and the Mozarabic rite (Toledo, Spain). Prior to the English Reformation, the Sarum (or Salisbury) rite was the most widespread rite in the British Isles. Following the Council of Trent (1545–1563), Pope St. Pius V allowed that those local Churches and religious orders whose rites could show a prescription of at least two hundred years should be permitted to keep them, although they could, if they wished, adopt the new Roman Missal of 1570.

# CHAPTER II

# THE REFORMIST POSITION IN BRIEF

It is mistaken to think that the only way to redeem the liturgy from its unhappy state is to return to preconciliar forms of the Roman rite. The traditionalist premise, that since the Council there has been a complete breach with tradition, is exaggerated: what traditionalists often call novelties and impurities are in fact elements retrieved from the Church's past. The traditionalist agenda is wed to a nonhistorical view of the liturgy (and of the Church in general) that romanticizes and "absolutizes" a particular epoch in the Church's life, namely, the four centuries between Trent and Vatican II. In addition, much of the traditionalist propaganda unfairly equates contemporary liturgical abuses with the reformed liturgy itself. Despite its problems, the liturgical renewal has yielded good fruit (most notably, the recovery of a corporate sense of worship), the seeds of which were planted well before the Council. Finally, for those Catholics born in the last thirty years or so, the "new" liturgy is not "new" at all; it is their only experience.

What we need is not a return to the past (as if reality has not changed since 1962), but an implementation of the Council's Constitution on the Sacred Liturgy (*Sacrosanctum Concilium*, December 4, 1963) according to the letter of the Constitution itself. This entails the recovery

of certain elements and patterns of prayer that have been
all but lost since the 1960s (for example, Latin and Gregorian chant) and, in the light of postconciliar experience, a critical reassessment (if not suppression) of some
practices that now enjoy official approbation (for example, Communion in the hand, female altar servers, the celebration of the whole Mass facing the people).[1] A new
liturgical reform—better, a "reform of the reform"—
would also require an enrichment of the current Missal so
that its continuity with the past can be more easily shown.
Of course, this is no overnight project. Its success will
depend largely on the willingness of the bishops and their
liturgical offices to carry it out, while avoiding the same
mistakes made in implementing the conciliar reforms.[2]

---

[1] From the mission statement of the Adoremus Society: "Adoremus believes liturgical changes approved since the Council should be reviewed and
measured against a deeper understanding of the Council's teaching. We believe the Church should reflect carefully on these changes, and... evaluate them
in the light of the original conciliar texts and of the experience of Catholic
faithful since the Council. Thus, when necessary, Adoremus will propose to
Church authorities changes more in harmony with the authentic renewal of
the liturgy expressed in the Council documents."

[2] James Hitchcock's analysis is of interest: "The process of liturgical change
was handled badly from a number of points of view: the people were never
consulted as to their wants and needs; there was insufficient education in the
new ways prior to their introduction; change was often presented as a hierarchical command to be obeyed; there were conflicting signals about the ratio-
nale for the changes (for example, was it to restore the ancient liturgy or to
come to terms with modern culture?); change was piecemeal and hence dou-
bly confusing" (*The Recovery of the Sacred* [San Francisco: Ignatius Press, 1995],
pp. 144–45).

# CHAPTER III

## RETURN TO THE OLD RITE, OR FIX THE NEW? A DIALOGUE

Our study of the restoration/reform controversy will take the form of a dialogue between fictitious representatives of the traditionalist and reformist movements: "T." and "R.", respectively.[1] Bear in mind that there is no predetermined "solution" toward which the discussion winds its way. My intention, rather, is to analyze the arguments put forth by traditionalists and reformists with a view to clearing up misunderstandings, elucidating the complexity of the situation (hence the folly of mutual anathematizing), and coming up with a reasonable strategy for achieving a more satisfactory liturgical life in the Latin Church. (While the sacred liturgy includes not only the rite of Mass but also the Divine Office, the sacraments, and sacramentals, we will focus on the Mass, the jewel in the crown of the liturgy.) If this work should incite a fruitful conversation among real people, then I believe it will have proved worthwhile.

---

[1] Given the many shades of traditionalism, on the one hand, and, on the other, the many possible alternative implementations of the Constitution on the Liturgy, *T.* and *R.* cannot possibly speak for every traditionalist and every reformist. Based on the wealth of material I have compiled over the past decade, I have no doubt that these fictitious spokesmen articulate the thoughts, concerns, and goals of the majority of people involved in their respective movements. The reader will be spared the polemics of conspiracy theorists, cultists, sedevacantists, and other extremists.

## Renewal or Rupture?

*R.:* The chief premise of the traditionalist movement is that "the post-conciliar liturgical reform, by its extension and brutality, represents a disturbing upheaval, as a radical rupture from the traditional Roman liturgy." [2] You traditionalists would have us believe that the Roman rite had always taken the form by which it was known just before Vatican II. Expressions such as "the traditional Mass" or "the ancient Mass" or "the Mass of all time" imply that the Roman Missal fell from heaven ready-made somehow and that Vatican II intervened to break this long, uninterrupted tradition. But this view does not square with the historical facts, as Cardinal Ratzinger explains:

> The Missal which appeared in 1570 by order of Pius V differed only in tiny details from the first printed edition of the Roman Missal of about a hundred years earlier. Basically the reform of Pius V was only concerned with eliminating certain late medieval accretions and the various mistakes and misprints which had crept in.... In 1614 [*sic*], under Urban VIII, there was already a new edition of the Missal, again including various improvements. In this way each century before and after Pius V left its mark on the Missal. On the one hand, it was subject to a continuous process of purification, and on the other, it continued to grow and develop, but it remained the same book

---

[2] Bishop Bernard Fellay, S.S.P.X, "Letter to Pope John Paul II", in *The Problem of the Liturgical Reform: A Theological and Liturgical Study* (Kansas City, Mo.: Angelus Press, 2001), p. I.

throughout. Hence those who cling to the "Tridentine Missal" have a faulty view of the historical facts.[3]

Note what His Eminence says about Pius V wanting to remove accretions and to restore noble simplicity in areas where it had become obscured. This is essentially the same language found in *Sacrosanctum Concilium*, which sought additionally to reintroduce practices that had disappeared, despite the fact that they represented a true source of richness for divine worship:

The rite of the Mass is to be revised in such a way that the intrinsic nature and purpose of its several parts, as well as the connection between them, may be more clearly manifested, and that devout and active

---

[3] Joseph Cardinal Ratzinger, *The Feast of Faith: Approaches to a Theology of the Liturgy*, trans. Graham Harrison (San Francisco: Ignatius Press, 1986), pp. 85–86. (Pope Urban VIII revised the Missal in 1634, not 1614. The first revision of the Tridentine Missal, however, was that of Pope Clement VIII in 1604.) Cf. Msgr. Klaus Gamber, *The Reform of the Roman Liturgy: Its Problems and Background* (San Juan Capistrano, Calif.: Una Voce Press, and Harrison, N.Y.: Foundation for Catholic Reform, 1993), pp. 23–24: "In the strict sense there is no 'Tridentine Mass', for, at least at the conclusion of the Council of Trent, there was no creation of a new Mass order; and the 'Missal of St. Pius V' is nothing else but the Missal of the Roman Curia, which had seen the light in Rome centuries earlier, and which had been introduced by the Franciscans into many Western countries. The changes made at the time by St. Pius V were so minimal that they can be noticed only by a specialist." Also, Prof. Laszlo Dobszay, "Ordo Antiquus: The 'Tridentine' Movement and 'Reform of the Reform'", *Sacred Music* 128, no. 3 (fall 2001): 13: "It [the 'traditional Roman liturgy'] is the liturgical practice of Rome continuously living and organically developing from the 4th century at the latest (if its basic features are meant) and fixed in the 8th/9th centuries; which preserved its identity during diffusion both geographical (in cathedrals) and institutional (in orders), as also admits the local and temporal variations regulated by the liturgical hierarchy."

participation by the faithful may be more easily achieved.

For this purpose the rites are to be simplified, due care being taken to preserve their substance. Parts which with the passage of time came to be duplicated, or were added with little advantage, are to be omitted. Other parts which suffered loss through accidents of history are to be restored to the vigor they had in the days of the holy Fathers, as may seem useful or necessary.[4]

Now, if a priest is unfaithful to "tradition" because he celebrates Mass according to the new Missal[5] instead of the 1962 Missal (or an earlier version), could the same charge be made against those priests who used the revised Missal of 1614 instead of the 1570 Missal? Was Pope Urban VIII wrong to modify the 1570 Missal, considering that his predecessor, Pope Saint Pius V, in his bull *Quo primum tempore*, established "in perpetuity" the right to use the 1570 Missal?[6] Who would seriously insist that the Missal should be frozen at some particular point in time, never again to be modified? Yet that is exactly what one occasionally hears: "Pius XII was wrong to reform the rites

[4] *Sacrosanctum Concilium* [hereafter SC], no. 50. All quotations from SC are from the translation of Austin Flannery, O.P., general ed., *Vatican Council II: The Conciliar and Post Conciliar Documents*, new rev. ed., Vatican Collection series, vol. 1 (Northport, N.Y.: Costello Publishing Co., 1992), pp. 1–40.

[5] The Roman Missal promulgated by Pope Paul VI in 1970 was revised in 1975 and again in 2000. The third *editio typica* (April 20, 2000) is now the normative Missal.

[6] *Quo primum tempore* (July 9, 1570) authorized the Roman Missal codified by the Council of Trent. It was published in the 1570 Missal and in all subsequent editions of the Roman Missal until 1970.

of Holy Week"... "John XXIII should have retained the second *Confiteor*"... "The 1965 Missal was the beginning of the end"... "The Council never mandated changes to the traditional Mass", and so on. Which *is* the "traditional" Mass: the one codified by the Missal of 1570 (Saint Pius V) or 1604 (Clement VIII) or 1634 (Urban VIII) or 1962 (Blessed John XXIII)? The answer is: *all* of these, of course. Yet, traditionalists deny that the Missal of Paul VI is traditional. How do you make sense of that?

*T.:* You have attacked a straw man. No traditionalist actually thinks that the Roman rite came prepackaged from on high, with orders never to be tampered with. Informed Catholics know that the old Roman liturgy, wrongly called "Tridentine", goes back in important respects (Ordinary, Canon, Proper of the Time, and much else) 1500 years to Pope Saint Gregory the Great (590–604) and, more rudimentarily, to Pope Saint Damasus (366–384). Expressions such as "the Mass of all time" and "the ancient liturgy" are meant to underscore that essential continuity with Christian antiquity and to insinuate the revolutionary character of the *Novus Ordo*.

Portraying traditionalists as historical illiterates conveniently diverts attention from what ought to be the *real* focus of the debate, namely, whether or not the new Mass is in continuity with the natural and legitimate development of the Roman rite. Paul VI's revisions cannot be put on a par with the relatively modest modifications introduced into the Missal by the popes from 1604 to 1962, as Monsignor Klaus Gamber explains: "The popes, until Paul VI, made no change in the Order of the Mass properly so-called, whereas, especially after the Council of Trent, they introduced new Propers for new feasts. That no more suppressed the 'Tridentine Mass' than, for example, additions to the civil law would cause it to lapse."[7] In other words, the Supreme Pontiffs from Clement VIII to Blessed John XXIII were intent on revisions and not revolution. That a revolution occurred in the wake of the Council is made painfully evident upon comparing the Missal of 1962 with that of 1970.

## Guiding Principles of the Reform

*R.:* The question whether or not the reformed liturgy represents a break from organic liturgical development has been the subject of so much debate that the possible citations are numerous.[8] Before comparing the 1962 and 1970 Missals, we ought to consider what the Fathers of the Second Vatican Council had in mind concerning the renewal of the liturgy. The Council intended the purest possible restoration of the ancient and long-lived Roman rite. According to article 50 of *Sacrosanctum Concilium*, the Order of the Mass was to be revised so that "the intrinsic nature and purpose of its several parts, as well as the connection between them, may be more clearly manifested"

---

[7] Gamber, *Reform*, p. 24.

[8] Suffice it to recommend just a few scholarly works. On the traditionalist side: Michael Davies, *The Liturgical Revolution*, vol. 3, *Pope Paul's New Mass* (Kansas City, Mo.: Angelus Press, 1980), and John W. Mole, O.M.I., *Whither the Roman Rite?* (Ottawa: Word of God Hour, 2000). On the reformist side: the proceedings of the 1996 Oxford Liturgy Forum, compiled by Stratford Caldecott, ed., *Beyond the Prosaic: Renewing the Liturgical Movement* (Edinburgh: T&T Clark, 1998). Nearly twenty years before the crystallization of the "reform of the reform" movement, James Likoudis and Kenneth D. Whitehead dealt with the standard traditionalist objections to the Missal of Paul VI in their book *The Pope, the Council, and the Mass* (West Hanover, Mass.: Christopher Publishing House, 1981).

and so that the faithful may be led to a "devout and active participation" in the liturgical action. This was to be achieved, on the one hand, by eliminating those "parts which with the passage of time came to be duplicated, or were added with little advantage" and, on the other hand, by restoring other "parts which suffered loss through accidents of history".[9] Hence some of the priest's private prayers, certain ritual actions, and the so-called Last Gospel were dropped, while the General Intercessions (or Prayer of the Faithful), the Presentation of the Gifts, and a wider selection of Prefaces were added.

*T.*: But article 50 of *Sacrosanctum Concilium* is vague and thus interpretable in many ways. "One man's junk is another man's treasure" is an adage that applies to the topic at hand. What one liturgist deems a useless accretion, another sees as an enrichment. How much can one rearrange, subtract from, or add to a rite without destroying or mutilating it? At what point does revision become transmutation? Could not these changes have been made to the traditional liturgy without the creation of the *Novus Ordo*? Gamber posits that "the type of revision of the liturgy of the Mass envisioned by the Council was the *Ordo*

---

[9] Cf. Joseph Cardinal Ratzinger, *Milestones: Memoirs 1927–1977*, trans. Erasmo Leiva-Merikakis (San Francisco: Ignatius Press, 1998), p. 123: The liturgical reform sought "to overcome certain tendencies of Baroque liturgy and nineteenth-century devotional piety and to promote a new humble and sober centering of the authentic mystery of Christ's presence in his Church." A cynical, if not sarcastic, view of this objective is that of Thomas E. Woods, Jr., "Old Pride, New Wineskins", *The Latin Mass*, fall 2000, p. 64: "The 1962 Missal isn't perfect, you see. We need to recover discarded traditions. Of course, this [is] the premise of every liturgical modernist. They all agree that the liturgy reached its apogee in 1132, or 631, or 207 or 1335, and that the benighted faithful who love the 1962 Missal really need a little dose of reeducation. No thanks."

*Missae* published in 1965." [10] This revision did not drastically remodel the traditional rite, whereas Pope Paul VI's *Ordo Missae* of 1969 created a new rite. The Tridentine Mass must therefore be preserved if the classical Roman rite is to survive.

**R.:** We are *both* interested in the survival of the Roman rite. However, I do not accept the hard-line traditionalist postulate that the new Order of Mass is a complete and irremediable break with tradition. Rather, I concur with the opinion of Monsignor Arthur Calkins of the Pontifical Commission *Ecclesia Dei*: "The continuity between our liturgical past and the present is far greater than any discontinuity." [11] Herein, I think, lies the rub: Whereas traditionalists advocate a return to the preconciliar Missal as an end in itself, I see it as the reference point for the reform of the Roman rite ordered by the Council. [12] By way of analogy, think of a student working on a mathematical problem who realizes he has made a mistake somewhere: he must go back, step by step, to find where he went wrong. He corrects the error and starts over from there. Similarly, we cannot simply go back to the old Missal and remain there. We should not scrap the positive aspects of the conciliar renewal. That would be like cutting off the nose to spite the face.

**T.:** What good has come out of the renewal?

---

[10] Gamber, *Reform*, p. 33.

[11] Msgr. Arthur B. Calkins, "The Latin Liturgical Tradition: Extending and Solidifying the Continuity", address to the Latin Liturgy Association, June 23, 2001, at St. John Cantius Parish in Chicago.

[12] Cf. Gamber, *Reform*, p. 114.

*R.:* For starters, there is a greater measure of common participation in the Mass and other sacramental rites (although participation ought not be measured in decibels).[13] The priest does not monopolize the rites as he has done for so long; rather, the people receive their proper place in the liturgical books, saying (or singing) the readings, responses, psalms, and prayers of various kinds that belong to them.[14] The new liturgy makes more extensive use of Scripture than did the old.[15] Concelebration, which previously was seen only at ordinations (and in a very different form), manifests the fraternity of the priesthood and is especially appropriate when the bishop is present.[16] There is a simpler classification of feasts, with preeminence given to Sunday, the *primordialis dies festus*, the "foundation and kernel of the whole liturgical year".[17] The sacrificial and

---

[13] SC, no. 14. Before the Council, the participation of the whole congregation in the liturgical action was endorsed by Pius XII's encyclical *Mediator Dei* of 1947 and facilitated by the so-called "dialogue Masses" of the 1950s.

[14] SC, nos. 26–32. Lectors and commentators were first mentioned in an instruction of the Sacred Congregation of Rites on Sacred Music and the Liturgy (September 3, 1958).

[15] SC, no. 35. The biblical readings, of which there were only two in the old rite, now number three at Sunday Mass; they are separated from one another by the Gradual (or Responsorial Psalm) and by the Alleluia (or Tract). Before the Council, a very small portion of the Bible was covered in the course of a year.

[16] SC, no. 41. Before Vatican II, each *ordinand* had his own chalice, paten, and Missal and said Mass at his own station (kneeling before a Missal stand) simultaneously with the bishop, who stood at the main altar and prayed the Canon aloud so that the *ordinandi* could follow along.

[17] SC, no. 106. This process of simplification was already beginning under Pius XII. In 1955 nearly all octaves were abolished and the classification of days greatly simplified. A completely fresh set of general rubrics for the Breviary and Missal was published in 1960, before the Council, on lines that were afterward followed.

sacramental dimensions of the Eucharist are more closely held together in the reformed liturgy, at least in practice.[18] Some use of the vernacular (in the Proper of the Mass) is desirable, I think, provided that the Latin text is faithfully translated and that at least the Ordinary of the Mass remains in Latin.[19] Ironically, the revised rite allows greater use of chant and incense than did the old rite.[20] Another improvement has been the allowance for certain adaptations according to circumstances.[21] Surely, these changes do not amount to a destruction of the traditional Roman liturgy.

---

[18] Nowadays Holy Communion is ordinarily received within Mass, not from the reserved Sacrament outside the Mass (which was a common practice in the past). Certain other practices, however, instruct against a proper understanding of the Eucharist as sacrifice, especially the offering of Mass facing the people and the use of a cross without a *corpus*. Concerning the latter, the most recent *General Instruction of the Roman Missal* (2000) prescribes a *crucifix* on or near the altar (nos. 122, 308).

[19] SC, no. 36: "The use of the Latin language, with due respect to particular law, is to be preserved in the Latin rites. But since the use of the vernacular, whether in the Mass, the administration of the sacraments, or in other parts of the liturgy, may frequently be of great advantage to the people, a wider use may be made of it, especially in readings, directives and in some prayers and chants." Also SC, no. 54: "A suitable place may be allotted to the vernacular in Masses which are celebrated with the people.... Nevertheless care must be taken to ensure that the faithful may also be able to say or sing together in Latin those parts of the Ordinary of the Mass which pertain to them."

[20] For example, the entire Eucharistic Prayer may be chanted, whereas in the old rite it was said inaudibly. In point of fact, the current Missal provides musical notation for the entire Order of Mass, from the sign of the cross and greeting to the final blessing and dismissal. Moreover, whereas the preconciliar Missal restricted the use of incense to certain forms of Mass, the new Missal allows its use at any Mass.

[21] Cf. SC, nos. 37–40. For example, the texts of the Masses for the dead provide for every kind of particular situation, from the death of a pope to the death of an unbaptized child.

*T.:* The relatively modest revisions ordered by *Sacrosanctum Concilium* could have been implemented without any substantial change to the traditional rite.

*R.:* I agree. Earlier you mentioned Monsignor Gamber's thesis, that the Missal of 1965 fulfills the changes envisioned by the Council Fathers in *Sacrosanctum Concilium*. Why, then, do traditionalists speak as if the 1962 Missal is the last of the "pure" Roman Missals, perfect in every way? They choose to ignore what Gamber said in favor of the 1965 Missal and even question the good faith of those who would use it. Says one writer: "To move traditional Catholics in the direction of the 1965 *Ordo Missae* is merely a means to try to do away once and for all with the Mass in which Christ was clearly recognized as King and Our Lady was honored as Queen." [22] Who can take that rhetoric seriously?

*T.:* It is possible to get carried away. However, you should not have been so selective in your quotation. The skittishness that traditionalists feel toward the 1965 Missal reflects the wisdom of hindsight, as that same writer explains:

> It is clear in retrospect that the *Ordo Missae* of 1965, though certainly not the *Novus Ordo* of 1969, was itself a means of introducing instability and uncertainty into the Roman rite. The prayers at the foot of the altar were made optional (and could be recited in the vernacular), the first step toward a

[22] Thomas A. Droleskey, "Enduring Ritual: Witness to the Divine", *The Latin Mass*, spring 2001, p. 29.

liturgy with more legitimate options and adaptations than there are approved rites within the universal Church. The wording of many of the formularies of the various parts of the Mass (collects, secrets, communion, postcommunion) were changed, beginning the process by which the Church would begin to express her unchanging doctrine less clearly, more ambiguously.[23]

Farther on, he states:

The institutionalization of instability by the *Novus Ordo* (and by the devolution of liturgical decision-making to national episcopal conferences and to agencies such as the International Commission on English in the Liturgy) could not have been possible unless there had been a gradual transition away from the traditional Latin Mass to that which was totally new and innovative, all gratuitous claims to the contrary notwithstanding.[24]

*R.:* So, the 1965 Missal was the proverbial camel's nose in the tent?

*T.:* That seems to be his point.

*R.:* This kind of talk can only fuel the general suspicion among mainstream Catholics that the so-called traditionalists reject the Council itself, and not merely its poor implementation. But this is not a legitimate option for Catholics. I fail to see how you can reconcile the obe-

---

[23] Ibid., p. 28.
[24] Ibid., pp. 28–29.

dience due to the Council with an insistence on the exclusive and perennial use of the 1962 Missal. The indisputable fact is that Vatican II ordered changes to the Roman liturgy in accordance with the general principles of *Sacrosanctum Concilium*. Among these principles are: allowance for the vernacular, especially in the readings and certain chants (but not to the exclusion of Latin);[25] a simplification of the rites;[26] and the promotion of the full and active participation of the faithful.[27]

*T.:* Are you certain that the application of these principles necessitated the publication of the 1965 Missal? The dominant principle, I maintain—call it the principle of principles—is stated in article 23: "There must be no innovations unless the good of the Church genuinely and certainly requires them." I cannot see how eliminating the prayers at the foot of the altar and the Last Gospel, for example, were for the "good of the Church". Actually, the only ritual change in the Mass mentioned in the Constitution is the restoration of the Prayer of the Faithful after the Gospel (or sermon).[28]

*R.:* We can dispute specific applications of *Sacrosanctum Concilium* until the Second Coming. Incidentally, as important as article 23 is, I maintain that the foundational principle of *Sacrosanctum Concilium* is stated in article 14: "Mother Church earnestly desires that all the faithful should

---

[25] SC, no. 36; cf. no. 54.
[26] SC, no. 34.
[27] SC, no. 14.
[28] SC, no. 53.

be led to that full, conscious, and active participation in liturgical celebrations which is demanded by the very nature of the liturgy." (The Constitution insists almost wearisomely on the essential part the faithful have in the whole range of the liturgy: in the Mass, in the sacraments and sacramentals, and in the Divine Office.) I am not suggesting that the 1965 Missal is the only conceivable materialization of the Constitution's general norms. I *am* saying that to leave the 1962 Missal entirely unaltered is to disregard the Council. The Liturgy Constitution is not optional. Its immediate result was the Missal of 1965, whatever one may think of it. Pope Paul VI evidently did not think it went far enough, so he promulgated a new Missal five years later.

## The 1962 and 1970 Missals Compared

*T.:* Having considered the principles of liturgical renewal, let us now compare the normative *Missale Romanum* of 1962 with that of 1970.[29] This will cast more light on the renewal-or-rupture question.

---

[29] Our historical information relies substantially on Adrian Fortescue, *The Mass: A Study of the Roman Liturgy* (1912; reprint, Albany, N.Y.: Preserving Christian Publications, 1997), and Joseph A. Jungmann, S.J., *The Mass of the Roman Rite: Its Origin and Development* (Missarum Sollemnia), trans. Francis A. Brunner, C.SS.R., 2 vols. (New York: Benziger Brothers, 1951 and 1955) [hereafter *MRR*]. On the new Eucharistic Prayers, see Louis Bouyer, *Eucharist: Theology and Spirituality of the Eucharistic Prayer*, trans. Charles Underhill Quinn (Notre Dame, Ind.: University of Notre Dame Press, 1968), pp. 446–61 [French original: *Eucharistie: Théologie et spiritualité de la prière eucharistique* (Paris: Desclée, 1966)].

*R.:* If your intention in contrasting the two Missals is to prove that the reform following Vatican II went far beyond what the Council authorized, we need not waste our time. I remind you of the substantial agreement that already exists between us with regard to the derailment of the liturgical movement after the Council. Furthermore, neither of us is competent to judge whether or not this or that specific alteration can be justified by *Sacrosanctum Concilium*, since that Constitution contained few specific directives for its implementation.[30] What, then, can we hope to achieve by a comparison of the old and new Missals?

*T.:* I believe a comparison of the two Missals will show that the *Novus Ordo* is no mere revision of the traditional Mass, but the product of a committee consumed with false ecumenism and naïve romanticism. Neither the reformists nor all the king's horses and all the king's men can salvage this sorry fabrication.

*R.:* Without wanting to understate the damage that occurred after the Council, I think that a comparison of the two Missals will reveal more continuity with tradition than discontinuity, thereby providing hope for the reformist agenda. Let's have a look at the Order of Mass as well as certain ceremonial actions, rubrics, and prayers that together comprise the Church's supreme act of worship, the Eucharistic Sacrifice.

---

[30] The first instruction on the implementation of the Liturgy Constitution, *Inter Oecumenici*, was promulgated by the Sacred Congregation of Rites on September 26, 1964. Among other things, this instruction makes more specific what *Sacrosanctum Concilium* expressed in general terms.

THE ORDINARY OF THE MASS (*Ordo Missæ*)[31]

*Introductory Rites (Ritus Initiales)*

*1962 Missal.*    Mass begins with the "prayers at the foot of
the altar."[32] (At High Mass, the *Asperges*, or sprinkling of
holy water, precedes these prayers and is not considered
part of the Mass itself.) At the entrance to the sanctuary,
the priest makes the sign of the cross and alternates with
his assistants in reciting the verses of Psalm 42 (*Iudica me*),
which is framed by the recitation of the antiphon "*Introibo ad altare Dei, ad Deum qui lætificat iuventutem meam.*"
(On some occasions, the psalm is omitted.) After this psalm,
the priest prays the *Confiteor*, which is then repeated by
the assistants, the response each time being the *Misereatur*.
The priest then recites the *Indulgentiam*. Finally, the priest
ascends to the altar while praying silently the *Aufer a nobis*
and kisses the altar saying the *Oramus te, Domine*. He again
makes the sign of the cross, reads the Introit, and says the

---

[31] The headings for the four principal divisions of the Mass correspond to
the 1970 Missal and subsequent editions. The prayers are referred to by the
Latin words with which they begin. (Thus, the embolism after the Lord's Prayer
is called the *Libera nos*.) From the viewpoint of external ceremony, it was the
custom before Vatican II to speak of "High Mass" and "Low Mass". A High
Mass is sung; a Low Mass is one in which the priest and people recite in a
speaking tone the parts that are sung in a High Mass. A High Mass is called
"Solemn Mass" when it is celebrated with the assistance of a deacon and subdeacon. (Thus, all "solemn" Masses are "high", but not all "high" Masses are
"solemn".) The reader will occasionally encounter these terms throughout
this study.

[32] These prayers were omitted at Requiem Masses and from Passion Sunday
to Holy Saturday. It should also be noted that other ancient liturgies in the
West (including the Ambrosian rite of Milan and the Mozarabic rite of Toledo
as well as the rite of the Carthusians) did not have these prayers.

*Kyrie* alternately with the assistants. (At a High Mass, the choir sings the Introit and the *Kyrie* while the priest incenses the altar.) Finally, he says or sings the *Gloria* (if prescribed), followed by the Collect (Opening Prayer).

*1970 Missal.* The 1970 Missal drops the prayers at the foot of the altar as well as the *Aufer a nobis* and *Oramus te.* It retains the Introit and puts it in its proper place, namely, during the entrance procession, not during the priest's recitation of private prayers. The priest approaches the altar and venerates it with a kiss. After making the sign of the cross and greeting the people with one of the approved biblical formulas, the priest leads the Penitential Rite, of which there are three forms. (On Sundays, the Rite of Blessing and Sprinkling Holy Water may replace the Penitential Rite.) Penitential Rite A, the form most consistent with the old Missal, consists of one recitation of the *Confiteor* by the priest and faithful together; Rite B, the shortest of the three, consists of two brief invocations said by the priest, each followed by the people's response; Rite C consists of three invocations said by the priest (or deacon), to which the people respond *Kyrie eleison* after the first and third invocation and *Christe eleison* after the second. All three Penitential Rites conclude with the *Misereatur,* said only by the priest. The *Indulgentiam* is dropped. As for the rest, everything was kept: the *Kyrie,*[33] the *Gloria,* the Collect, and so on. (If incense is used, the priest incenses the altar during the singing of the Introit or Entrance Hymn; the Penitential Rite is said once he is

---

[33] In the 1970 Missal the former ritual of 3 × 3 invocation (*Kyrie eleison,* three times; *Christe eleison,* three times; *Kyrie eleison,* three times) is simplified to a simple threefold invocation and its repetition.

finished.) The 1970 Missal leaves essentially intact the traditional outline for the opening of Mass without a congregation (*Ordo Missæ sine Populo*).[34]

## Liturgy of the Word (Liturgia Verbi)

*1962 Missal.* There are nearly always two readings, the first taken from either the Old Testament, from the apostolic Epistles, or from the Apocalypse (Book of Revelation); the second is always taken from the Gospels. The Sunday Epistle and Gospel are read by the priest facing the altar, unless these are chanted by the subdeacon and deacon, as in the case of Solemn Mass.[35] The Gospel is read from the left side of the altar ("left" as you face the altar) or the "Gospel side", as opposed to the right or "Epistle side". Between the Epistle and Gospel is the Gradual and (usually) the Alleluia verse. There is no recognizable *lectio continua* throughout the year. Provision is made only for Sundays and for these readings to be repeated on ferial days.

---

[34] Having arrived at the entrance of the sanctuary, the priest and server genuflect (if the Blessed Sacrament is reserved on the altar) or bow. They make the sign of the cross and, from the foot of the altar, recite the *Confiteor*, whereupon the priest says the *Misereatur*, proceeds to the altar, reverences it with a kiss, says the Introit, alternates with the server in saying the *Kyrie*, and then reads the Collect. (The Missal of 2000 eliminates the difference between the opening of Mass with and without a congregation.)

[35] Prior to Pope John XXIII's reform of the rubrics in 1960, the priest read the Epistle and Gospel silently at the altar while the subdeacon and deacon sang these. The 1962 Missal incorporated these reforms and put an end to this. Astonishingly, even the 1962 Missal is denounced by some traditionalists (for instance, the sedevacantist Society of St. Pius V) because it is based on the principles of the "modernist" liturgical movement.

*1970 Missal.* The readings follow a two-year cycle for weekdays and a three-year cycle for Sundays. The reading of the first (and second) Scripture reading(s) and assistance with the book by the side of the celebrant, once assigned to the subdeacon as his special function, are now performed by other ministers. The readings are read from the lectern. The responses after the readings (*"Deo gratias"* and *"Laus tibi, Christe"*), formerly reserved for the Mass server, are said by the people. On Sundays and feast days, two readings precede the Gospel: the first from the Old Testament (except during Easter), the second (corresponding to the Epistle of the old rite) from the Acts or Epistles of the apostles. The Responsorial Psalm follows the first reading and relates to it: the cantor (or the lector) intones (or reads) the psalm, and the people respond by singing (or reciting) a refrain from the psalm. The Alleluia verse occurs between the first (or second, as the case may be) reading and the Gospel and is omitted during Lent. A homily is prescribed for Sundays and feast days. The Liturgy of the Word concludes with the Prayer of the Faithful, or General Intercessions (*Oratio universalis*), a prayer of petition for the Church and for the world, with provision for the addition of special intentions. The Scripture readings are not published in the Roman Missal properly so-called (the sacramentary); rather, they are contained in a separate book called the lectionary.

### Liturgy of the Eucharist (Liturgia Eucharistica)

*1962 Missal.* The Offertory rite begins with the priest offering the bread while praying the *Suscipe, sancte Pater.* Then, having poured a small amount of water into the chalice

(*Deus, qui humanæ*), he offers the wine (*Offerimus tibi*). He then prays the *In spiritu humilitatis*, followed by a brief invocation of the Holy Spirit (*Veni, Sanctificator*). At this point, the gifts and altar are incensed (at High Mass). Next, the priest washes his hands while reciting Psalm 25:6–12 (*Lavabo*), after which he says the prayer *Suscipe, sancta Trinitas*. All of these prayers are spoken quietly. The *Orate fratres* and its response (*Suscipiat*) precede the prayer over the gifts (the "Secret Prayer"), which also is said quietly except for its conclusion ("... *per omnia sæcula sæculorum*").

The only Eucharistic Prayer in the 1962 Missal and in all preconciliar Roman Missals is the Roman Canon, said quietly. Substantially fixed in the so-called Gelasian Sacramentary of the sixth century, this Canon was slightly modified by Pope Saint Gregory the Great (590–604) and left untouched until 1962, when Pope John XXIII on his own initiative inserted Saint Joseph's name into the first list of saints.

The Communion of the priest is separate from that of the faithful. Following the *Libera nos* and *Pax* (said silently), the priest says aloud the *Agnus Dei* and, silently, the three prayers before Communion: the *Domine Iesu Christe, qui dixisti* (this followed by the Kiss of Peace at Solemn Mass), the *Domine Iesu Christe, Fili Dei vivi*, and the *Perceptio Corporis tui*. He says aloud three times "*Domine, non sum dignus*" and (each time) continues silently "*ut intres sub tectum meum*," and so on. Then he communicates himself. Before distributing Communion to the faithful,[36] he says aloud "*Ecce Agnus Dei*," and so on,

---

[36] Prior to the new rubrics of the Roman Missal issued by the Holy See in 1960, the *Confiteor* was said (again) by the servers and people before their Communion. The second *Confiteor* is omitted in the 1962 Missal.

and "*Domine, non sum dignus*" (the latter three times). The formula for administering Communion is "*Corpus Domini nostri Iesu Christi custodiat animam tuam in vitam æternam. Amen.*"

*1970 Missal.* The Offertory, or Presentation of the Gifts, is considerably simpler. The *Suscipe, sancte Pater*, the *Offerimus tibi*, the *Veni, Sanctificator*, and the *Suscipe, sancta Trinitas* have all been abolished. The prayers accompanying the offering of the bread and wine are substantially different: each time the celebrant receives one of the elements, he says, "*Benedictus es, Domine, Deus universi, quia de tua largitate accepimus panem [vinum], quem [quod] tibi offerimus, fructum terræ [vitis] et operis manuum hominum, ex quo nobis fiet panis vitæ [potus spiritalis]*"; the people reply to both, "*Benedictus Deus in sæcula.*" The incensing of the gifts and altar remains in the new rite, although the prayers that accompanied the blessing of the incense and the censing of the gifts and altar have been eliminated. The prayer as the priest washes his hands has been reduced to just the first verse of Psalm 25, followed by the prayer *In spiritu humilitatis*, all spoken quietly. The *Orate fratres* and its response have been retained. The prayer over the gifts is said aloud in its entirety. Moreover, the presentation of the bread and wine by members of the congregation is encouraged.

The 1970 Missal provides more Prefaces, especially for feast days, liturgical seasons, and special occasions. On Sundays, the Preface of the Most Holy Trinity, in use since the thirteenth century but not prescribed until 1759, has been replaced by Prefaces that stress the Paschal Mystery.

The Eucharistic Prayer (*Prex eucharistica*) is said audibly. In the Roman Canon (Eucharistic Prayer I) of the

1970 Missal, some of the saints in the two parallel series are in brackets to indicate that they may be omitted. The ending *"Per Christum Dominum nostrum. Amen"* concluding each individual section may be omitted. The *epiclesis*[37] has been transferred from the *Hanc igitur* to the *Quam oblationem*. The important change is the actual institution narrative, where the clause *"quod pro vobis tradetur"* has been added after the consecration of the bread. As regards the consecration of the wine: *"Hæc quotiescumque feceritis, in mei memoriam facietis"* is replaced by *"HOC FACITE IN MEAM COMMEMORATIONEM"* (in capitals), no longer preceded but followed by the *"Mysterium fidei"*, which cues the people's memorial acclamation: *"Mortem tuam annuntiamus, Domine..."* (or other forms).

Three new Eucharistic Prayers (II, III, and IV), promulgated in 1968, appear in the 1970 Missal, all of which have some common features. These are: a consecratory *epiclesis* (invocation of the Holy Spirit) before the institution narrative, uniform wording for the Consecration, and intercessions with an invocation of the saints. Eucharistic Prayer II is substantially the one Saint Hippolytus of Rome composed around A.D. 215. Eucharistic Prayer III combines the Roman tradition with certain formularies of the Gallican and Mozarabic liturgies. Eucharistic Prayer IV was modeled on the Eastern liturgies of Saint Basil and Saint James.

The third part of the Liturgy of the Eucharist, the Communion rite, has been considerably rearranged in the 1970 Missal. What was once the priest's private, preparatory

---

[37] The *epiclesis* is the prayer asking God (the Father) to send the Holy Spirit to change the bread and wine into the Body and Blood of Christ. During this invocation, the priest extends his hands over the bread and wine.

prayer leading up to the sign of peace (*Domine Iesu Christe, qui dixisti*) is now prayed aloud. This is then followed by the benediction, *Pax domini* (which in the 1962 Missal came right after the *Libera nos*). Next comes the (optional) Sign of Peace, followed by the *Agnus Dei*. In contrast to the 1962 Missal, the public invitation to receive Communion (*Ecce Agnus Dei*) is issued before the priest's Communion, and the *Domine non sum dignus* is said only once. Before communicating himself, the priest prays silently either the *Domine Iesu Christe, Fili Dei vivi* or the *Perceptio Corporis* (not both). The form for administering Holy Communion is simply "*Corpus Christi*", to which the communicant replies, "*Amen.*"

## Concluding Rite (Ritus Conclusionis)

*1962 Missal.* After the Postcommunion prayer, the priest says "*Dominus vobiscum*" and gives the dismissal, "*Ite missa est.*" He then says silently the *Placeat tibi*, after which he blesses the people before returning to the side of the altar in order to read the Last Gospel, usually a pericope from the Gospel of John (1:1–14).

*1970 Missal.* After the Postcommunion prayer, the priest says "*Dominus vobiscum*" and then blesses the people. He then says the "*Ite missa est.*" There is no *Placeat tibi* or Last Gospel.

### Ritual Actions

Fourteen *genuflections* are prescribed in the preconciliar Missal. Generally, there are no more than three genuflections in the Missal of 1970: after the elevations of the Host and chalice and before the priest's Communion. The celebrant and his ministers genuflect upon entering and leaving the sanctuary if the Blessed Sacrament is reserved therein; otherwise they bow to the altar. (Curiously, the old Missal calls for the server to genuflect even if the Blessed Sacrament is not present, in which case only the priest bows.) Whereas the old Missal prescribes a genuflection while saying (or singing) the *Et incarnatus est* of the Creed, the new Missal calls for a bow.

The *kissing of the altar* no longer occurs, as in the past, each time the priest voices a greeting (*Dominus vobiscum*, *Orate fratres*). It is the essential rite of greeting and farewell that the celebrant addresses to the altar; thus it is done at the beginning and end of Mass.

In the preconciliar Missal, the *sign of the cross* is multiplied abundantly. (For example, during the Canon, the priest makes nearly twenty signs of the cross over the chalice and the host.) In the 1970 Missal, the sign of the cross is prescribed only at the following times: at the beginning of Mass, at the blessings of holy water and incense, at the blessing of the deacon who proclaims the Gospel, at the *epiclesis* (except for the Roman Canon, when it is done much earlier), and before the dismissal. Consistent with the 1962 Missal, the sign of the cross is also made on the Gospel and then on the forehead, lips, and breast prior to the proclamation of the Gospel.

In the traditional Mass the priest keeps his *thumbs and forefingers* joined from the time of the Consecration onward to the final ablution, out of respect for particles of the consecrated Host. The 1970 Missal contains no such directive; gone, too, is the requirement to purify the fingers during the ablutions. The new Missal provides the option of *purifying the sacred vessels* either immediately after Communion or immediately after Mass, whereas the old Missal prescribed the purifications immediately after Communion.

## PRAYERS

The 1962 Missal contains 1182 orations (Collects, Secrets, Postcommunions, and certain blessings), about 760 of which were dropped entirely. Of the approximately 36 percent that remained, over half were altered before being introduced into the Missal of 1970. Thus, only some 17 percent of the traditional orations made it untouched into the 1970 Missal.[38] The *Dominus vobiscum* before each oration has been eliminated in the new Missal.

Aside from the orations, the following prayers of the 1962 Missal have been suppressed altogether: the *Judica me* psalm (at the foot of the altar); the *Aufer a nobis* (as the priest ascends to the altar); the *Oramus te, Domine* (as the priest kisses the altar); the Offertory prayers (with the exception of the *In spiritu humilitatis* and an extract from the *Deus, qui humanæ*); the prayers for the blessing of incense and the incensation of the gifts and altar); and the *Placeat tibi* (at the end of Mass). Other prayers have been truncated: the *Confiteor* no longer explicitly invokes the intercession of Saints Michael the Archangel, John the Baptist, Peter, and Paul; the *Munda cor meum* no longer makes reference to the Prophet Isaiah; the *Libera nos* no longer appeals for any saintly aid (not even that of our Lady), and a new ending (*Quia tuum est regnum*) has been added.

---

[38] These statistics are taken from Anthony Cekada, *The Problems with the Prayers of the Modern Mass* (Rockford, Ill.: TAN Books, 1991), p. 9.

The priest and people together say (or sing) the *Pater noster*, whereas in the old Missal it is recited by the priest alone until *"sed libera nos a malo"*, which is said by the people.

## Commentary

*T.:* Having compared the traditional Mass to the new, I have no doubt that the reforms were aimed at making the Catholic liturgy more palatable to Protestants and Modernists.[39] This is apparent right from the very opening of the Mass, at the Introductory Rites. Those prayers that were either truncated or eliminated expressed distinctively Catholic beliefs, such as the intercession of the saints (the *Confiteor* and the *Oramus te*), the sacredness of the sanctuary and altar (the *Aufer a nobis*), and the priestly forgiveness of sins (the *Indulgentiam*). The elimination of the prayers at the foot of the altar "greatly weakens the sense that the priest is about to enter a holy place, before

---

[39] Protestantism rejects the Catholic (and Orthodox) theology of the Mass as a propitiatory sacrifice offered to God for the living and the dead, even though Catholicism teaches that the Mass is none other than the Church's offering to the Father of the unique sacrifice of the Cross in sacramental form. Even those Protestant communities affirming a "real" presence of Christ in the Eucharist (viz., Lutherans and Anglicans) have historically eschewed the Catholic theology of eucharistic sacrifice.

Modernism, a term for the attempt to bring Catholic thought in line with rationalism and liberalism, would eviscerate the Christian religion of supernatural and metaphysical concepts (divine revelation, miracles, the intercession of the angels and saints, the soul, sanctifying grace, and so on). Pope St. Pius X, in his encyclical *Pascendi Dominici Gregis* (September 8, 1907), condemned Modernism as the "synthesis of all heresies".

which he has paused to prepare himself".[40] What is more, the shortening of the triple "*mea culpa*" in the English translation of the *Confiteor* is most regrettable:

> This was one of the most familiar, almost archetypal, moments of the entire Mass, and in the Latin it had become virtually a proverb. An important opportunity to maintain continuity was lost. The psychological effect of the triple recitation was overlooked, and the result is flat and pedestrian.[41]

**R.:** Prior to the reforms of the Council of Trent, the psalm *Iudica me* was frequently said in the sacristy or, in the older mediaeval rites, on the way to the altar. Penitential Rites in various forms appear in the Missals published on the eve of the Protestant Reformation. They were standardized in the Missal of 1570, but were not regarded as a proper part of the rite itself. As for the *Confiteor*, I agree that the removal of the invocations of the saints was of no benefit, but these invocations were not originally part of that prayer: the oldest formulas phrased the invocation of saints only in general terms: "and all the saints" (*et omnibus sanctis*). With regard to the triple "*mea culpa*", we should be careful to consider only the *normative* editions of the two Missals, lest we compare apples to oranges: the Latin *Missale Romanum* of 1970 retains the triple "*mea culpa*". Finally, the *Indulgentiam* had served for centuries as the

---

[40] James Hitchcock, *The Recovery of the Sacred* (San Francisco: Ignatius Press, 1995), p. 149.
[41] Ibid.

formula of sacramental absolution; perhaps it was dropped to avoid a sacramental interpretation.

*T.:* Moving on to the Liturgy of the Word, my critique pertains more to content than to form. Few would object to hearing the word of God in the mother tongue, something for which there is precedence in the Roman rite.[42] However, the use of lay readers has been criticized, and there is some uneasiness even with the Liturgy of the Word being carried out *versus populum* (facing the people):

> The traditional Mass is a seamless whole. The Scriptural passages at Mass doubtless perform a didactic function, but in reading them the priest is also proclaiming God's great works and thus performing an act of adoration. In that sense the tradition of priest and faithful facing East throughout the entire rite, and not merely during the "Liturgy of the Eucharist", stands on solid theological ground from a theological perspective.[43]

*R.:* The 1962 Missal allowed a lector to read the Epistle at Mass, when no subdeacon was present, although this seldom occurred.[44] With regard to the position of the reader, article 50 of *Sacrosanctum Concilium* states that the intrinsic nature and purpose of the various Mass parts should be clearly

---

[42] For example, in the ninth century the missionary brothers Saints Cyril and Methodius used a Slavic translation of the Latin Gospels.

[43] Thomas E. Woods, Jr., "Cardinal Ratzinger on the Liturgy", review of *The Spirit of the Liturgy*, by Joseph Cardinal Ratzinger, in *The Latin Mass*, spring 2001, p. 57. Woods takes issue with His Eminence's positive appraisal of the new Liturgy of the Word.

[44] *Missale Romanum* (1962), *Ritus servandus in celebratione Missæ*, VI, no. 8.

manifested. For the priest, deacon, or lector to stand at the ambo and face the people when reading to them seems wholly in keeping with this directive. Long before the Council, it was acknowledged that the former practice obscured the distinction between the service of the Word and that of the Eucharist.[45] As for the *content* of the Liturgy of the Word, what objections are there?

*T.:* Monsignor Gamber finds nothing wrong, in principle, with enriching the lectionary of the Roman Missal by adding more texts and Sunday cycles. He objects, however, to the wholesale replacement of the traditional corpus of biblical readings, which dates back, at least in parts, to Saint Jerome (d. 420). Moreover, he and others have noted the pedagogical difficulties posed by the use of three annual cycles.[46]

---

[45] Cf. Fortescue, *Mass*, p. 215: "The essential division of the Mass is between that of the Catechumens and that of the Faithful. This division is now so hidden in the Roman rite that most people hardly think of it. There is little to mark the end of one and the beginning of the other; in fact the later Creed which just overlaps the transition covers it completely. Nevertheless, historically, this is the most important distinction of all." (The divisions of the Mass known as the "Mass of the Catechumens" and the "Mass of the Faithful" roughly correspond to the "Liturgy of the Word" and the "Liturgy of the Eucharist" in the postconciliar rite of Mass.) An exception was the Pontifical Mass: the bishop was at his throne during the first part and went to the altar at the Offertory.

[46] Gamber, *Reform*, p. 71: "It is obvious that exegetes, not liturgists, developed the new Order of Readings. What the exegetes apparently failed to consider is that most among the faithful simply do not have the necessary background and knowledge to understand, let alone appreciate, certain passages from Scripture; that they know little about salvation history prior to Christ; and that, therefore, there is little in the Pentateuch or in the Book of Kings that would have any real meaning to them." Cf. Romano Amerio, *Iota Unum: A Study of Changes in the Catholic Church in the XXth Century*, trans. Rev. John P. Parsons (Kansas City, Mo.: Sarto House, 1996), pp. 642–43: "The policy of putting as

*R.:* The revisions to the Liturgy of the Word were prompted by article 51 of the Liturgy Constitution, which states: "The treasures of the Bible are to be opened up more lavishly so that a richer fare may be provided for the faithful at the table of God's word." I agree that the new arrangement presents challenges both for the congregation and for the homilist. Most people cannot assimilate three readings in one sitting, especially considering that the second reading (Epistle) is usually unrelated thematically to the others. An alternative implementation of article 51, one that is not only pedagogically better but also accommodates the traditional Order of Readings, should not be too difficult to realize.[47] Shall we move on to the Preparation of the Gifts, or Offertory?

*T.:* Here we find a veritable showcase of evidence supporting the traditionalist claim that the new Mass was de-

---

much as possible of the treasures of the Bible before the people of God during worship runs into a serious difficulty, inasmuch as it frustrates the use of the memory as an educational principle. In the traditional rite, in the course of the liturgical year the people would hear on Sundays a single annual cycle of Gospel passages.... The annual recurrence of these readings, with an accompanying sermon, eventually had the effect of stamping no small part of the Master's teaching upon the minds of the faithful. The principal element in remembering something is the repetition of a single impression. Because man's knowledge comes to very little without memory, the knowledge of the Bible produced by the new lectionary is very slight, inasmuch as the same thing only recurs every third year, and thus cannot become clearly stamped in one's memory."

[47] Cf. Rev. Brian W. Harrison, O.S., "What Do We Do Now? Part III: The Gamber Proposal as Long-Term Solution", *Adoremus Bulletin* 1, no. 3 (January 1996): 7; reprinted in Appendix III, below, pp. 151–93. Harrison proposes that the Epistle and Gospel of the old Missal be retained as the lessons for Year A of a different three-year cycle, while redistributing for Years B and C only the most pastorally and catechetically valuable readings from the new rite.

signed to conciliate Protestants. The revised Offertory rite represents a practical undermining of the theology of the Mass as the renewal of the sacrifice of the Cross for the remission of sins. Note how all the unambiguous references to the sacrificial nature of the Mass have been excised: the two *Suscipe* prayers, the *Offerimus tibi*, and the *Veni, Sanctificator*. The prayers accompanying the offering of the bread and wine are fine examples of equivocation: the expressions *panis vitæ* (bread of life) and *potus spiritalis* (spiritual drink) could mean anything. The new Offertory prayers no longer explicitly express Catholic doctrine concerning the sacrifice of the Mass. The suppression of any reference to a sacrificial victim (*hostia*) before the *Orate, fratres* means that even the reference to sacrifice in this prayer could be interpreted in a Protestant sense, as a sacrifice of praise and thanksgiving. Small wonder that high-ranking churchmen protested to Paul VI that the new *Ordo Missae* "represents, both as a whole and in its details, a striking departure from the Catholic theology of the Mass as it was formulated in Session XXII of the Council of Trent".[48]

---

[48] Letter of Alfredo Cardinal Ottaviani and Antonio Cardinal Bacci to Pope Paul VI, September 25, 1969, known in English-speaking countries as *The Ottaviani Intervention*. Ottaviani formerly headed the Vatican's Holy Office (now the Sacred Congregation for the Doctrine of the Faith). Bacci during this time served on the Vatican Congregations for Religious, Causes of Saints, and Catholic Education. The Council of Trent taught in its 22nd Session that the Mass is the unbloody renewal of the Lord's bloody sacrifice offered on the Cross: "For, it is one and the same Victim, the same one now offering by the ministry of the priests as He who then offered Himself on the Cross, the manner of offering alone being different" (*The Sources of Catholic Dogma*, trans. Roy J. Deferrari from the 30th ed. of Henry Denzinger's *Enchiridion Symbolorum* [St. Louis: B. Herder Book Co., 1957], no. 940).

*R.:* The Offertory prayers in the preconciliar Missals are all importations from other texts (mostly Gallican) into the Roman Mass during the first centuries of the Middle Ages. From the standpoint of liturgical evolution, even Gamber finds no fault with the new prayers: the formulas are from ancient times, probably the words used at the blessing of bread and wine in a Jewish meal at the time of Christ. More to the point, however, the vocabulary of the Tridentine Offertory prayers was too sacrificial given their location: we should not speak of the unconsecrated bread and wine as the "spotless victim" (*immaculatam hostiam*) and "chalice of salvation" (*calicem salutis*). Father James Crichton, in his commentary on *Sacrosanctum Concilium* published soon after its promulgation, explains:

> The offertory, far from being a simple rite of presenting the offerings of the people, in which they took their part... has become an almost purely private act of the priest, accompanied by a number of prayers which are positively misleading. They speak of the bread and wine as if they were already consecrated and all the ingenuity of commentary in the world cannot remove faulty impressions. That is why it was once called "the Little Canon." [49]

*T.:* As "positively misleading" as Father Crichton finds the Tridentine Offertory prayers, any half-educated Catholic knows that the bread and wine do not become the Savior's Body and Blood until the Consecration. He and

---

[49] J. D. Crichton, *The Church's Worship: Considerations on the Liturgical Constitution of the Second Vatican Council* (New York: Sheed & Ward, 1964), p. 141.

the other critics of the old Offertory seem to have unwittingly adopted an extreme literalism. There is another perspective on the matter:

> What...[they] know is that what are on the altar until the Consecration are bread and wine. What they fail to appreciate is what they are there as: symbolically, already the Body and Blood of Christ. During the action of offering the "host" and "chalice" at the Tridentine offertory, the priest says prayers of sacrificial offering, which all admit refer to the Body and Blood of Christ, not to bread and wine. In that sense critics and defenders of the Tridentine offertory rightly refer to it as "anticipatory"; the one group to discredit it, the other to defend it.[50]

Those who fail to appreciate the anticipatory character of these prayers—an idea not exclusive to the traditional Roman Mass[51]—need to step back from the trees to see the forest:

> [Their] thinking...is so preoccupied with the fact of transubstantiation itself, that they do not go on to relate transubstantiation to the Eucharistic Sacrifice. If one's concern is to teach transubstantiation, one will emphasize that on the altar, until the Consecration, are bread and wine, and that afterwards, by the

---

[50] W.J. Morgan, "The Theology of Sacrifice", *The Latin Mass*, fall 2000, p. 56.

[51] The Byzantine Cherubic Hymn, sung while the gifts are brought in solemn procession to the altar (the so-called Great Entrance), calls the bread and wine "the king of all things". The corresponding *Sigêsatô* hymn of the Antiochian liturgy says: "The king of kings, Christ our God comes."

total conversion of their substances, one has the Body
and Blood of Christ together with His soul and Divinity. If one is primarily concerned—as one should
be in expounding the Mass prayers—with the Sacrifice being offered, one will give due attention to
the symbolic role (prior to the Consecration) of the
bread and wine as signs of the Body and Blood of
Christ separated in sacrificial death; which sacrifice
one wishes to offer to God.[52]

*R.:* It is unlikely that anyone preoccupied with transubstantiation would want to devise a rite acceptable to Protestants. Yet you allege that the new Mass was created
precisely for that purpose.

    *T.:* You are missing the point. The Real Presence of
the Lord's Body and Blood under the species of bread and
wine—the Eucharist as *sacrament*—is but one dimension
of the eucharistic mystery. The Eucharist is *first and foremost* the sacrifice of the Cross, re-presented sacramentally
on the altar. When this is forgotten or obscured, the Mass
is viewed simply as a ceremony for producing the Blessed
Sacrament, and not as the means that Christ gave us in
order to unite ourselves with him in the very act by which
he redeemed the world. I fear that this truth is simply
unknown to many, if not most, Catholics today:

    Even among the older generations the indications are
    that any concept of the Mass as being *offered* is lim-
    ited to the sense in which any act of worship or pi-
    ety, for example a decade of the Rosary, can be offered
    for a certain intention. The fact that Christ our Me-

---

[52] Morgan, "Theology", p. 57.

diator has given to His Church a perpetual means by which we can make our own effective offering of His sacrificial death through the ministry of the ordained priesthood is fast fading from consciousness.[53]

In their ecumenical zeal, the architects of the new Mass muted the theology of sacrifice by decimating the Tridentine Offertory. Even your fellow reformist Father Brian Harrison seems to be of this opinion.[54] What is more, the anomaly of offering Mass facing the people only makes matters worse: the Mass is made to appear as a commemorative meal at which the "presider" repeats a narrative for the people to hear. The congregation focuses unduly on the human celebrant and upon itself. The impression is given that the Mass is essentially the representation of the Last Supper, whereas in fact the Mass is the unbloody renewal of Calvary.

    *R.:* I wholeheartedly concur with you that the practice of celebrating toward the people obscures not only the sacrificial but, as Cardinal Ratzinger has shown,[55] also the eschatological and cosmic dimensions of the Eucharist.

---

[53] Ibid., p. 59.

[54] "Gamber maintains that 'Nothing is to be said against new offertory prayers' (although he admits that 'the recently developed texts are less than satisfactory'), because originally there were practically no offertory prayers, anyway. Many of us, on the contrary, believe there is much 'to be said against new offertory prayers' because those which the Church used for over half a millennium before Vatican II expressed so perfectly the sacrificial nature of the Mass, and because their suppression now cannot but appear as an attempt to downplay that essential characteristic of the Eucharist" (Brian W. Harrison, O.S., "Excellent Contribution", review of *The Reform of the Roman Liturgy*, by Msgr. Klaus Gamber, in *The Latin Mass*, March–April 1994, pp. 38–39).

[55] Ratzinger, *Feast of Faith*, pp. 139–45; and idem, *The Spirit of the Liturgy*, trans. John Saward (San Francisco: Ignatius Press, 2000), pp. 74–84.

But let us leave the question of orientation aside for now. You assert that the changes to the Offertory rite amount to a tacit denial of the sacrifice of the Mass in order to appeal to Protestants. I'm not quite convinced of that. There is another way of accounting for the revised Offertory, which requires a brief historical review.

*T.:* Please go on.

*R.:* During the late Middle Ages, the connection between the sacrifice of the Cross and the sacrifice of the Mass was largely misunderstood. Particular abuses further obscured a correct understanding of the eucharistic sacrifice. For fear of undercutting the unique sacrifice of the Cross, the Protestant Reformers denied the sacrificial nature of the Mass and even went so far as to call the Mass idolatrous (Heidelberg Catechism) and abominable (Smalcaldian Articles). The Council of Trent clarified the relation between the eucharistic sacrifice and the sacrifice of the Cross: In the Mass, Christ's all-sufficient sacrifice offered on the Cross is rendered present sacramentally. The Mass, in other words, is a representation (literally, a making present again) and an application of the sacrifice of Calvary and, thus, is neither a repetition of the unique event of the crucifixion nor a new sacrificial action of Christ. Theologians after Trent endeavored to explain exactly how this is so. One of the good fruits of the preconciliar liturgical movement has been a renewed understanding of the biblical concept of memorial (Hebrew=*zikkaron*; Greek=*anamnêsis*) as the making present of a past event in salvation history: The Eucharist is the sacrament of Christ's unique redemptive sacrifice; that is to say, the Eucharist actualizes throughout history the Lord's eternal sacrifice on Calvary.[56] This recovery lies at the heart of the theology of the Paschal Mystery and has proved very helpful in clearing up misunderstandings between Catholics and Protestants. I suppose the concern to respect the indissolubility of the Eucharist as sacrament and as sacrifice is what motivated the excision of sacrificial language from the Offertory rite. In other words, there is no sacrifice until the sacrament has been confected.

*T.:* The Paschal Mystery theology interprets the ideas of eucharistic sacrifice and Real Presence within the central category of memorial. It has been argued recently—and compellingly, to my satisfaction—that this "renewal" of eucharistic theology is chiefly responsible for the liturgical reform's abandonment of Trent's definition of the Mass.[57]

---

[56] Especially influential in bringing about this shift were two Benedictine theologians, Dom Anscar Vonier, *A Key to the Doctrine of the Eucharist* (1925), and Dom Odo Casel, *The Mystery of Christian Worship* (1932). Whereas post-Tridentine theological manuals treated the sacramental and sacrificial aspects of the Eucharist separately, these and other *ressourcement* theologians adopt a more holistic view: The Eucharist is the sacrament of Christ's Body and Blood and of Christ's sacrifice. This begs the question: How can past historical events be made present now? Only if that past event contains a metahistorical reality, specifically, the Divinity and glorified Humanity of Christ.

[57] Society of St. Pius X, *Problem of the Liturgical Reform*, passim. What makes this treatise unique among the numerous critiques of Paul VI's liturgical reform is its thesis that the theology of the "Paschal Mystery"—a term popularized by the twentieth-century theological and liturgical movements—constitutes a new understanding of Redemption that is incompatible with the traditional teaching of the Church. Therefore, "whatever distinguishes the Paschal mystery from the Redemption—the change of name corresponds to the radical change of ideas—will distinguish the new missal from the traditional missal" (p. 36). Moreover (so the thesis), it was this heterodox view of the redemption that led to the reform's diminution of the classic conception of the eucharistic sacrifice.

*R.:* The thesis merits consideration, inasmuch as the liturgical movement was shaped by the results of biblical research, liturgical theology, a patristic renewal, and ecumenical discussions. After all, a house is only as sound as its foundation. Is the foundation thoroughly bad, or is it simply a matter of repairing a few cracks in it? Does the problem concern the Paschal Mystery theology per se or, rather, some mistaken inferences drawn from it? I suspect that those who denounce the Paschal Mystery theology are doing the wrong thing for the right reason. They reject the idea of memorial because they interpret it in the modern sense of that word—a mere commemoration. Unfortunately, there is no word in the English language to convey the biblical sense of memorial. The word "memorial" as it is commonly used implies that the eucharistic liturgy is merely a remembrance of the events of the Upper Room and Calvary. So the problem is essentially one of terminology, just as the early christological and trinitarian disputes owed largely to language.

*T.:* Notwithstanding the critique of the Paschal Mystery theology, one is entitled to doubt that the good of the Church warranted a drastic revision of the Offertory rite. Moving on to the heart of the Mass, we find that the three new Eucharistic Prayers, from a stylistic standpoint, "constitute a complete break with the traditional rite: they have been newly created using Oriental and Gallican texts as models." [58] In no way, then, do they represent a natural development from the classical Roman rite. Nor is there warrant for them in *Sacrosanctum Concilium*. If anything, their introduction violates article 38, which requires that

---

[58] Gamber, *Reform*, p. 55.

the substantive unity of the rite be safeguarded. Even if I were to concede to you on the Offertory question, you would have to admit, on the evidence of these fabricated canons alone, that Paul VI's *Ordo Missae* constitutes a new rite of Mass and not merely a renewed or "touched up" form of the former rite.

*R.:* How curious that you would object to the new Eucharistic Prayers on the basis of their non-Roman origins, considering that much of the Tridentine Mass, as we have seen, borrows from non-Roman liturgies. At any rate, the 1970 Missal retains the Roman Canon as "Eucharistic Prayer I", thereby preserving continuity with tradition.

*T.:* That's only because Paul VI didn't let the Consilium[59] have its way: it wanted to drop the Roman Canon altogether![60] Besides, the celebrant is not required to use

---

[59] The Consilium was the commission established by Paul VI in 1964 to implement *Sacrosanctum Concilium*. It ceased as a separate entity in 1970.

[60] See Davies, *Pope Paul's New Mass*, pp. 46 and 329, both times citing Douglas Woodruff's pamphlet, *Paul VI* (London: Catholic Truth Society, 1974), p. 11. Vincentian Father (later Archbishop) Annibale Bugnini, the Consilium's secretary from 1964 to 1969, admits that the Consilium deemed the Roman Canon problematic on account of its structural defects and limitations; but nowhere in his posthumous chronicle of the reform does he substantiate the claim that the traditional Canon's suppression was desired. See Annibale Bugnini, C.M., *The Reform of the Liturgy, 1948–1975*, trans. Matthew J. O'Connell (Collegeville, Minn.: Liturgical Press, 1990) [the authorized English translation of *La riforma liturgica, 1948–1975* (Rome: Centro Liturgico Vincenziano—Edizioni Liturgiche, 1983)]. Additional confutation of the charge comes from Oratorian Fr. Louis Bouyer, also a member of the Consilium: "Along the way the *Consilium* naturally came across those pseudo-critical interpretations of the Roman canon which tended either to cast it aside altogether or to refashion it fancifully.... [T]he *Consilium* rightly refused to involve itself in such a disastrous deadlock" (*Eucharist*, p. 446). In the summer of 1966, the Pope ruled against drastic revisions to the Canon, while permitting the composition of new Eucharistic Prayers to be used as alternatives (see Bugnini, *Reform*, pp. 449–50).

the Roman Canon, which is why most Catholics seldom hear it anymore. So the "continuity" of the new Missal with the liturgical tradition of the Latin Church depends on whether or not the celebrant uses the Roman Canon. How preposterous!

*R.:* You do have a point. While there is more to a liturgical rite than its Eucharistic Canon, we should not understate the degree to which the Canon is the defining feature of a rite, at least in the West. As an aside, you may be interested to know that the Jesuit liturgical scholar Father Josef Jungmann (a member of the Consilium) finds in the Liturgy Constitution vague justification for the new Eucharistic Prayers. The Roman Canon, he observes, is almost exclusively a prayer of sacrifice and petition, having little connection to the Prefaces (the various introductions to the Canon), wherein the dominant note is that of thanksgiving. While containing no explicit regulations concerning the Canon, the Constitution decrees that the rites and prayers of the Mass facilitate the people's active participation in the mystery thereby signified. From this general principle, Jungmann syllogizes:

> It was clear from the start that if the Canon was to help the people understand the mystery of redemption that becomes present in the Mass, a mere translation of the Roman Canon into the mother tongue would not be of much use. So the reform was faced with two alternatives: either to revise the text of the Canon itself, in which case the move would be in the direction of enriching the Preface and, above all, of shifting all intercessions to bring them together at the end of the Canon; or to introduce alongside the

traditional Roman Canon other forms of the Eucharistic Prayer. Pope Paul VI decided upon the latter alternative.[61]

The logic is tenuous, but it does furnish a background for understanding the insertion of these new Eucharistic Prayers into the Roman Missal.

*T.:* Quite a stretch, that! At any rate, the new prayers are fabrications placed alongside the 1500-year-old Roman Canon, the very substance of the Roman rite. Equally noteworthy is the apparently senseless relocation of the words *"Mysterium fidei"* (the mystery of faith), which had been part of the Consecration formula since the seventh century. In the new *Ordo*, the phrase comes *after* the words of Consecration and serves as a cue for the memorial acclamation— something alien to all rites of the Church save the Coptic. "Besides," says Gamber, "it is an abrupt change from addressing God the Father to addressing God the Son."[62]

*R.:* I agree that the memorial acclamation, which is addressed to Christ, seems out of place in the Eucharistic Prayer, which as a whole is addressed to the Father *through* the Son. Contrary to the claims of some traditionalists, however, the phrase *"Mysterium fidei"* is not required for a valid Consecration.

*T.:* Still, we should not underestimate the impact of so seemingly trivial a change. A recent addition to the flood of literature critical of the new liturgy explains how

---

[61] Josef A. Jungmann, S.J., *The Mass: An Historical, Theological and Pastoral Survey*, ed. Mary Ellen Evans, trans. Julian Fernandes, S.J. (Collegeville, Minn.: Liturgical Press, 1976), p. 199.

[62] Gamber, *Reform*, p. 56.

the relocation of the *Mysterium fidei* is emblematic of the reform's devaluation of the sacrificial aspect of Holy Mass:

> The traditional missal places the expression "*Mysterium fidei*" amid the very words of consecration in order to solicit an act of faith in the real presence of Christ brought about through transubstantiation, and also to mark the culminating point of the Mass. Here is the sacrifice; Christ is present in an immolated state wherein the species of bread and wine signify the separation of His Body and Blood during His Passion. In the new Missal the "Mystery of Faith" is no longer the sacrificial consecration, but all the mysteries of Christ's life proclaimed and remembered together. "Let us proclaim the mystery of faith: dying you destroyed our death, rising you restored our life. Lord Jesus, come in glory."[63]

*R.:* The critique is specious. First of all, the words "Let us proclaim" do not precede the phrase "*Mysterium fidei*" in the Latin Missal. More to the point, there is no historical basis for asserting that the *Mysterium fidei* was intended to bolster faith in the Real Presence. The phrase is taken from 1 Timothy 3:9, where it occurs in a different context, namely, that the deacons must sincerely believe in "the mystery of faith". It *may* have become associated with the Consecration of the wine by reason of the fact that the preparation of the chalice was the deacon's task. We simply do not know how or when or

---

[63] Society of St. Pius X, *Problem of the Liturgical Reform*, p. 12.

why the phrase was inserted.[64] As for its indicating the
"culminating point of the Mass", one could argue that
the *Per ipsum* doxology, rather than the Consecration, is
the pinnacle of the Mass. If the purpose of the Mass
were solely to make Christ present in the Blessed Sacrament, then the Consecration would indeed be its culmi-
nation. But since the Consecration is ordered toward the
offering of sacrifice—the immolation of Christ our Priest
and spotless Victim—the doxology crowns the sacrifice,
as it were: "*Through him [Christ], with him, in him, in the
unity of the Holy Spirit, all glory and honor is yours [Father].*"
The new rite expresses this more clearly than the old by
having the celebrant raise the chalice and paten as he
says or sings the doxology.

*T.:* Since you are eager to affirm the primacy of the
sacrificial nature of the Mass, what do you have to say
about the suppression of the *Placeat tibi*? This final prayer
of the Mass was unacceptable to the Protestant Reformers
because of its unequivocal reference to the priest having
offered sacrifice. Like the traditional Offertory prayers, it,
too, was a casualty of the conciliar reform.

*R.:* Like so many of the prayers in the 1962 Missal,
the *Placeat tibi* was originally a private prayer that was later
incorporated into the Order of Mass. It was initially said
by the priest privately after Mass.

*T.:* And what need was there of rearranging the conclusion of the Mass and eliminating the Last Gospel?

---

[64] Jungmann, *MRR*, 2:199–201, rejects the popular explanation that the
phrase was originally spoken by the deacon to indicate to the congregation
the consecration of the wine.

*R.:* Before the Tridentine reform, the Last Gospel was read as a private devotion by the priest immediately after Mass, having left the altar. By dropping the Last Gospel and swapping the locations of the dismissal and blessing, the 1970 Missal restores proper order to the end of Mass. The reading of the Last Gospel undercut the dismissal: the people were told to go (*Ite, missa est*), yet more followed. In the new rite, Mass is truly finished when the dismissal is given. In line with this logic, not even a final hymn is envisioned. Recessional hymns, though commonplace, are not (and never were) an integral part of the Mass.

*T.:* Now let us consider the orations and other prayers of the Mass. Father Anthony Cekada compared the texts of many of the Collects contained in the Missal of Paul VI with those of the Tridentine Missal and discovered a lengthy list of Catholic doctrines neglected in the new Missal, even in its official Latin edition: judgment, punishment for sin, the wickedness of sin as the greatest evil, detachment from the world, Purgatory, the souls of the departed, the Church Militant, the evils of heresy and schism, the merits of the saints, and miracles.[65] Each of these realities, as you well know, is rejected, redefined, or ignored by "progressive" or Modernist Catholics. The virtual elimination of these concepts from the orations of the Pauline Missal is tantamount to an attack on the integrity of the Catholic faith. To shroud a substantial portion of these truths in obscurity or silence is to invite their denial. The alteration and elimination of many of the traditional prayers parallels the changes made by the Protestant Reformers. For example, they suppressed the

---

[65] Cekada, *Problems with the Prayers of the Modern Mass.*

*Libera nos* after the *Pater noster* because it invoked the intercession of the saints. The version of this prayer adapted for the new *Ordo* has the invocation of the saints removed. Is the Missal of 1970 doctrinally sound? Yes— but only if you subscribe to a minimalist understanding of orthodoxy. The absence of explicit heresy no more betokens a sound rite than the absence of arsenic betokens a nourishing and tasty meal.

*R.:* I have read Father Cekada's treatise and find it incontrovertible. Vatican II never even hinted at the wholesale replacement of the ancient Collects. Indeed, many of these venerable prayers were abolished or expurgated because they expressed ideas unpopular with liberal Catholics. A recovery of these traditional Collects, even if they were to be made options alongside the new ones, would go a long way in augmenting the continuity of the reformed rite with tradition.

*T.:* Cannot much the same be said of the multiple signs of the cross and genuflections that were done away with? These gestures communicated the faith without words and helped foster a sense of adoration and contemplation. The *Novus Ordo*, however, is affectively sterile. It attempts to express the faith through an inflation of words, explanations, and commentaries—which makes it all the more difficult for the people to *pray*.

*R.:* I agree that, in many ways, the new rite is symbolically impoverished compared to the old. As James Hitchcock has pointed out:

Although religious ritual needs to be intelligible to worshipers in at least its fundamental meanings and its major contours, too great a concern with the intelligibility of the rites tends to be counter-productive. . . . The "fallacy of explicitness" has been responsible for much liturgical impoverishment, since some liturgists (and some worshipers) appeared to assume that once the symbols had been "explained" there was no longer any need for them. The goal of some liturgical reform appeared to be that of translating as many symbols as possible into words, with the eventual elimination of symbols altogether.[66]

While keeping in mind the Council's desire to replace extravagance with "noble simplicity",[67] Hitchcock's suggestions for improvement deserve to be taken seriously:

The puritan mentality should be recognized as, on the whole, a destructive feature of contemporary liturgical life. Every effort should be made to restore a worship which is rich, complex, and even occasionally ornate. The use of incense, bells, candles, and traditional gestures should be revived where it has lapsed. Signs of the cross, genuflections, and striking the breast should be reinstated while they still have meaning for many worshipers.[68]

---

[66] Hitchcock, *Recovery*, p. 176.

[67] SC, no. 124.

[68] Hitchcock, *Recovery*, p. 175. Cf. Dietrich von Hildebrand, *Trojan Horse in the City of God: The Catholic Crisis Explained* (Manchester, N.H.: Sophia Institute Press, 1993), p. 237: "The faithful are not drawn into the world of Christ only by their faith or by strict symbols. They are also drawn into a higher world by the beauty of the church, its sacred atmosphere, the splendor of the altar, the rhythm of the liturgical texts, and by the sublimity of the Gregorian chant or other truly sacred music—for example, a mass by Mozart or by Bach. Even the odor of incense has a meaningful function to perform in this direction. The use of all channels capable of introducing us into the sanctuary is

*T.:* Agreed. Vatican II wasn't the only council to call for the simplification of the rubrics and ritual actions; Trent did the same. Noble simplicity, however, does not mean bleakness but rather clarity of form and intention. Authentic ritual developments no more contradict simplicity than doctrinal developments compromise doctrinal purity. Now that we have compared the prayers and ritual actions of the two Missals, I'll let Michael Davies voice my assessment of the reform:

> Examine the changes that have been made, and find one—just one—that the good of the Church *genuinely and certainly required.* You will search in vain. Find one—just one—that has made us better and more spiritual Catholics. You will search in vain. Fine one that has contributed to the unity of the Church. You will search in vain. Find one that has grown organically from forms already existing. You will search in vain. Did the *Judica me* really have to go? Was the beautiful double *Confiteor* truly a cause of spiritual atrophy? Did kneeling at the *Incarnatus* cause great harm to the cause of doctrinal orthodoxy? Were those sublime Offertory prayers alienating young Catholics from the Faith? Did the good of the Church genuinely and certainly require that the inspired words of the Last Gospel no longer be read at the conclusion of every Mass?

Traditional Catholics are often accused of disobedience to the Council. There has indeed been

---

deeply realistic and deeply Catholic. It is truly existential and plays a great role in helping us lift up our hearts." For a more recent critique along these lines, see David Torevell, *Losing the Sacred: Ritual, Modernity and Liturgical Reform* (Edinburgh: T&T Clark, 2000).

disobedience to the Council, disobedience on a massive scale, but it has been on the part of those who took it upon themselves to defy the Council's Liturgy Constitution and destroy the most venerable rite in Christendom, which it had commanded should be preserved and fostered in every way.[69]

*R.:* I think the good of the Church certainly *did* require a recovery of a communal sense of worship. That was a chief aim of the Liturgy Constitution. You and I may share Mr. Davies' dim appraisal of the Consilium's work, but I do not agree with his attribution of most (if not all) of the changes to a deliberate protestantization of the liturgy: a table instead of an altar, Mass facing the people, Communion in the hand and under both species, the removal of Offertory prayers and prayers at the foot of the altar, ambiguity in the Eucharistic Prayers. As he sees it, the Consilium sought to make the Mass resemble a Protestant (specifically, Calvinist) communion service. I submit, however, that many of the changes that seem to represent concessions to non-Catholics were in fact motivated by the desire to reproduce the worship of the early Church, or at least what was thought to be primitive Christian worship. For the Consilium, everything primitive was "pure" and therefore normative, while everything late mediaeval or Baroque was decadent and therefore had to go.[70] Hence,

---

[69] Michael Davies, "The New Mass: An Ecumenical Compromise", *The Latin Mass*, January–February 1993, p. 39.

[70] Cf. Joseph Cardinal Ratzinger, *Spirit of the Liturgy*, p. 82: "As I see it, the problem with a large part of modern liturgiology is that it tends to recognize only antiquity as a source, and therefore normative, and to regard everything developed later, in the Middle Ages and through the Council of Trent, as decadent. And so one ends up with dubious reconstructions of the most an-

the removal of so many prayers, gestures, and signs that had accrued to the Roman rite during the Middle Ages. Even though Pope Pius XII roundly condemned this primitivism in his encyclical *Mediator Dei* (November 20, 1947)— "archaeologism" was the word he used—its influence on the conciliar reform is undeniable. That there is not a single reference to *Mediator Dei* in *Sacrosanctum Concilium* is quite telling. Archaeologism was more a trend or an ideology than a formal heresy, but it was just as devastating to Catholic worship as iconoclasm or Protestantism. To put it another way: if the new liturgy seems "less Catholic" than the old, it is because the Consilium sought to replicate the worship of the early Christians according to some false archaeological ideal, not because they subscribed to the heretical views of Luther, Calvin, Zwingli, and Cranmer.

*T.:* Yet six Protestant "observers" advised the Consilium in the formulation of the new liturgical rites! This fact is well documented.[71] How do you explain that?

*R.:* Father Francis Clark, an authority on the English Reformation and Anglican Orders, offers the proper perspective on this. Even though he was responding to criticisms of the revised Catholic ordination rite of 1968, his remarks have broader import and help to avert extremism:

---

cient practice, fluctuating criteria, and never-ending suggestions for reform, which lead ultimately to the disintegration of the liturgy that has evolved in a living way."

[71] For example, Davies, *Pope Paul's New Mass*, appendix 3. But cf. Bugnini, *Reform*, p. 200: "What was the role of the observers at the Consilium? Simply to 'observe'. Their attitude at the meetings of the Consilium was one of great reserve and unobtrusiveness. They never took part in the discussions, never asked to speak."

Even if some of the promoters of the new Roman rites in the decade following Vatican II were animated by a questionable theological liberalism, even if Protestant "observers" were accorded a role which enabled them to influence (informally but effectively) the deliberation of the Roman *Consilium* which drafted the new rites, there is not the slightest doubt that the supreme authority that sanctioned the changes, the Holy See, was determined to maintain intact the full doctrine of the Mass and the priesthood. The new forms, liturgically impoverished though they are, are nevertheless still vested with the sacred significance which the supreme authority of the Catholic Church attaches to its sacraments, ministry, and rites. The documents of the Second Vatican Council and the teaching of Pope Paul VI are the contemporary overall context which objectively supplies the due meaning which is no longer explicit in the ritual forms. This is the overriding *determinatio ex adiunctis* which safeguards the sacramental significance and validity of the new rites.[72]

Let me add that at least one of these Protestant observers, Frère Max Thurian of the French ecumenical Taizé community, was ordained a Catholic priest in 1987 and actually endorsed a return to the celebration of Mass *ad orientem*, that is, with priest and people facing the same direction,

---

[72] Quoted in Michael Davies, *The Order of Melchisedech: A Defence of the Catholic Priesthood*, 2d ed. (Harrison, N.Y.: Roman Catholic Books, 1993), p. xxi. The *"determinatio ex adiunctis"* can be translated as the "determination from its setting", that is, from the connotation of the ceremony as a whole or from the traditional teaching of the Church.

toward the East.[73] Does this sound like someone who rejects the traditional Catholic theology of the Eucharist?

*T.:* "No longer explicit in the ritual forms", Clark says. In other words, the ritual no longer clearly expresses the theology. Isn't that incriminating enough? But to answer your question: One can support a return to the traditional, *ad orientem* celebration and still not believe in the sacrificial nature of the Mass. The eastward position signifies the transcendent and "cosmic" dimensions of the liturgy. I wonder if Brother Thurian would have become a Catholic priest if he had had to celebrate the Tridentine Mass, with its explicit references to offering sacrifice, its invocations of our Lady and the saints, its multiple kisses of the altar and genuflections?

*R.:* Conjecture of that sort is futile. Judging from the documents he either edited or wrote personally, it is evident that Thurian accepted the Catholic understanding of the Eucharist as both sacrament and sacrifice.[74]

---

[73] Fr. Max Thurian, "The Liturgy and Contemplation", *L'Osservatore Romano* (English ed.), July 24, 1996, pp. 2, 4.

[74] See, for example, *Baptism, Eucharist and Ministry*, Faith and Order paper no. 111 (the "Lima Document"), ed. Max Thurian (Geneva: World Council of Churches, 1982), no. E8: "The Eucharist is the sacrament of the unique sacrifice of Christ, who ever lives to make intercession for us. It is the memorial of all that God has done for the salvation of the world. What it was God's Will to accomplish in the incarnation, life, death, resurrection and ascension of Christ, God does not repeat. These events are unique and can neither be repeated nor prolonged. In the memorial of the Eucharist, however, the Church offers its intercession in communion with Christ, our great High Priest."

The commentary following this paragraph reads: "It is in the light of the significance of the Eucharist as intercession that references to the Eucharist in Catholic theology as 'propitiatory sacrifice' may be understood. The understanding is *that there is only one expiation, that of the unique sacrifice of the cross, made actual in the Eucharist* and presented before the Father in the intercession

*Distinguishing between the Rite and Its Common Usage*

*T.:* Perhaps it comes down to what is called the *sensus fidei*, the supernatural sense of the faith: we traditionalists prefer the old Mass because the new Mass looks and feels Protestant—a Communion table instead of an altar of sacrifice, the "presider" facing the people and reciting a narrative, lay persons in the sanctuary (if there even *is* a clearly defined sanctuary), Communion received in the hand. We should consider the matter from the perspective of the average man in the pew, who is, after all, the alleged beneficiary of the liturgical reforms. It has been said that:

> Someone from 1862 would not have had any problem recognizing the Mass celebrated according to the Missal of 1962, promulgated by Pope John XXIII. To be sure, there had been some changes made (feasts added, the insertion of St. Joseph's name into the Canon, making the prayers after Low Mass optional, Pope Pius XII's reformation of the Holy Week liturgies). However, the Mass, *in se*, would have been

---

of Christ and of the Church for all humanity. In the light of the biblical conception of memorial, all churches might want to review the old controversies about 'sacrifice' and deepen their understanding of the reasons why other traditions than their own have either used or rejected this term" [italics added].

Thurian presided over the steering group that drafted this and other documents of the Faith and Order Commission of the World Council of Churches. Many evangelical Protestants took issue with *BEM*'s affirmation of the Eucharist as an "actualization" of Christ's sacrifice. Notwithstanding *BEM*'s decidedly Catholic tone, it does seem to equate the notion of propitiation with "intercession", thus possibly compromising the full Catholic doctrine of the Mass; cf. the Vatican Response to *BEM* in *Origins* 17 (November 19, 1987): 409–10.

recognizable in 1962 to one who had lived in the previous century.[75]

Let us transport our hypothetical time traveler to today. Would he be able to recognize and feel at home with the contemporary rite of Mass?

*R.:* I believe he *would*, provided that the celebration were performed exactly as prescribed in the Roman Missal, with the priest and people facing the same direction for the prayers.[76] Lamentably, such celebrations of the Eucharist are rare, causing many people to equate abuses and problematic practices with the new rite itself. It should not be necessary to point out that liturgical abuses and questionable pastoral practices occurred before the Council as well as after. Father Peter Stravinskas' recollections echo what I have heard others say:

> Everything wasn't perfect in the "good old days." As an altar boy for 10 years under the pre-Conciliar liturgy, I personally witnessed hundreds of Masses which were sloppily and even sacrilegiously celebrated, with parts left out or mumbled over. The only difference

---

[75] Droleskey, "Enduring Ritual", p. 27.

[76] Cf. Denis Crouan, *The Liturgy Betrayed* (San Francisco: Ignatius Press, 2000), p. 16: "For many [traditionalists], all it takes for them to believe that they are assisting at an 'old Mass' is for the liturgy to be celebrated in Latin and at the high altar, that is to say, with the priest's back to the people. For example, many of the faithful who flock to the Abbey of Fontgombault in the belief that there they are going to find the ancient liturgy in all its completeness are totally unaware that the Benedictine monks have made 'adaptations' and are not therefore entirely faithful to the so-called rite 'of Saint Pius V' such as it was experienced in the past in the parishes. This example given in passing is a good illustration of the fuzziness that surrounds the question of liturgy in the present day."

between then and now is the fact that before the Council such irregularities were unknown to the average parishioner because the priest did not face the people and offered the liturgy in a language not familiar to most listeners. Chances are that priestly violators of liturgical norms today would have been (and some were) similarly disrespectful [of the] rubrics then.[77]

One might also recall the frequent (in some places, almost daily) Requiem Masses.[78] I think you'll agree that it is wrong to judge the pre-Vatican II liturgy on the basis of these anomalies, just as it is false to equate the reformed liturgy with contemporary abuses. Nevertheless, so much of the traditionalist criticism of the *Novus Ordo* concerns matters that are not inherent to the rite itself as codified in the liturgical books.

*T.:*  For instance?

*R.:*  Consider the things that trouble us both: ugly, inaccurate, and "politically correct" translations of Scripture and Mass texts (especially in the English-speaking countries); the priest offering sacrifice to God while eyeballing the people; Holy Communion given in the hand

---

[77] Peter Stravinskas, "Why I Oppose a Tridentine Prelature", *The Catholic World Report*, February 1992, p. 38.

[78] Requiem Masses, popularly called "black" Masses because of the liturgical color, were permitted (as they are today) on most ferial days (weekdays for which there was no observance of a feast or memorial). Many priests celebrated a "low" Requiem Mass at every available opportunity because it was considerably shorter than other Masses (e.g., the prayers at the foot of the altar were truncated, and the Last Gospel omitted). Although this practice did not violate any liturgical norm, it was symptomatic of a minimalism that pervaded many sectors of the Church and that persists today.

by "lay ministers" (sometimes while the celebrant is seated or while other priests are on hand); cloying informality and spontaneity. Traditionalists cite these practices to justify their rejection of the new Mass. Yet, these things have nothing to do with the Missal of Paul VI. The dreadful English translation of the Latin *editio typica* dates to 1973.[79] Communion in the hand was permitted by indult[80] in the United States only in 1977[81] and is nowhere mentioned in the 1970 Missal. The 1970 Missal and its subsequent revisions (1975 and 2000) take for granted that the celebrant is facing away from the congregation during the Liturgy of the Eucharist; otherwise, the rubrics would not direct him to face the people at various times.[82] Ecclesiastical law still prohibits the habitual use of extraordinary ministers of Holy Communion.[83]

---

[79] In most of the English-speaking world, the task of translating liturgical texts has (until quite recently) been monopolized by the International Commission on English in the Liturgy.

[80] An indult is a faculty granted by the Holy See to deviate from the common law of the Church.

[81] On June 17, 1977, the Congregation of Sacraments and Divine Worship approved the request of the National Council of Catholic Bishops to permit the option of receiving Communion in the hand.

[82] *Missale Romanum* (2000): Order of Mass, nos. 29, 127, 132, 141; General Instruction, nos. 107, 112, 115, 122 (paragraph numbers sometimes differ from the 1970 and 1975 editions). Gamber, *Reform*, chaps. 12–15, demonstrates convincingly that the precedents for freestanding altars with Mass "facing the people" have been highly exaggerated. Cf. my article, "[Re]Turn to the East?", *Adoremus Bulletin* 5, no. 8 (November 1999): 5, 8; also, Thomas V. Vaverek, "Celebration of Mass *ad Orientem* in a Parish Setting", *Homiletic and Pastoral Review* 100, no. 1 (October 1999): 26–32.

[83] Code of Canon Law (1983), can. 230, §§ 2 and 3. The interdicasterial Instruction on Certain Questions regarding the Collaboration of the Non-Ordained Faithful in the Sacred Ministry of Priests, *Ecclesiae de mysterio* (August 15, 1997), art. 8, §2, reiterates the "supplementary and extraordinary"

In the same vein, much of what people identify with the Tridentine Mass is *not* prohibited in the new rite of Mass. No Roman directive forbids the reception of Holy Communion on the tongue. Mass may be celebrated entirely in Latin. The priest may stand in front of the altar throughout the Offertory and Canon, facing the same direction as the people.[84] Take away the abuses and employ all the traditional options, and our hypothetical time traveler would feel at home with the reformed liturgy. As Cardinal Ratzinger observes: "The differences in the liturgy with the new liturgical books, as it is actually practiced and celebrated in various places, is often much greater than the differences between the old and new liturgies when celebrated according to the rubrics of the liturgical books."[85]

*T.:* The disparity among celebrations of the new Mass from place to place is a result of the new *Ordo* itself. Its loose structure invites both abuse and heterogeneity. The multiple options for Penitential Rites, Eucharistic Prayers, acclamations, and even language make it possible for two priests to celebrate the *Novus Ordo* strictly by the book,

---

nature of lay administration of the Eucharist. Laymen were first granted the faculty to distribute Holy Communion in extraordinary circumstances by the Sacred Congregation for the Discipline of the Sacraments in the Instruction *Immensae Caritatis* (January 29, 1973).

[84] Technically, the orientation of the celebration is not inherent to either rite. The rubrics of the 1570 Missal allow for the possibility of an altar facing the people, with the priest standing behind it, but this practice was very rare. In Europe, some priests celebrated Mass facing the people as early as the 1920s and 1930s.

[85] Conference in Rome held on October 24, 1998, commemorating the tenth anniversary of Pope John Paul II's Motu Proprio *Ecclesia Dei adflicta*.

and yet, because of the great leeway for personal preferences and adaptation, those two celebrations can look and feel very different. Two contrasting ways of perceiving the Church and her liturgy, the "liberal/progressive" and the "conservative/traditional", are equally at home in the new liturgy. This is a fact readily acknowledged even by those who do not advocate the traditionalist proposal.[86] In a word, the unity of the rite has been lost.

Say what you will about the possibility of celebrating the new Mass in Latin, with Gregorian chant and all the "traditional" options. Such celebrations are the exception, not the norm: the new Mass "on paper" does not correspond to reality—which is why the terms "Latin Mass" and "traditional Mass" are virtually synonymous with the *preconciliar* rite of Mass, the Tridentine Mass.[87]

With regard to your claim that our visitor from the nineteenth century could not tell the difference between the

---

[86] Rev. Brian W. Harrison, O.S., "Planning a 'Reform of the Reform'. Part II: Some Inadequate Solutions to the Eucharistic Liturgy Crisis", *Adoremus Bulletin* 1, no. 2 (December 1995): 1, 8; reprinted in Appendix III, below, pp. 151–93.

[87] "There are instances of the Novus Ordo being celebrated in a manner resembling the Roman rite, but they are relatively rare. What is generally seen everywhere and exclusively is a Novus Ordo characterized by practices utterly untypical of the Roman rite. Moreover, because of the so-called 'creativity' which varies from one so-called 'presider' to another, the Novus Ordo appears to be quite amorphous" (John W. Mole, O.M.I., "Liturgy and Peace", *The Latin Mass*, fall 2000, p. 28). Some of these "untypical" practices are now officially approved or at least tolerated (female altar servers, lay Eucharistic ministers, white vestments at Requiem Masses, "overlay" stoles worn over the chasuble, celebration *versus populum*), while others are not approved (sand in the holy water fonts for Lent, blue vestments for Advent, lay homilists, inviting small congregations to enter the sanctuary and gather around the altar).

old Mass and a Latin, "traditional style" *Novus Ordo* Mass: That may be true, but he would have to be deaf. The Canon of the new Mass is spoken aloud, whereas in the traditional Mass it is whispered. And were he to compare the Latin texts side by side, even without knowledge of Latin, he would find that several of the prayers of the former Missal have been senselessly truncated or omitted altogether in the new and that the *Ordo* has been dramatically rearranged in several places, as we have seen. To be sure, the new Mass can be celebrated with reverence and solemnity; but it is *not*, as its orthodox defenders claim, a normal development from the traditional liturgy. This is precisely why the ancient liturgy must be made widely available: to ensure the survival of a rite that expresses the fullness of the Catholic faith, the rite to which the Roman Catholic Church owes her identity.

## Other Considerations

*T.:* Apart from the liturgical texts and ritual actions, I can cite other examples of a real break with tradition. First, there is no tradition allowing those who are not in ecclesiastical orders to perform special liturgical roles. Even he who locked and unlocked the church had to be received into the minor order of porter.

*R.:* Even before the Council, most "acolytes" serving Mass and other liturgical functions in parish churches were not actually clerics in the minor order of acolyte; they were "altar boys". Laymen also served as subdeacons at Solemn Mass in the absence of an ordained subdeacon. The Council of Trent envisioned the conferral of minor orders on laymen not bound for the priesthood to be exercised in a stable and permanent fashion, but this did not happen.[88] Except in the seminaries, the minor orders had become more symbolic than real, which is why Paul VI abolished them in his 1972 Apostolic Letter *Ministeria Quaedam*. This document, together with the 1973 Instruction of the Sacred Congregation for the Discipline of the Sacraments, *Immensae Caritatis*, permits laymen to function as extraordinary ministers of Holy Communion when needed; but the Roman Missal does not treat this practice as normal. Parenthetically, what was *truly* out of keeping with the Church's long-standing liturgical tradition was the phenomenon of Solemn Mass carried out by three *priests*, one acting as celebrant, the others ministering as deacon and subdeacon. There was, furthermore, the unliturgical custom of the celebrant reading in a low voice those parts of the Mass that were simultaneously sung by others.[89] Liturgical incongruities are nothing new.

---

[88] Council of Trent, Session 23 (July 15, 1563), chap. 17 de ref. *The Canons and Decrees of the Sacred and Œcumenical Council of Trent*, ed. and trans. J. Waterworth (London: Dolman, 1848), pp. 186–87.

[89] With the advent in the thirteenth century of the *Missale plenarium*, which combined and replaced the sacramentary, the lectionary, and the choir books, we find the priest reading all the texts of the Mass, including the reader's part. This became the rule even at Solemn Mass, where readers, subdeacon, deacon, and choir were available. Moreover, the development at this time of the Low Mass as the norm (with the choir and assistants as optional extras) led to the increasing isolation of the celebrant and the loss of a sense of the liturgy as a corporate action of the whole Church singing and *doing*. The Tridentine reform missed this problem. Cf. Fortescue, *Mass*, p. 190: "Originally the celebrant said or sang his part and listened, like everyone else, to the other parts— the lessons, gradual and so on. Later, having become used to saying these other parts at Low Mass (in which he had to take the place of ministers and choir himself), he began to say them at High Mass too. So we have our present

*T.:* The custom of individuals performing liturgical roles not proper to them was a problem before the Council as well as after, the difference being that, whereas the priest monopolized the liturgy before the reform, the laity have taken over the sanctuary today. I think far greater harm is caused by the "clericalization of the laity" (as Pope John Paul II puts it) than by having priests function as deacons or read the *Gloria* while the *schola* sings it.

*R.:* I won't dispute that, but I would add that the common denominator is the failure to appreciate the hierarchical nature of the liturgy and the variety of liturgical roles. What other instances of a break with tradition would you cite?

*T.:* There is no tradition of casualness in the liturgy of any Catholic rite. The tradition of the Church has always moved in the direction of ever-greater formality, born of awe.

*R:* You imply that casualness and informality are integral to the rite itself. This is simply untrue. The Pauline Missal does allow for introductory remarks about the Mass of the day, which usually amounts to a tedious greeting. Nowhere, however, is the celebrant instructed to be irreverent or casual. Very early in our conversation, you accused me of attacking a straw man because I picked on the vocabulary used by traditionalists. Now *you* have set up a straw man.

---

arrangement that the celebrant also repeats in a low voice at the altar whatever is sung by the ministers and choir." Cf. Jungmann, *MRR*, 1:230; Dom Gregory Dix, *The Shape of the Liturgy* (London: A&C Black, 1945), pp. 599–600. The 1962 Missal did away with this anomaly.

*T.:* Fair enough. Let me qualify my remarks. Insofar as the new Missal allows the celebrant to address the people in his own words at various times, informality is built into the rite. Finally, there is no tradition of constructing a liturgical rite and imposing it on the faithful while forbidding the previous rite.

*R.:* Father Stravinskas' clarification on this point is instructive:

> Yes, never before has a rite been constructed as the 1969 Missal [*sic*], but with good reason. Prior to the Council of Trent, liturgical change occurred naturally and organically. Thus a practice would surface in a diocese and be incorporated into the liturgy of that diocese, sometimes spreading to an ecclesiastical province and beyond. Not infrequently, over a period of decades or centuries, that practice would be incorporated into the liturgy of Rome. The Fathers of Trent were so concerned about the contagion of heresy that they decided to regulate the Sacred Liturgy much more carefully and rigidly. As a result, forms of the Mass unique to individual dioceses, regions or religious orders were suppressed (unless they were more than 200 years old), and all future deviations from the standard Roman text were prohibited. In other words, organic development was stopped (and I would say, with very good reason), but that automatically meant that future development would have to be done "on the computer," in the sense that local experimentation would be replaced by historical study and construction of rites,

with immediate submission to the proper Roman authority for approval—before their use could be
sanctioned.[90]

So you see, it was the Tridentine reform that created a precedent for future reforms, as Paul VI implied in his Apostolic Constitution *Missale Romanum* (April 3, 1969). Organic
liturgical development actually ceased with Saint Pius V, not
Paul VI. Jungmann puts it vividly: "After fifteen hundred
years of unbroken development in the rite of the Roman
Mass, after the rushing and the streaming from every height
and out of every valley, the Missal of Pius V was indeed a
powerful dam holding back the waters or permitting them
to flow through only in firm, well-built canals." [91]

*T.:* But there is one way in which the Vatican II
reform differed sharply from that of Trent: "Unlike the
Reform of St. Pius V, which showed respect for cher-
ished local liturgies, that of Paul VI standardized a single
rite (excluding all others) by an 'executive fiat' with complete ruthlessness and a total disregard for the feelings of
the faithful." [92] Traditionalists are no longer the only
ones saying that this was a mistake.[93] Perhaps now we

---

[90] Fr. Peter Stravinskas, *The Catholic Answer*, November-December 2000,
p. 25. Although the revised *Ordo Missæ* and the Apostolic Constitution *Missale
Romanum* were published on Holy Thursday, April 3, 1969, the entire Missal
was not definitively approved and officially published until Holy Thursday,
March 26, 1970.

[91] Jungmann, *MRR*, 1:140.

[92] Michael Davies, "Non-Historical Liturgists", *Una Voce America news*, summer 2000, p. 11.

[93] For example, Msgr. Calkins: "On the pastoral and psychological level, I
believe that it was a serious mistake to suppress it virtually overnight. For
those who were less accustomed to using a hand missal in assisting at Mass and
who were less formed in certain forms of liturgical piety, the changes in the

are better positioned to discuss the status of the traditional Latin Mass in the Church today.

## What Place Ought the Preconciliar Roman Liturgy to Have?

### Is There a Right to the Old Rite?

*R.:* I think it is false to maintain (as some traditionalists do) that the preservation of the old liturgy is a *right*. Neither the Council nor the Supreme Pontiff makes an allowance for the perpetual preservation of the old rite.

*T.:* You are mistaken. Article 4 of the Constitution on the Liturgy states: "The sacred Council declares that holy Mother Church holds all lawfully recognized rites to be of equal right and dignity; that she wishes to preserve them in the future and to foster them in every way."

---

celebration of the Mass and the introduction of the vernacular were fairly readily received. For those whose piety had long been nourished by the solemn celebration of the Roman liturgy, there was more trauma. In my opinion this was primarily an error in judgment; it did not touch doctrine, but it is understandable that it caused uneasiness, discomfort and at times disorientation" (Address to Latin Liturgy Association, June 23, 2001).

Brian W. Harrison, O.S., "What Do We Do Now?", p. 8: "Vatican II never even hinted at the composition of new Eucharistic Prayers, not even as options.... They represent in effect the creation of a new rite, not the revision of the old. Gamber makes the telling point that to change anything so central as the 1500-year-old Canon, the very heart of the Roman rite and the fundamental defining point of its very identity in comparison with other rites, 'is synonymous with the destruction of the rite in its entirety.' And the Council certainly never dreamed of any such abolition of the old rite in order to replace it with a newly invented one."

Nichols, *Looking at the Liturgy*, p. 122: "The mistake to which poor advice led Paul VI of depriving many of the faithful of a hitherto canonical, indeed mandatory, rite to which they were attached must not be made again."

*R.:* But that article needs to be read in the light of the preceding one, which states: "Among these principles and norms there are some which can and should be applied both to the Roman rite and also to all the other rites. The practical norms which follow, however, should be taken as applying only to the Roman rite." Obviously, the Council intended changes to the "traditional" Roman rite. Article 4 was referring to rites other than the Roman: the Eastern rites of the Church were to be respected as equals to the Roman rite. Your interpretation of that article, however, implies that the Council Fathers merely *suggested* the implementation of the Constitution. The false idea that *Sacrosanctum Concilium* never intended to touch the existing Roman rite is frequently advanced in traditionalist propaganda.

*T.:* If you find my appeal to the Liturgy Constitution unpersuasive, what do you have to say about Pope John Paul II's indication that the old liturgy is indeed a *right*? In his motu proprio[94] *Ecclesia Dei adflicta* (July 2, 1988), he instructed the bishops to respect what he terms the "rightful aspirations" of traditionalists by permitting the use of the 1962 Missal and other liturgical books under certain conditions. Clearly the Holy Father deems the traditional Latin liturgy to be a right.

*R.:* But Rome's support for the Tridentine Mass has been equivocal at best. If the Pope had been truly enthusiastic about preserving the old rite, why did he not celebrate the Tridentine Mass for the faithful who gathered

---

[94] A *motu proprio* is a rescript issued by the pope on matters initiated by himself.

in Rome to commemorate the tenth anniversary of the *Ecclesia Dei* indult? Why does he not allow the celebration of the Tridentine Mass in Saint Peter's Basilica? Even if he personally takes no interest in the old rite, why did he not simply remove all restrictions from its use, leaving it entirely up to priests and faithful so disposed? This has not happened.

*T.:* Most bishops have been disobedient to the Holy Father in that they have chosen to ignore or stonewall *Ecclesia Dei*. (And who is to say that the removal of all restrictions will not happen?) You ask why the Pope has not simply given blanket approval for the use of the old rite. I would argue that he *has* effectively done so by calling for "a *wide and generous* application of the directives already issued some time ago by the Apostolic See for the use of the Roman Missal...of 1962."[95] To put a spin on your question: Why did the Pope not simply remind us that Latin and Gregorian chant, key characteristics of the "Latin liturgical tradition", are not forbidden in the new rite (quite the opposite!), and therefore we should forget once and for all about the old rite? Could it be that he is acknowledging, albeit tacitly, that the Latin liturgical tradition is scarcely to be found, except in traditionalist churches and chapels?

It is said that the "argument from authority" is the weakest of all arguments. But when that authority is Petrine, its pronouncements should be decisive for loyal Catholics on both sides of the aisle. Furthermore, not only the Holy

---

[95] *Ecclesia Dei adflicta*, no. 6c. The earlier directive was the indult *Quattuor abhinc annos* (October 3, 1984).

Father but also Cardinal Ratzinger has said that the time has come to reach out to a long-neglected contingent of marginalized Catholics, namely the traditionalists. They desire the traditional Latin Mass, and not simply the *Novus Ordo* in Latin, because of the distinctive features of the old rite: the prayers at the foot of the altar, the ancient Collects, the whispered Canon, Communion received kneeling and distributed only by those in Holy Orders, and so on.[96]

*R.:* I am of the opinion that the Vatican's qualified support—toleration is more like it—of the preconciliar liturgy reflects a genuine pastoral concern for disenfranchised Catholics, coupled with a commitment to the authentic renewal endorsed by the Council. The fact that the Pontifical *Ecclesia Dei* Commission was given "no clear road map"[97] for the execution of its charge, namely, oversight of the *Ecclesia Dei* indult, is quite telling in this regard. I remain convinced—and I believe this is the position of the Holy See—that the authorization of the use of the "Tridentine" liturgy is nothing more than a stopgap to

---

[96] "I am of the opinion, to be sure, that the old rite should be granted much more generously to all those who desire it. It's impossible to see what could be dangerous or unacceptable about that. A community is calling its very being into question when it suddenly declares that what until now was its holiest and highest possession is strictly forbidden and when it makes the longing for it seem downright indecent. Can it be trusted any more about anything else? Won't it proscribe again tomorrow what it prescribes today?" Joseph Cardinal Ratzinger, *Salt of the Earth: An Interview with Peter Seewald*, trans. Adrian Walker (San Francisco: Ignatius Press, 1997), pp. 176–77.

[97] Msgr. Arthur B. Calkins, Address to Latin Liturgy Association, June 23, 2001.

the current liturgical debacle. My interest in (and support of) the old rite extends only insofar as it relates to what is truly needed today, namely, the reform of the Roman liturgy *ad mentem Ecclesiae* as expressed at Vatican II.[98]

## Other Considerations

*T.:* Given the current crisis of faith in the West and the overall climate of secularism and agnosticism, your dedication to upholding non-negotiable principles of liturgical renewal seems misplaced if not insane. Monsignor Gamber's counsel in this regard may well be prophetic:

> We are living in a time when there is little faith left. The call grows louder and louder to save what we can.... In the final analysis, this means that in the future the traditional rite of the Mass must be retained in the Roman Catholic Church, and not only as a means to accommodate older priests and lay people, but as the primary liturgical form for the celebration of Mass. It must become once more the norm of our faith and the symbol of Catholic unity

---

[98] Cardinal Ratzinger: "For some time now, in various quarters and for different reasons, the possibility of a revision of the Missal promulgated by Pope Paul VI in 1970 has been a topic of discussion. If such a revision were contemplated, the criterion to be followed should be that of maximum fidelity to the indications of the Constitution *Sacrosanctum Concilium*. Consequently, such a revision should make evident the continuity and identity of the Roman rite before and after the reform. It is clear that the proposal of a 're-form of the reform' refers to the Missal of 1970 and not to that of 1962, even if the ultimate aim of this reform would be a liturgical reconciliation" (*The Latin Mass*, spring 1997, p. 8).

throughout the world, a rock of stability in a period of upheaval and never-ending change.[99]

The English Dominican Aidan Nichols believes that, because of the striking differences between the 1962 and 1970 Missals, it is not possible to use the reformed liturgy as a basis for restoring an "adequate continuity" with the "ritual integrity" of the traditional Roman rite.[100] The "reform of the reform", in other words, is impossible without the preconciliar liturgy as its basis. Practically speaking, what does this mean? It means that it is not enough to have the old rite as a normative reference point for renewal "on paper", to be studied by academics and commissions. No, there must be an experiential encounter with the "Tridentine" rite. The old liturgical books must be used as well as studied. The ancient liturgy must be celebrated regularly and universally if it is to be a viable alternative to the *Novus Ordo*. Only then will we begin to reconnect with the tradition in a living and meaningful way. And only then will true renewal begin.[101]

**R.:** Even if Rome should give unconditional approval for the old rite, do you think that is the whole

---

[99] Gamber, *Reform*, p. 114.

[100] Nichols, *Looking at the Liturgy*, p. 119. Evidently, Nichols subscribes to a mitigated form of the traditionalist rupture theory. His proposals for reforming the reform essentially amount to what was codified in the Missal of 1965, although curiously he makes no mention of that Missal.

[101] Cf. Dobszay, "Ordo Antiquus", p. 19: "The Tridentine movement may maintain in the Church a responsible way of thinking about the liturgy, and transmit the dogmatic and liturgical principles which have formed and educated many generations in the correct approach to the liturgy."

answer? There would be a lot more to consider than simply which Missal to use. For instance, in parishes where both the old and new rites are celebrated, there is the question of altar placement (unless, of course, the same altar is used for both rites) as well as the difficulty of following two liturgical calendars.[102]

*T.:* That is why I think it is best to set aside parishes where the traditional rite would be celebrated exclusively. This could be done either by creating a personal prelature for traditionalist clergy and faithful or by granting a universal indult permitting all Latin-rite priests to celebrate the traditional Mass and sacraments (according to the liturgical books in force in 1962) without having to ask permission of their bishops.

*R.:* There are some who believe that this would actually be detrimental to the cause of genuine reform and orthodoxy. Listen to Father Stravinskas' caveat:

Creation of a personal prelature for traditionally-minded Catholics would take them out of the mainstream, leaving no one to do battle with the strong secularizing forces that still form the core of "middle-management" in many American dioceses and parishes. This effort would have divisive repercussions, in effect, building a church within the Church. . . .

The practical effect of their organization of a personal prelature would be to concede the ultimate

---

[102] Cf. Jeffrey Tucker, "What Does a General Indult Portend?", *The Latin Mass*, winter 2001, pp. 40–42.

victory to the hardcore, radical left in the Church in this country. Where would we be today if St. Athanasius had contented himself with gathering around him a band of faithful souls who, against the rest of the Church, held to the true Faith? What if he had refused to fight the cause of orthodoxy in the heart of the Church? [103]

*T.:* I wonder if the good Father opposes the existence of the various Eastern-rite Churches in union with Rome. Are these not distinct Churches within the one Catholic Church? At any rate, we are not proposing the establishment of a *sui iuris* Church for "Tridentine" Catholics, akin to, say, the Armenian or Maronite or Greek-Melkite Catholic Churches. We are *Roman* Catholics who simply want those same bishops and pastors who tout pluralism and diversity to practice what they preach when it comes to us. In the final analysis, it is not so much that "the cause" must be fought *in* the heart of the Church; rather, the cause is *for* the heart of the Church: the Holy Sacrifice of the Mass and an orthodox understanding thereof. "The ancient rite", Father Mole says, "is also needed as a standard to save the liturgical reform from being pushed into complete discontinuity with what the Mass has always been and must substantially remain." [104] His subsequent counsel, if heeded, should assuage any anxiety about traditionalist isolationism:

---

[103] Stravinskas, "Why I Oppose a Tridentine Prelature", pp. 37–38.

[104] John W. Mole, O.M.I., "The Traditional Mass Movement", *Homiletic and Pastoral Review* 95, no. 1 (October 1994): 62–63.

The Traditionalist Mass movement must not give the impression that as long as its members have what they want, it does not matter what happens to the Novus Ordo and the rest of the Church. It is wrong to want the Traditional Mass merely as a matter of personal preference. We must make it absolutely clear that our reason for preserving the Mass of all ages is for the good of all, whatever rite one prefers. Those who fail to see the matter in that light are likely to sink into a ghetto mentality.[105]

*R.:* But liturgical rites do not exist in a vacuum, divorced from theology, spirituality, and ecclesiastical discipline. As we well know, there was an authentic, orthodox liturgical movement that began in the nineteenth century and received endorsement from the Roman pontiffs from Saint Pius X on.[106] This movement was part of a larger program of *ressourcement* (a return to the sources of Christian faith, especially patristic theology), which brought about significant changes in the liturgy even before the Council—most notably Pius XII's revision of the rites of Holy Week. The post-Vatican II confirmation rite reflects a renewed emphasis on the Holy Spirit in the West, and the sacrament's

---

[105] Ibid., p. 63.

[106] The liturgical movement was launched by Dom Prosper Guéranger, the founder and first abbot of the Benedictine Abbey of Solesmes (1833). It received further impetus from the reforms of Pope Pius X at the beginning of the twentieth century and was in full force by the time Vatican II opened. Another Benedictine, Dom Virgil Michel of St. John's in Collegeville, Minnesota, is credited with bringing the liturgical movement to the United States in 1925.

relationship with the process of Christian initiation is made clearer. The revised rite of anointing of the sick marks a return to the older view of this sacrament as a sacrament of healing.

What happens to this renewed theology and practice in traditionalist parishes? Would the anointing of the sick return to extreme unction? For how long would the faithful be obliged to fast before receiving Communion: One hour? Three hours? From midnight? Would new Propers be incorporated into the 1962 Missal, or would traditionalist communities just pretend that no saints have been canonized since the Council?

*T.:* The Mass and sacraments, and the norms governing their celebration, would be observed as prescribed in the old Missal and Roman Ritual. Extreme unction, then, would remain just that: the anointing of the dying. This should not pose an insufferable problem, since the Catholic Church has always accommodated a multiplicity of rites, disciplines, and sacramental theologies. (Contrast, for example, the Latin and Eastern theologies of confirmation and matrimony.) As for the inclusion of new Propers: this can be done without the need for a new edition of the Missal; alternatively, the priest need only use one of the Commons if he wishes to commemorate a saint not found on the pre-1970 Calendar.

*R.:* Assuming that all these details can be cleared up, what would you propose be done with the current Missal?

*T.:* Father Aidan Nichols proposes dubbing the new Order of Mass the *"ritus communis"* (common rite) with a threefold purpose in view: first, for use as a basis for developing new rites for young (non-Western) Churches;

secondly, for facilitating reunion with Catholic-minded separated Western Christians who are unaccustomed to "high" liturgy;[107] thirdly, for use by those communities who prefer the reformed, vernacular liturgy. Thus, in the Western Church there would be two principal rites: the traditional (or classical) Roman rite (the *ritus Romanus*) and the common rite, just as in the first millennium the Roman and Gallican rites coexisted in the West.

The reformists can work on improving the *ritus communis*, although such an undertaking seems futile even under the conservative pontificate of John Paul II. The problem is that:

> Every new edition of the Missal, or the instructions implementing the Missal, is (on balance) worse than the previous one—or at least implicitly enshrines practices that would once have been shocking to Catholic sensibilities. For example, the new General Instruction declares unequivocally that the tabernacle may not be attached to the altar, thus forbidding the new rite to be said in the manner in which the Mass has been said throughout most of Christian history. It further discourages genuflection during Mass and declares that Mass facing the people is to be preferred to the traditional manner of facing East *with* the people. These changes may not have much practical

---

[107] Nichols, *Looking at the Liturgy*, pp. 121–22. The implication here is that the new liturgy is decidedly and characteristically "low". This is ironic, since (a) the early reformers bewailed the supplanting of the once-normative Solemn Mass by the Low Mass, and (b) the new rite contains practically no restrictions on the use of incense and plainchant, as there is no sharp distinction between "High" and "Low" Mass.

import since Novus Ordo Masses mostly follow these Instructions. It's the trendline that is bothersome: today's innovation always seems to become tomorrow's imposition. For any priest with conservative sensibilities, all of this is madness.[108]

So, traditionalists aren't the only ones who have to contend with Rome. And who knows how long until the "reform of the reform" begins to bear fruit? A priest who celebrates both rites offers what I think is the most realistic assessment of the situation:

> Of course, Ratzinger has given wide encouragement to the several organizations desiring a reform of the reform, which is all well and good. But while their contributions are most necessary to the life of the Church, their effects shall not be seen for generations. The same animus meeting the Tridentine Mass awaits them as well. With one difference. Catholics may find respite now, in the Tridentine Masses being celebrated today, all throughout the world. What Ratzinger is saying... is that the "reform of the reform Mass" must await both the demise of the Liturgical Apparatus (controlling almost every Liturgy Office in the world) and the glacial movement of the Holy See. Yes, let a hundred orthodox flowers bloom. But let us not forget that one is already in full blossom.[109]

---

[108] Tucker, "What Does a General Indult Portend?", pp. 40–41.

[109] Fr. John Perricone, "A Rumbling—Part Two", *Excelsis*, May 1999. *Excelsis* is the newsletter of ChristiFideles, an association of Catholic faithful based in New York City.

*R.:* His point is well taken. We seem to have come full circle. Each of us has reason to deem the other's agenda problematic or even unrealistic.

*T.:* Yes. You reformists can try to harness a liturgical revolution that has gone out of control and to devise a rite of Mass more in keeping (as you see it) with the intentions of Vatican II.

*R.:* And you traditionalists can try to coordinate the use of pre-Vatican II liturgical books with a renewed (restored) sacramental theology and the 1983 Code of Canon Law. A square peg in a round hole, it seems. Since I began our conversation, you should have the last word.

*T.:* You are committed to "moving beyond" the Missal of 1962 and devising the "authentic" Vatican II Mass because, as you see it, not to do so would be to betray the Council. I am committed to the preservation of the 1962 Missal because, as I see it, that is our only link with the Mass of the classical Roman rite, the Mass to which the Latin Church owes her identity. I see no other way around this stalemate than to permit the unrestricted use of both rites—or, if you prefer, both forms of the Roman rite. Who knows where Divine Providence will lead the Church from there? If Church history has taught us anything, it is that the Holy Ghost can make use of our discord and mistakes in order to make more intelligible the mysteries of the faith, and *the* Mystery of Faith.

# CONCLUSION

Pivotal to the traditionalist/reformist debate is the question of the Pauline reform's continuity with liturgical tradition. This question evades a categorical answer, because in the reformed Roman rite there exist elements of both continuity and discontinuity with the classical Roman liturgy, completed in its essentials by Pope Saint Gregory the Great (590–604), augmented over the centuries by Gallican or other elements, and codified by Pope Saint Pius V in 1570. Perhaps the description of the modern rite as the "forlorn stump" of the traditional rite is on the mark.[110] Throughout the last four decades, we have seen the devastation caused by the antithetical ideologies of progressivism and archaeologism—the one idealizes (and idolizes) modernity; the other, antiquity. Paradoxically, the liturgical movement adopted both errors, schizophrenically behaving one moment as if a Huxleyan Brave New Church emerged in the 1960s, the next moment as if the Church reached her maturity sometime around the third century.

Catholicism's genius is (and always has been) its ability to preserve the inner equilibrium of revealed truth in an organic unity of tensions.[111] The Church has always eschewed false oppositions because she thinks in terms of "both/and" rather than "either/or": reason *and* revelation, Scripture *and* tradition, grace *and* free will, faith *and* good works, hierarchy *and* charism, marriage *and* celibacy,

---

[110] Mole, *Whither the Roman Rite?*, p. 54.
[111] Cf. St. Thomas Aquinas, *Summa Theologiæ* II–II, q. 1, a. 2.

and so forth. A new liturgical reform should aim at a more obvious balance of the "Tridentine" and "Vatican II" accents: sacrifice *and* supper, cross *and* resurrection, priest *and* assembly, exterior participation *and* interior recollection, sacrament *and* word, regularity *and* versatility. This will entail, on the one hand, retrieving those elements whose abolition was unwarranted by the Council and, on the other hand, suppressing practices that, in the light of experience, have obscured or subverted Catholic orthodoxy. All this, of course, presupposes that the reformists will have gained influence in the liturgical establishment as well as the support of the bishops. As if this were not challenging enough, a new reform must not repeat the mistake of treating the liturgy as a concoction by a committee rather than as the fruit of organic development. Whether or not this ambitious program is theoretically sound and practically possible remains to be seen.

The turbulent postconciliar years have seen terrible wounds inflicted on the Mystical Body of Christ, not least of which was the Lefebvrist schism. Surely, traditionalists and reformists are free to debate the cure. Meanwhile, the wounds fester. With each passing year, the rich liturgical patrimony of the Latin Church diminishes, making it increasingly difficult to maintain what little connection remains with the "classical" Roman rite.[112] Because there is strength in numbers, a traditionalist-reformist coalition of some form might well be the urgently needed first aid (perhaps a scholarly association comprising both traditionalists and reformists,

---

[112] The third *editio typica* of the postconciliar Roman Missal (2000) disappointed those who had hoped for a judicious restoration of certain Tridentine prayers and rubrics.

into which some existing smaller organizations would be subsumed).[113] Pooling the "brightest and best" of both movements would create a redoubtable bloc of scholars (laity and clergy) with enough clout to facilitate a consensus in the hierarchy on the direction the renewal should take.

For the present time, each movement should let the other pursue its aims peacefully, without polemics and antagonism. This, it seems, is the wisest and most pastoral approach to reviving a genuinely catholic (and Catholic) understanding and experience of the liturgy. When I asked Father James McLucas (editor of *The Latin Mass* magazine) his opinion of the "reform of the reform", he replied that the old and new rites should exist side by side, thereby providing traditional Catholics a sure refuge in the old liturgy while the reformists work on improving the new. "Then, in twenty years or so," he said with a smirk, "we'll see which of them is left standing." Prognostications aside, maybe a peaceful (if somewhat uneasy) coexistence of the old and new rites is exactly what is needed to provide a new generation of Catholics the opportunity to appreciate what was and to imagine what might be. At least it could make liturgical stability in Roman Catholicism seem something other than an eschatological concept.

---

[113] For this hypothetical consortium to do well, its members will have to affirm certain suppositions. Traditionalist members must accept the authority of *Sacrosanctum Concilium*—some do not, claiming that the document is inherently flawed due to its unsound philosophical underpinnings (see n. 3 above)—and therefore the untenability of holding fast to the 1962 liturgical books until the Second Coming. Reformists, for their part, must acknowledge that a lived experience of the "Tridentine" liturgy can actually promote and facilitate a true renewal.

# EPILOGUE

*The Reverend Peter M. J. Stravinskas*

What kind of liturgy will bring stability to the Church's worship and peace to her ongoing, daily life? Will the Tridentine indult "work"? What about Cardinal Ratzinger's "reform of the reform"? In some sense, the Lord's question to Saint Peter is apropos here: *Quo vadis, Ecclesia?* Our author has asked me to look into my crystal ball and to suggest where we might want to go and where we might be able to go.

In undertaking this project of giving some kind of form or vision to what Father Kocik has provided in such depth and in so scholarly a fashion, I feel somewhat like Saint Luke as he launched out on his effort to produce the Third Gospel, realizing that many had engaged in similar programs before him. In the current context, I am put in mind of men such as Fathers Brian Harrison, O.S., Joseph Fessio, S.J., Aidan Nichols, O.P., and John Parsons, as well as groups such as Adoremus and CIEL (Centre International d'Études Liturgiques).

As Father Kocik has documented so well, while many are dissatisfied with the state of Catholic worship today, nothing close to unanimity exists for a remedy. Indeed, the divisions are often as deep between "reformists" and "traditionalists" as between Tridentine devotees and members of the "erector-set" school of liturgics. I think we need to begin with people who agree that something has to be done and then try to find "common ground". Of course, that is precisely where it gets sticky. What should the starting point be? No matter what one thinks of the Missal of Pope Saint Pius V, I cannot imagine the Church returning to that incarnation of Catholic worship in a thousand years. That it could—and probably should—be the point of departure for future development is not unrealistic, simply because that was the text the Vatican II Council Fathers had in mind when they mandated and encouraged various changes.

At the same time, it seems to me that the most realistic course to adopt would be to look at the Missal of 1970. Those of a more "adventuresome" stripe (that is, pushing for either the 1962 or 1964 Missals) should recall that even the Missal of 2000 experienced not a few problems in "tightening up" that of 1970 and, to the dismay of not a few observers, the Congregation for Divine Worship ended up giving indults after the fact for certain practices that the new *editio typica* sought to control. In other words, the liturgical mentality of the 1960s is not dead by any means, and the Holy See itself has difficulty at times in dealing with that phenomenon. Add to it the disunity among "conservatives" and the rather united front of "the Left", especially the liturgical bureaucracy around the world, which makes it almost impossible to encounter opposition toward any liberalizing program from that quarter.

Furthermore, for the vast majority of Catholics—even those generally upset with the direction things have taken liturgically—I do not find the Missal of 1970 to be a major problem. I come to this conclusion from two sources.

First, as the founding editor of *The Catholic Answer*, with fifteen years of experience under the belt, with a readership of approximately a quarter of a million, and with several hundred liturgical inquiries every month, I have a good sense of the pulse of the Catholic scene in America. Very few subscribers have ever suggested that they cannot pray the Mass since the prayers at the foot of the altar were eliminated or because new Offertory prayers have replaced the old ones. No, the difficulties for them revolve around priests and liturgists "making it up as they go along".

Second, for two years now, I have celebrated the only vernacular Mass for the week in an otherwise "Tridentine" parish. Initially, the indult-Mass folks who chose to attend the Vigil Mass were quite skeptical. What do we do? We use the high altar (in fact, there is no other altar, anyway) and thus have an *ad orientem* celebration. The entire Mass is sung, with good vernacular hymnody and generous portions of Latin Gregorian chant. Incense fills the air. Communicants are given the option to kneel or stand. Eucharistic Prayers I, III, and IV are regularly rotated (II is not employed because this is a Sunday Mass). Lay lectors serve, but no altar girls and no extraordinary ministers of Holy Communion. With the passage of time, die-hard "old Mass" faithful have said repeatedly, "Father, if it were done like this in all the parishes, I wouldn't have a problem with the new Mass." Hence, my conclusion that the "new Mass" is not an insurmountable obstacle for most dissatisfied Catholics.

If we go back to *Sacrosantum Concilium*, we find the Council Fathers calling for several developments: an expanded lectionary, the reintroduction of the Offertory procession, the reinstatement of the General Intercessions (or

Prayer of the Faithful), some limited use of the vernacular, and the streamlining of texts and ceremonies that had lost their meaning with the passage of time. The Council also called for the restoration of priestly concelebration in the Latin Church as well as the provision of Communion under both species for certain special occasions.

Combining the various liturgical changes from 1964 through 1970, we would thus come up with a liturgy that looked like this: some vernacular (for example, the variable parts of the Mass?); an expanded lectionary (Father Harrison has suggested allowing the old annual cycle of readings to serve as Cycle A in any reform); an *ad orientem* celebration (although, as Father Kocik has noted, the "old Mass" could also be offered *versus populum*, even as the new rite can still be celebrated *ad orientem*); an Offertory procession; General Intercessions; priestly concelebration for the situations envisioned by the Council; the opportunity for Communion under both species for the circumstances delineated in *Sacrosanctum Concilium;* and the streamlining of gestures and ceremonies (for example, the elimination of multiple signs of the cross, either on the celebrant himself or over the gifts, especially after they have been consecrated).

What should have remained from the 1962 Missal are those prayers that had an intensely biblical foundation. One thinks immediately of the *Lavabo* (even if one might wish to cut it somewhat short of its original) or the blessing of the incense or the prayer of the deacon (or priest) before the Gospel reading. Ironically, as the Council stressed a return to biblical theology, many of the liturgical reformers gutted those very references that were so apparent in the earlier texts and now are barely hinted at. Thirty years into a profound bow at the *Credo*, I think it fair to say that it is noted in the breach more than in the observance, probably because people find such a gesture to be awkward or contrived, whereas the old genuflection seemed to come more naturally.

There should be no problem with an audible Eucharistic Prayer, especially since the old ordination rite included that practice for the newly ordained (as it did concelebration as well, albeit in a rather odd form). Given the track record of the past three decades, it would seem prudent to consign to the dustbin of liturgical history the possibility for celebrants to interject their own comments (for example, at the beginning of Mass, to introduce the Communion Rite, and at the end of Mass); these are nearly always ancillary homilies, poorly thought out, rambling and not infrequently filled with dubious theological content (not necessarily intentionally). The worst part of these ongoing remarks is that it makes for an overly cerebral, cognitive event and likewise can have the effect of encouraging priests to improvise even where not permitted.

No change introduced after 1970 would pass muster in our reformed rite. Thus, there would be no Communion in the hand, no female altar servers, no extraordinary ministers of Holy Communion—all of which have caused great confusion among the faithful and no small amount of scandal to our Orthodox brethren. If someone wished to adopt a change beyond 1970, the burden would be on him to justify such a development, which is no more than what the Council said, to begin with, regarding decisions to add to or subtract from the existing liturgy.

At times, one hears critics of the "new Mass" say that an ungodly percentage of the classical Roman orations were "butchered" in the revision process. There is no question that many of those prayers were edited—and seriously at times, but not always imprudently or malevolently. For example, once the discipline surrounding Lent changed, could we continue to pray Collects that took for granted that every weekday of Lent was a day of fast? Now, one can make the case that the discipline of Lent should not have changed; but once it did, we have to pray with integrity, thus demanding adaptations to the ancient texts. The same can be said about prayers that reflected certain outmoded theological concepts (for example, an unhealthy despisal of this earthly city). Beyond that, many prayers in the Missal of Paul VI are beautiful enrichments, coming from sacramentaries long gone at the time of the Tridentine codification.

A question not directly related to the text of a missal is the calendar, but there is surely a connection. While most observers agree that the former calendar needed dramatic reform, especially in regard to octaves upon octaves and rankings of celebrations—a reform undertaken in phases between 1955 and 1960—the cold, clinical cut-and-paste approach of the calendar revision could only be seen as unwarranted in the extreme. A saint who had a feast for hundreds of years on one particular date found his or her day moved (sometimes by only a day), in the name of bringing about a greater correspondence between dates of death and liturgical observance. But what about people who had been named for such a saint because they were born on that day, or towns and villages named for a saint whose feast was now moved, thus breaking a wonderful and important link between faith and culture? Surely, transferring non-holy-day solemnities to the nearest Sunday was well motivated but unhelpful in the event. How many Americans joke and ask how many days of Christmas there will be this year—eight, ten, fourteen? But rarely twelve any more! Perhaps we need to take a second look at restoring some octaves, thus allowing for the traditional observance (for example, January 6 for Epiphany), all the while giving a particularly strong celebration to the solemnity on the Sunday within the octave.

Another innocuous development would be to reinsert several prayers that were dropped as options to existing texts or where silence now prevails. One could easily allow for the old Offertory prayers as an option to the current ones. Similarly, the *Perceptio Corporis tui*, the *Panem cælestem*, and the *Quid retribuam* before the priest's Communion, as well as the *Corpus tuum, Domine* as an alternative to the single possibility of the *Quod ore sumpsimus*.

These are my musings as I have just completed twenty-five years of priestly service, most of which have been spent trying to recapture a lost sense of the sacred. I would die a happy priest if I could simply celebrate the Mass of Pope Paul VI without any accretions or harassment. I am not sure my dream will be fulfilled. The biggest reason I am not so sanguine about this hope is that it would require strong episcopal direction. Unless and until the bishops resume control of the sacred liturgy and wrest its control from the liturgical tinkerers, no liturgical peace will be possible and thus no ecclesial peace, either.

In the interim, I would make a plea for Father Kocik's "reformists" and "traditionalists" to begin an earnest conversation, taken up with respect and charity and evincing as much unity as possible, lest our efforts be wasted on unavailing argumentation that will ultimately give the field to those who wish for nothing more than yet another generation of liturgical chaos. Those of us who see the liturgical action as essentially about adoration need to keep that in focus about one another (in other words, what unites us is far more significant than what divides us), realizing that the alternative ("liturgy is about me/us") has strong proponents ready to inject massive doses of their secular agenda when we are too busy fighting each other instead of fighting secularists' defective brand of worship.

Father Kocik has given us ample material for an intelligent and even spirited conversation to start. With Saint Paul, we need to pray that "the God who has begun this good work... would also bring it to perfection".

# APPENDIX I

## ORDER OF MASS

## 1962 MISSAL

The people's responses, as well as prayers said/sung by the priest and people together, are printed in **bold** type. Requiem and "High" Masses will vary somewhat from this Order.

✠ In nomine Patris et Filii, et Spiritus Sancti. **Amen.**

✠ In the name of the Father, and of the Son, and of the Holy Spirit. **Amen.**

Introibo ad altare Dei. **Ad Deum qui lætificat iuventutem meam.**

I will go in unto the altar of God. **To God, Who gives joy to my youth.**

*Psalm 42:1–5*
Iudica me, Deus, et discerne causam meam de gente non sancta: ab homine iniquo, et doloso erue me.

*Psalm 42:1–5*
Judge me, O God, and distinguish my cause from the nation that is not holy; deliver me from the unjust and deceitful man.

**Quia tu es, Deus, fortitudo mea: quare me repulisti, et quare tristis incedo, dum affligit me inimicus?**
Emitte lucem tuam, et veritatem tuam: ipsa me deduxerunt, et adduxerunt in montem sanctum tuum, et in tabernacula tua.

**For You are, God, my strength; why have You cast me off? And why do I go sorrowful while the enemy afflicts me?**
Send forth Your light and Your truth: they have conducted me and brought me unto Your holy hill, and into Your tabernacles.

Et introibo ad altare Dei:
ad Deum qui lætificat
iuventutem meam.
Confitebor tibi in cithara,
Deus, Deus meus: quare tristis
es, anima mea, et quare
conturbas me?
Spera in Deo, quoniam
adhunc confitebor illi:
salutare vultus mei, et
Deus meus.
Gloria Patri, et Filio, et
Spiritui Sancto.
Sicut erat in principio, et
nunc, et semper, et in
sæcula sæculorum. Amen.

Introibo ad altare Dei.
Ad Deum qui lætificat
iuventutem meam.

Adiutorium nostrum ✠ in
nomine Domini.
Qui fecit cælum et terram.

Confiteor Deo omnipotenti,
beatæ Mariæ semper Virgini,
beato Michaeli Archangelo,
beato Ioanni Baptistæ, sanctis
Apostolis Petro et Paulo,
omnibus Sanctis, et vobis,
fratres, quia peccavi nimis
cogitatione, verbo et opere:
mea culpa, mea culpa, mea
maxima culpa. Ideo precor
beatam Mariam semper
Virginem, beatum Michaelem
Archangelum, beatum
Ioannem Baptistam, sanctos

And I will go in unto the
altar of God: to God Who
gives joy to my youth.
To You, O God, my God, I will
give praise upon the harp: why
are you sad, O my soul, and why
do you disquiet me?
Hope in God, for I will still
give praise to Him, the
salvation of my countenance
and my God.
Glory be to the Father, and to
the Son, and to the Holy Spirit.
As it was in the beginning, is
now, and ever shall be, world
without end. Amen.

I will go in unto the altar of God.
To God, Who gives joy to my
youth.

Our help ✠ is in the name of the
Lord.
Who made heaven and earth.

I confess to almighty God, to
blessed Mary ever-Virgin, to
blessed Michael the Archangel,
to blessed John the Baptist, to
the holy Apostles Peter and Paul,
to all the Saints and to you,
brethren, that I have sinned
exceedingly in thought, word,
and deed: through my fault,
through my fault, through my
most grievous fault. Therefore, I
beseech blessed Mary ever
Virgin, blessed Michael the
Archangel, blessed John the

Apostolos Petrum et Paulum,
omnes Sanctos, et vos, fratres,
orare pro me ad Dominum
Deum nostrum.

Misereatur tui omnipotens
Deus, et, dimissis peccatis
tuis, perducat te ad vitam
æternam.
Amen.

Confiteor Deo omnipotenti,
beatæ Mariæ semper
Virgini, beato Michæli
Archangelo, beato Ioanni
Baptistæ, sanctis Apostolis
Petro et Paulo, omnibus
Sanctis et tibi, Pater, quia
peccavi nimis cogitatione,
verbo, et opere: mea culpa,
mea culpa, mea maxima
culpa. Ideo precor beatam
Mariam semper Virginem,
beatum Michaelem
Archangelum, beatum
Ioannem Baptistam, sanctos
Apostolos Petrum et
Paulum, omnes Sanctos,
et te, Pater, orare pro me
ad Dominum Deum
nostrum.
Misereatur vestri omnipotens
Deus, et, dimissis peccatis
vestris, perducat vos ad vitam
æternam.
Amen.

Indulgentiam, ✠
absolutionem, et remissionem
peccatorum nostrorum,

Baptist, the holy Apostles Peter
and Paul, all the Saints, and you,
brethren, to pray for me to the
Lord our God.

May almighty God have
mercy on you, and, having
forgiven you your sins, bring
you to life everlasting.
Amen.

I confess to almighty God, to
blessed Mary ever-Virgin, to
blessed Michael the
Archangel, to blessed John
the Baptist, to the holy
Apostles Peter and Paul, all
the saints, and to you, Father,
that I have sinned
exceedingly in thought,
word, and deed: through my
fault, through my fault,
through my most grievous
fault. Therefore I beseech
blessed Mary ever-Virgin,
blessed Michael the
Archangel, blessed John the
Baptist, the holy Apostles
Peter and Paul, all the Saints,
and you, Father, to pray for
me to the Lord our God.
May almighty God have mercy
on you, and, having forgiven you
your sins, bring you to life
everlasting.
Amen.

May the almighty and merciful
Lord grant us pardon, ✠ absolution and remission of our sins.

tribuat nobis omnipotens et
misericors Dominus.
**Amen.**

Deus, tu conversus vivificabis
nos.
**Et plebs tua lætabitur in
te.**

Ostende nobis, Domine,
misericordiam tuam.
**Et salutare tuum da nobis.**

Domine, exaudi orationem
meam.
**Et clamor meus ad te
veniat.**

Dominus vobiscum.
**Et cum spiritu tuo.**

Oremus.
Aufer a nobis, quæsumus,
Domine, iniquitates nostras:
ut ad Sancta sanctorum puris
mereamur mentibus introire.
Per Christum Dominum
nostrum. Amen.

Oramus te, Domine, per
merita Sanctorum tuorum,
quorum reliquiæ hic sunt, et
omnium Sanctorum: ut
indulgere digneris omnia
peccata mea. Amen.

[✠*Introit*]

Kyrie, eleison.
**Kyrie, eleison.**
Kyrie, eleison.
**Christe, eleison.**

**Amen.**

You will turn again, O God, and
quicken us.
**And Your people will rejoice
in You.**

Show us, O Lord, Your mercy.

**And grant us Your salvation.**

O Lord, hear my prayer.

**And let my cry come unto
You.**

The Lord be with you.
**And with your spirit.**

Let us pray.
Take away from us our iniquities,
we beseech You, O Lord: that,
being made pure in heart we
may be worthy to enter into the
Holy of Holies. Through Christ
our Lord. Amen.

We beseech You, O Lord, by the
merits of those of Your saints
whose relics are here, and of all
the saints, that You would
vouchsafe to pardon me of all my
sins. Amen.

[✠*Introit*]

Lord, have mercy.
**Lord, have mercy.**
Lord, have mercy.
**Christ, have mercy.**

Christe, eleison.
**Christe, eleison.**
Kyrie, eleison.
**Kyrie, eleison.**
Kyrie, eleison.

Christ, have mercy.
**Christ, have mercy.**
Lord, have mercy.
**Lord, have mercy.**
Lord, have mercy.

**Gloria in excelsis Deo. Et in terra pax hominibus bonæ voluntatis.** Laudamus te, benedicimus te, adoramus te, glorificamus te, gratias agimus tibi propter magnam gloriam tuam. Domine Deus, Rex cælestis, Deus Pater omnipotens. **Domine Fili unigenite, Iesu Christe, Domine Deus, Agnus Dei, Filius Patris, qui tollis peccata mundi, miserere nobis; qui tollis peccata mundi, suscipe deprecationem nostram. Qui sedes ad dexteram Patris, miserere nobis. Quoniam tu solus Sanctus, tu solus Dominus, tu solus Altissimus, Iesu Christe, cum Sancto Spiritu, in gloria Dei Patris. Amen.**

Glory to God in the highest. And on earth peace to men of good will. We praise You, we bless You, we adore You, we glorify You, we give You thanks for Your great glory. O Lord God, heavenly King, God the Father almighty. **Lord Jesus Christ, the only-begotten Son, Lord God, Lamb of God, Son of the Father, Who take away the sins of the world, have mercy on us; Who take away the sins of the world, receive our prayer. Who sit at the right hand of the Father, have mercy on us. For You alone are the Holy One, You alone are the Lord, You alone are the Most High, Jesus Christ, with the Holy Spirit, in the glory of God the Father. Amen.**

Dominus vobiscum.
**Et cum spiritu tuo.**
Oremus.

The Lord be with you.
**And with your spirit.**
Let us pray.

[ *Collect* ]
**Amen.**

[ *Collect* ]
**Amen.**

[ *Epistle* ]
**Deo gratias.**

[ *Epistle* ]
**Thanks be to God.**

[ *Gradual and Alleluia / Tract* ]

Munda cor meum, ac labia
mea, omnipotens Deus, qui
labia Isaiæ Prophetæ calculo
mundasti ignito: ita me tua grata
miseratione dignare mundare,
ut sanctum Evangelium tuum
digne valeam nuntiare. Per
Christum Dominum
nostrum. Amen.

Iube, Domine, benedicere.
Dominus sit in corde meo, et
in labiis meis: ut digne et
competenter annuntiem
Evangelium suum. Amen.

Dominus vobiscum.
**Et cum spiritu tuo.**
✠ Sequentia (Initium) sancti
Evangelii secundum *N.*

**Gloria tibi, Domine.**

[ *Gospel* ]
**Laus tibi, Christe.**
Per evangelica dicta, deleantur
nostra delicta.

*On Sundays and solemnities:*

**Credo in unum Deum,
Patrem omnipotentem,
factorem cæli et terræ,
visibilium omnium et
invisibilium.**
    **Et in unum Dominum,
Iesum Christum, Filium
Dei unigenitum, et ex Patre
natum ante omnia sæcula.**

[ *Gradual and Alleluia / Tract* ]

Cleanse my heart and my lips,
almighty God, Who did cleanse
with a burning coal the lips of
the Prophet Isaiah; and vouchsafe
in Your loving kindness so to
purify me that I may be enabled
worthily to announce Your holy
Gospel. Through Christ our
Lord. Amen.

Vouchsafe, O Lord, to bless me.
The Lord be in my heart and on
my lips, that I may worthily and
becomingly announce His
Gospel. Amen.

The Lord be with you.
**And with your spirit.**
✠ The continuation (Beginning)
of the holy Gospel according
to *N.*
**Glory be to You, O Lord.**

[ *Gospel* ]
**Praise be to You, O Christ.**
May our sins be blotted out by
the words of the Gospel.

*On Sundays and solemnities:*

**I believe in one God, the
Father almighty, maker of
heaven and earth, of all
things visible and invisible.**

    **And in one Lord, Jesus
Christ, the only-begotten Son
of God, born of the Father
before all ages. God from**

Deum de Deo, lumen de lumine, Deum verum de Deo vero. Genitum, non factum, consubstantialem Patri: per quem omnia facta sunt. Qui propter nos homines et propter nostram salutem descendit de cælis. Et incarnatus est de Spiritu Sancto ex Maria virgine: et homo factus est. Crucifixus etiam pro nobis sub Pontio Pilato, passus et sepultus est. Et resurrexit tertia die, secundum Scripturas. Et ascendit in cælum: sedet ad dexteram Patris. Et iterum venturus est cum gloria, iudicare vivos et mortuos: cuius regni non erit finis.

Et in Spiritum Sanctum, Dominum et vivificantem: qui ex Patre Filioque procedit. Qui cum Patre et Filio simul adoratur et conglorificatur: qui locutus est per Prophetas.

Et unam sanctam, catholicam, et apostolicam Ecclesiam. Confiteor unum baptisma in remissionem peccatorum. Et exspecto resurrectionem mortuorum, et vitam ✠ venturi sæculi. Amen.

God, light from light, true God from true God. Begotten not made, consubstantial with the Father: through Whom all things were made. Who for us men and for our salvation came down from heaven. By the power of the Holy Spirit, He became incarnate of the Virgin Mary, and was made man. He was also crucified for us under Pontius Pilate, suffered unto death and was buried. On the third day He rose again, in accordance with the Scriptures. And He ascended into heaven: He sits at the right hand of the Father. He will come again with glory to judge the living and the dead, and of His kingdom there will be no end.

And in the Holy Spirit, the Lord and Giver of life, Who proceeds from the Father and the Son, Who together with the Father and the Son is adored and glorified: Who has spoken through the prophets.

And one, holy, catholic and apostolic Church. I confess one baptism for the remission of sins. And I await the resurrection of the dead, and the life ✠ of the world to come. Amen.

Dominus vobiscum.
**Et cum spiritu tuo.**
Oremus.

[*Offertory antiphon*]

Suscipe, sancte Pater,
omnipotens æterne Deus,
hanc immaculatam hostiam,
quam ego indignus famulus
tuus offero tibi Deo meo,
vivo et vero, pro
innumerabilibus peccatis, et
offensionibus, et negligentiis
meis, et pro omnibus
circumstantibus, sed et pro
omnibus fidelibus christianis
vivis atque defunctis: ut mihi,
et illis proficiat ad salutem in
vitam æternam. Amen.

Deus, qui humanæ substantiæ
dignitatem mirabiliter
condidisti, et mirabilius
reformasti: da nobis per huius
aquæ et vini mysterium, eius
divinitatis esse consortes, qui
humanitatis nostræ fieri
dignatus est particeps, Iesus
Christus, Filius tuus,
Dominus noster: Qui tecum
vivit et regnat in unitate
Spiritus Sancti Deus: per
omnia sæcula sæculorum.
Amen.

Offerimus tibi, Domine,
calicem salutaris, tuam
deprecantes clementiam: ut in

The Lord be with you.
**And with your spirit.**
Let us pray.

[*Offertory antiphon*]

Receive, O holy Father, almighty
and eternal God, this spotless
host, which I, Your unworthy
servant, offer unto You, my
living and true God, for my
countless sins, trespasses, and
failings; for all here present, and
for all faithful Christians,
whether living or dead, that it
may avail both me and them to
salvation unto life everlasting.
Amen.

O God, Who in creating man
did exalt his nature very
wonderfully and yet more
wonderfully did establish it anew:
by the mystery signified in the
mingling of this water and wine,
grant us to partake of the
divinity of Him Who has
vouchsafed to share our
humanity, Jesus Christ, your Son,
our Lord, Who lives and reigns
with You in the unity of the
Holy Spirit, God: for ever and
ever. Amen.

We offer unto You, O Lord, the
chalice of salvation, beseeching
Your clemency that it may

conspectu divinæ maiestatis tuæ, pro nostra, et totius mundi salute cum odore suavitatis ascendat. Amen.

In spiritu humilitatis, et in animo contrito suscipiamur a te Domine: et sic fiat sacrificium nostrum in conspectu tuo hodie, ut placeat tibi, Domine Deus.

Veni, sanctificator, omnipotens æterne Deus: et bene✠dic hoc sacrificium, tuo sancto nomini præparatum.

Lavabo inter innocentes manus meas: et circumdabo altare tuum, Domine: Ut audiam vocem laudis, et enarrem universa mirabilia tua. Domine, dilexi decorem domus tuæ, et locum habitationis gloriæ tuæ. Ne perdas cum impiis, Deus, animam meam: et cum viris sanguinum vitam meam. In quorum manibus iniquitates sunt: dextera eorum repleta est muneribus. Ego autem in innocentia mea ingressus sum: redime me, et miserere mei. Pes meus stetit in directo: in ecclesiis benedicam te, Domine. Gloria Patri...

Suscipe, sancta Trinitas, hanc oblationem, quam tibi

ascend as a sweet odor before Your divine majesty, for our own salvation, and for that of the whole world. Amen.

In a spirit of humility and with a contrite heart may we be received by You, O Lord, and may our sacrifice today be so rendered in Your sight, that it may please You, Lord God.

Come, Sanctifier, almighty and everlasting God: and bless ✠ this sacrifice which is prepared for the glory of Your holy name.

I will wash my hands among the innocent, and will compass Your altar, O Lord. That I may hear the voice of praise, and tell of all Your wondrous works. I have loved, O Lord, the beauty of Your house, and the place where Your glory dwells. Take not away my soul, O God, with the wicked; nor my life with men of blood. In whose hands are iniquities: their right hand is filled with gifts. But as for me, I have walked in my innocence; redeem me, and have mercy on me. My foot has stood in the right way; in the churches I will bless You, O Lord. Glory be to the Father...

Receive, O holy Trinity, this oblation offered up by us to You

offerimus ob memoriam passionis, resurrectionis, et ascensionis Iesu Christi Domini nostri: et in honorem beatæ Mariæ semper Virginis, et beati Ioannis Baptistæ, et sanctorum Apostolorum Petri et Pauli, et istorum, et omnium Sanctorum: ut illis proficiat ad honorem, nobis autem ad salutem: et illi pro nobis intercedere dignentur in cælis, quorum memoriam agimus in terris. Per eundem Christum Dominum nostrum. Amen.

in memory of the passion, resurrection, and ascension of our Lord Jesus Christ, and in honor of blessed Mary ever-Virgin, of blessed John the Baptist, of the holy Apostles Peter and Paul, of these, and of all the Saints: that it may be available to their honor and to our salvation; and may they whose memory we celebrate on earth vouchsafe to intercede for us in heaven. Through the same Christ our Lord. Amen.

Orate, fratres: ut meum ac vestrum sacrificium acceptabile fiat apud Deum Patrem omnipotentem.

Pray, brethren, that my sacrifice and yours may be acceptable to God the Father almighty.

**Suscipiat Dominus sacrificium de manibus tuis ad laudem et gloriam nominis sui, ad utilitatem quoque nostram, totiusque Ecclesiæ suæ sanctæ.**
Amen.

**May the Lord receive the sacrifice from your hands, to the praise and glory of His name, for our welfare and that of all His holy Church.**

Amen.

Oremus.
[ *'Secret' Prayer* ]

Let us pray.
[ *'Secret' Prayer* ]

Dominus vobiscum.
**Et cum spiritu tuo.**
Sursum corda.
**Habemus ad Dominum.**

The Lord be with you.
**And with your spirit.**
Lift up your hearts.
**We have lifted them up to the Lord.**

Gratias agamus Domino Deo
nostro.
**Dignum et iustum est.**
[*Preface*]

Let us give thanks to the Lord
our God.
**It is right and just.**
[*Preface*]

**Sanctus, Sanctus, Sanctus,
Dominus Deus Sabaoth.
Pleni sunt cæli et terra
gloria tua. Hosanna in
excelsis.** ✠ **Benedictus qui
venit in nomine Domini.
Hosanna in excelsis.**

**Holy, Holy, Holy, Lord God
of hosts. Heaven and earth
are full of Your glory:
Hosanna in the highest.** ✠
**Blessed is He Who comes in
the name of the Lord:
Hosanna in the highest.**

*Roman Canon*

*Roman Canon*

Te igitur, clementissime Pater,
per Iesum Christum, Filium
tuum, Dominum nostrum,
supplices rogamus ac petimus,
uti accepta habeas et
benedicas hæc ✠ dona, hæc ✠
munera, hæc ✠ sancta
sacrificia illibata. In primis,
quae tibi offerimus pro
Ecclesia tua sancta catholica:
quam pacificare, custodire,
adunare et regere digneris
toto orbe terrarum: una cum
famulo tuo Papa nostro *N.* et
Antistite nostro *N.* et
omnibus orthodoxis, atque
catholicæ et apostolicæ fidei
cultoribus.
Memento, Domine,
famulorum famularumque
tuarum *N.* et *N.* et omnium
circumstantium, quorum tibi
fides cognita est, et nota
devotio, pro quibus tibi

Therefore, most merciful Father,
we humbly pray and beseech
You, through Jesus Christ Your
Son, our Lord, to accept and
bless these ✠ gifts, these ✠
offerings, these ✠ holy, unspotted
sacrifices. We offer them unto
You, first, for Your holy Catholic
Church, which may it please You
to keep in peace, unite, and
govern throughout the world;
along with Your servant our
Pope *N.*, and our Bishop *N.*, and
for all true confessors of the
catholic and apostolic faith.

Be mindful, O Lord, of Your
servants and handmaids, *N.* and
*N.*, of all here present, whose
faith You know and whose
devotion You behold, for whom
we offer, or who themselves offer

offerimus: vel qui tibi offerunt hoc sacrificium laudis, pro se, suisque omnibus: pro redemptione animarum suarum, pro spe salutis et incolumitatis suæ: tibique reddunt vota sua æterno Deo, vivo et vero.

Communicantes, et memoriam venerantes, in primis gloriosæ semper Virginis Mariæ, genetricis Dei et Domini nostri Iesu Christi: sed et beati Ioseph, eiusdem Virginis Sponsi, et beatorum Apostolorum ac Martyrum tuorum, Petri et Pauli, Andreæ, Iacobi, Ioannis, Thomæ, Iacobi, Philippi, Bartholomæi, Matthæi, Simonis et Thaddei: Lini, Cleti, Clementis, Xysti, Cornelii, Cypriani, Laurentii, Chrysogoni, Ioannis et Pauli, Cosmæ et Damiani et omnium Sanctorum tuorum; quorum meritis precibusque concedas, ut in omnibus protectionis tuæ muniamur auxilio. Per eundem Christum Dominum nostrum. Amen.

Hanc igitur oblationem servitutis nostræ, sed et cunctæ familiæ tuæ, quæsumus, Domine, ut placatus accipias: diesque nostros in tua pace disponas, atque ab æterna damnatione

unto You this sacrifice of praise, for themselves and for all in their care, for the redemption of their souls, for the hope of their safety and salvation; and who render their homage unto You, the eternal God, living and true.

Joining in communion with, and venerating the memory, first of the glorious and ever-Virgin Mary, Mother of God and our Lord Jesus Christ; and also of blessed Joseph, the spouse of the same Virgin, and the blessed Apostles and Martyrs, Peter and Paul, Andrew, James, John, Thomas, James, Philip, Bartholomew, Matthew, Simon and Thaddeus; Linus, Cletus, Clement, Sixtus, Cornelius, Cyprian, Lawrence, Chrysogonus, John and Paul, Cosmas and Damian and of all Your Saints; through whose merits and prayers grant that in all things we may be strengthened by the help of Your protection. Through the same Christ our Lord. Amen.

We, therefore, beseech You, O Lord, graciously to accept this oblation of our service and of Your whole family; order our days in Your peace, deliver us from eternal damnation, and direct that we be numbered

nos eripi, et in electorum tuorum iubeas grege numerari. Per Christum Dominum nostrum. Amen.

Quam oblationem tu, Deus, in omnibus, quæsumus, bene✠dictam, adscrip✠tam, ra✠tam, rationabilem, acceptabilemque facere digneris: ut nobis Cor✠pus et San✠guis fiat dilectissimi Filii tui, Domini nostri Iesu Christi.

Qui pridie, quam pateretur, accepit panem in sanctas ac venerabiles manus suas, et elevatis oculis in cælum ad te Deum Patrem suum omnipotentem, tibi gratias agens bene✠dixit, fregit, deditque discipulis suis, dicens: Accipite, et manducate ex hoc omnes.

Hoc est enim Corpus meum.

Simili modo postquam cenatum est, accipiens et hunc præclarum Calicem in sanctas ac venerabiles manus suas: item tibi gratias agens, bene✠dixit, deditque discipulis suis, dicens: Accipite, et bibite ex eo omnes.

Hic est enim Calix Sanguinis mei, novi et æterni testamenti: mysterium

among the flock of Your elect. Through Christ our Lord. Amen.

This oblation, O God, we beseech You, vouchsafe in every way to make ✠ blessed, ✠ approved, ✠ ratified, reasonable, and acceptable; that it may become for us the ✠ Body and ✠ Blood of Your most dearly beloved Son, Jesus Christ our Lord.

Who, on the day before He suffered, took bread into His holy and venerable hands, and lifting up His eyes to heaven, to You, O God, His Father almighty, giving thanks He ✠ blessed it, and broke it, and gave it to His disciples, saying: Take this, all of you, and eat of it.

For this is My Body.

In the same way, when supper was ended, He took this precious Chalice into His holy and venerable hands, and when He had given You thanks, He ✠ blessed it and gave it to His disciples, saying: Take this, all of you, and drink of it.

For this is the Chalice of My Blood, of the new and everlasting covenant: the

fidei: qui pro vobis et pro
multis effundetur in
remissionem peccatorum.
Hæc quotiescumque
faceritis, in mei memoriam
facietis.

Unde et memores, Domine,
nos servi tui, sed et plebs tua
sancta, eiusdem Christi Filii
tui Domini nostri tam beatæ
passionis, nec non et ab inferis
resurrectionis, sed et in cælos
gloriosæ ascensionis: offerimus
præclaræ maiestati tuæ de tuis
donis, ac datis, hostiam ✠
puram, hostiam ✠ sanctam,
hostiam ✠ immaculatam,
Panem ✠ sanctum vitæ
æternæ, et Calicem ✠ salutis
perpetuæ.

Supra quæ propitio ac
sereno vultu respicere digneris: et accepta habere, sicuti
accepta habere dignatus es
munera pueri tui iusti Abel,
et sacrificium Patriarchæ
nostri Abrahæ, et quod tibi
obtulit summus sacerdos tuus
Melchisedech, sanctum
sacrificium, immaculatam
hostiam.

Supplices te rogamus,
omnipotens Deus: iube hæc
perferri per manus sancti
Angeli tui in sublime altare
tuum, in conspectu divinæ
maiestatis tuæ; ut, quotquot
ex hac altaris participatione

mystery of faith: which shall
be poured out for you and for
the many unto the remission
of sins. As often as you shall
do these things, you shall do
them in remembrance of me.

Therefore, O Lord, we Your
servants and Your holy people,
mindful of the ever-blessed
passion of the same Christ Your
Son our Lord, His resurrection
from the dead, and His glorious
ascension into heaven, offer unto
Your most glorious majesty, from
Your own gracious gifts, a pure ✠
offering, a holy ✠ offering, a
spotless ✠ offering, the holy ✠
Bread of eternal life, and the
Chalice ✠ of everlasting salvation.

Deign to look upon these gifts
with a gracious and kindly
countenance, and to accept
them, as it pleased You to accept
the gifts of Your righteous
servant Abel, and the sacrifice of
our Patriarch Abraham, and the
holy sacrifice, the spotless
offering which Your high priest
Melchisedech offered unto You.

We humbly beseech You,
Almighty God, to bid that these
gifts be carried by the hands of
Your holy angel to Your altar on
high, in the sight of Your divine
majesty, that those of us who
share in them at this altar and

sacrosanctum Filii tui Cor✠pus et San✠guinem sumpserimus, ✠ omni benedictione cælesti et gratia repleamur. Per eundem Christum Dominum nostrum. Amen.

Memento etiam, Domine, famulorum famularumque tuarum *N.* et *N.*, qui nos præcesserunt cum signo fidei, et dormiunt in somno pacis. Ipsis, Domine, et omnibus in Christo quiescentibus, locum refrigerii, lucis et pacis, ut indulgeas, deprecamur. Per eundem Christum Dominum nostrum. Amen.

Nobis quoque peccatoribus famulis tuis, de multitudine miserationum tuarum sperantibus, partem aliquam, et societatem donare digneris, cum tuis sanctis Apostolis et Martyribus: cum Ioanne, Stephano, Matthia, Barnaba, Ignatio, Alexandro, Marcellino, Petro, Felicitate, Perpetua, Agatha, Lucia, Agnete, Cæcilia, Anastasia et omnibus Sanctis tuis: intra quorum nos consortium, non æstimator meriti, sed veniæ, quæsumus, largitor admitte. Per Christum Dominum nostrum.

Per quem hæc omnia, Domine, semper bona creas, sancti✠ficas, vivi✠ficas, bene✠dicis, et præstas nobis.

receive the most sacred ✠ Body and ✠ Blood of Your Son may be filled with ✠ every heavenly grace and blessing. Through the same Christ our Lord. Amen.

Be mindful also, O Lord, of Your servants and handmaids, *N.* and *N.*, who have gone before us marked with the sign of faith, and who rest in the sleep of peace. To them, O Lord, and to all that rest in Christ, grant, we beseech You, a place of refreshment, light and peace. Through the same Christ our Lord. Amen.

To us also Your sinful servants, trusting in Your boundless mercies, vouchsafe to grant some share and fellowship with Your holy Apostles and Martyrs; with John, Stephen, Matthias, Barnabas, Ignatius, Alexander, Marcellinus, Peter, Felicity, Perpetua, Agatha, Lucy, Agnes, Cecilia, Anastasia and all Your saints; into whose company we beseech You to admit us, not weighing our merits, but pardoning our offenses. Through Christ our Lord.

Through Whom, O Lord, You ever create, ✠ sanctify, ✠ quicken, ✠ bless, and bestow upon us all these good things.

Per ip✠sum, et cum ip✠so,
et in ip✠so, est tibi Deo Patri
✠ omnipotenti, in unitate
Spiritus ✠ Sancti, omnis
honor et gloria. Per omnia
sæcula sæculorum.
**Amen.**

Oremus: Præceptis salutaribus
moniti, et divina institutione
formati, audemus dicere: Pater
noster...
**Sed libera nos a malo.**
Amen.

Libera nos, quæsumus,
Domine, ab omnibus malis,
præteritis, præsentibus, et
futuris; et intercedente beata,
et gloriosa semper Virgine
Dei Genetrice Maria, cum
beatis Apostolis tuis Petro et
Paulo, atque Andrea, et
omnibus Sanctis, ✠ da
propitius pacem in diebus
nostris: ut ope misericordiæ
tuæ adiuti, et a peccato simus
semper liberi, et ab omni
perturbatione securi. Per
eundem Dominum nostrum
Iesum Christum Filium tuum.
Qui tecum vivit et regnat in
unitate Spiritus Sancti, Deus,
Per omnia sæcula sæculorum.
**Amen.**

Pax ✠ Domini sit ✠ semper
vobis✠cum.
**Et cum spiritu tuo.**

Through ✠ Him, and with ✠
Him, and in ✠ Him, in the unity
of the Holy ✠ Spirit, to You,
God the Father ✠ almighty, all
honor and glory for ever and
ever.
**Amen.**

Let us pray: Taught by our
Savior's commands, and formed
by the word of God, we dare to
say: Our Father...
**But deliver us from evil.**
Amen.

Deliver us, we beseech You, O
Lord, from all evils, past, present
and to come, and by the
intercession of the blessed and
glorious ever-Virgin Mary,
Mother of God, together with
Your blessed Apostles Peter and
Paul, and Andrew, and all the
Saints, ✠ mercifully grant peace
in our days, that, assisted by the
power of Your merciful love, we
may always be both free from sin
and safe from all distress.
Through the same Jesus Christ,
Your Son our Lord, Who lives
and reigns with You in the unity
of the Holy Spirit, God, forever
and ever.

**Amen.**

The peace ✠ of the Lord be ✠
always ✠ with you.
**And with your spirit.**

Hæc commixtio, et
consecratio Corporis et
Sanguinis Domini nostri Iesu
Christi, fiat accipientibus
nobis in vitam æternam.
Amen.

May this mingling and hallowing
of the Body and Blood of our
Lord Jesus Christ bring eternal
life to us who receive it. Amen.

Agnus Dei, qui tollis peccata
mundi: miserere nobis.

Agnus Dei, qui tollis peccata
mundi: miserere nobis.

Agnus Dei, qui tollis peccata
mundi: dona nobis pacem.

Lamb of God, Who take away
the sins of the world: have mercy
on us.

Lamb of God, Who take away
the sins of the world: have mercy
on us.

Lamb of God, Who take away
the sins of the world: grant us
peace.

Domine Iesu Christe, qui
dixisti Apostolis tuis: Pacem
relinquo vobis, pacem meam
do vobis: ne respicias peccata
mea, sed fidem Ecclesiæ tuæ:
eamque secundum
voluntatem tuam pacificare et
coadunare digneris: Qui vivis
et regnas Deus per omnia
sæcula sæculorum. Amen.

Lord Jesus Christ, Who said to
Your Apostles: Peace I leave you,
my peace I give you: Look not
on our sins, but on the faith of
Your Church; and deign to grant
her peace and unity in
accordance with Your will, Who
live and reign, God, for ever and
ever. Amen.

Domine Iesu Christe, Fili Dei
vivi, qui ex voluntate Patris,
cooperante Spiritu Sancto,
per mortem tuam mundum
vivificasti: libera me per hoc
sancrosanctum Corpus et
Sanguinem tuum ab omnibus
iniquitatibus meis, et universis
malis: et fac me tuis semper
inhærere mandatis, et a te
numquam separari permittas:

Lord Jesus Christ, Son of the
living God, Who by the will of
the Father and the cooperation
of the Holy Spirit, brought life
to the world by Your death:
through this, Your most holy
Body and Blood, deliver me
from all my sins and from every
evil: make me always hold fast to
Your commandments, and never
permit me to be parted from

Qui cum eodem Deo Patre et
Spiritu Sancto vivis et regnas
Deus in sæcula sæculorum.
Amen.

Perceptio Corporis tui,
Domine Iesu Christe, non
mihi proveniat in iudicium et
condemnationem: sed pro tua
pietate prosit mihi ad
tutamentum mentis et corporis,
et ad medelam percipiendam:
Qui vivis et regnas cum Deo
Patre in unitate Spiritus
Sancti Deus, per omnia
sæcula sæculorum. Amen.

Panem cælestem accipiam, et
nomen Domini invocabo.

[*Three times:*] Domine, non
sum dignus, ut intres sub
tectum meum: sed tantum dic
verbo et sanibitur anima mea.

✠ Corpus Domini nostri Iesu
Christi custodiat animam
meam in vitam æternam.
Amen.

Quid retribuam Domino pro
omnibus quæ retribuit mihi?
Calicem salutaris accipiam, et
nomen Domini invocabo.
Laudans invocabo Dominum,
et ab inimicis meis salvus ero.

You. Who with the same God
the Father and the Holy Spirit
live and reign, God, for ever and
ever. Amen.

O Lord Jesus Christ, may the
reception of Your Body and
Blood not bring me judgment
and condemnation, but by Your
kindness may it be for me a
protection of mind and body and
an effective source of healing.
Who live and reign with God
the Father in the unity of the
Holy Spirit, God, for ever and
ever. Amen.

I will take the Bread from
heaven, and will call upon the
name of the Lord.

[*Three times:*] Lord, I am not
worthy that You should come
under my roof: but only say the
word and my soul shall be
healed.
✠ May the Body of our Lord
Jesus Christ preserve my soul
unto life everlasting. Amen.

What return shall I make to the
Lord for all the things he has
given unto me? I will take the
chalice of salvation, and call
upon the name of the Lord. I
will call upon the Lord and give
praise: and I shall be saved from
my enemies.

✠ Sanguis Domini nostri Iesu Christi custodiat animam meam in vitam æternam. Amen.

Ecce Agnus Dei, ecce qui tollit peccata mundi.

[*Three times:*] **Domine, non sum dignus, ut intres sub tectum meum: sed tantum dic verbo et sanabitur anima mea.**

Quod ore sumpsimus, Domine, pura mente capiamus: et de munere temporali fiat nobis remedium sempiternum.

Corpus tuum, Domine, quod sumpsi, et Sanguis, quem potavi, adhæreat visceribus meis: et præsta; ut in me non remaneat scelerum macula, quem pura et sancta refecerunt Sacramenta: Qui vivis et regnas in sæcula sæculorum. Amen.

[*Communion antiphon*]

Dominus vobiscum.
**Et cum spiritu tuo.**
Oremus.
[*Post-communion Prayer*]
**Amen.**
Dominus vobiscum.
**Et cum spiritu tuo.**
Ite, Missa est.
**Deo gratias.**

✠ May the Blood of our Lord Jesus Christ preserve my soul unto life everlasting. Amen.

Behold the Lamb of God, behold Him Who takes away the sins of the world.

[*Three times:*] **Lord, I am not worthy that You should come under my roof: but only say the word and my soul shall be healed.**

What we have received with our mouths, O Lord, may we take with pure minds, and from a temporal gift, may it become for us an eternal remedy.

May Your Body, O Lord, which I have received and Your Blood which I have drunk, cleave to my inmost parts, and grant that no stain of sin remain in me; whom these pure and holy Sacraments have refreshed. Who live and reign for ever and ever. Amen.

[*Communion antiphon.*]

The Lord be with you.
**And with your spirit.**
Let us pray.
[*Post-communion Prayer*]
**Amen.**
The Lord be with you.
**And with your spirit.**
Go, the Mass is ended.
**Thanks be to God.**

Placeat tibi, sancta Trinitas, obsequium servitutis meæ: et præsta, ut sacrificium quod oculis tuæ maiestatis indignus obtuli, tibi sit acceptabile; mihique et omnibus pro quibus illud obtuli, sit, te miserante, propitiabile. Per Christum Dominum nostrum. Amen.

May the tribute of my homage be pleasing to You, O most holy Trinity. Grant that the sacrifice which I, unworthy as I am, have offered in the presence of Your majesty, may be acceptable to You. Through Your mercy may it bring forgiveness to me and to all for whom I have offered it. Through Christ our Lord. Amen.

Benedicat vos omnipotens Deus, Pater, ✠ et Filius, et Spiritus Sanctus.
**Amen.**

May almighty God, the Father, and ✠ the Son, and the Holy Spirit, bless you.
**Amen.**

*Last Gospel*

*Last Gospel*

Dominus vobiscum.
**Et cum spiritu tuo.**

The Lord be with you.
**And with your spirit.**

✠ Initium sancti Evangelii secundum Ioannem.
**Gloria tibi, Domine.**

✠ The beginning of the holy Gospel according to John.
**Glory to you, O Lord.**

In principio erat Verbum, et Verbum erat apud Deum, et Deus erat Verbum. Hoc erat in principio apud Deum. Omnia per ipsum facta sunt: et sine ipso factum est nihil, quod factum est: in ipso vita erat, et vita erat lux hominum: et lux in tenebris lucet, et tenebræ eam non compre-henderunt. Fuit homo missus a Deo, cui nomen erat Ioannes. Hic venit in testimonium, ut

In the beginning was the Word, and the Word was with God, and the Word was God. The same was in the beginning with God. All things were made by Him, and without Him was made nothing that was made. In Him was life, and the life was the light of men: and the light shone in darkness, and the darkness did not comprehend it. There was a man sent from God, whose name was John. This man

testimonium perhiberet de lumine, ut omnes crederent per illum. Non erat ille lux, sed ut testimonium perhiberet de lumine. Erat lux vera, quæ illuminat omnem hominem venientem in hunc mundum. In mundo erat, et mundus per ipsum factus est, et mundus eum non cognovit. In propria venit, et sui eum non receperunt. Quotquot autem receperunt eum, dedit eis potestatem filios Dei fieri, his, qui credunt in nomine eius: qui non ex sanguinibus, neque ex voluntate carnis, neque ex voluntate viri, sed ex Deo nati sunt. Et Verbum caro factum est, et habitavit in nobis: et vidimus gloriam eius, gloriam quasi Unigeniti a Patre, plenum gratiæ et veritatis.

**Deo gratias.**

came for a witness, to bear witness to the light, that all men through him might believe. He was not the light, but was to bear witness to the light. That was the true light, which enlightens every man that comes into this world. He was in the world, and the world was made by Him, and the world knew Him not. He came unto His own, and His own received Him not. But as many as received Him, to them He gave power to become the sons of God; to them that believe in His name: who are born, not of blood, nor of the will of the flesh, nor of the will of man, but of God. And the Word was made flesh, and dwelt among us, and we saw His glory, the glory as of the Only-begotten of the Father, full of grace and truth.

**Thanks be to God.**

# APPENDIX II

## ORDER OF MASS

## 1970 MISSAL

| | |
|---|---|
| *Ritus initiales* | *Introductory rites* |
| [*Introit*] | [*Introit*] |
| ✠ In nomine Patris et Filii, et Spiritus Sancti. | ✠ In the name of the Father, and of the Son, and of the Holy Spirit. |
| **Amen.** | **Amen.** |
| [A] Gratia Domini nostri Iesu Christi, et caritas Dei, et communicatio Sancti Spiritus sit cum omnibus vobis. | [A] The grace of our Lord Jesus Christ, and the love of God, and the communion of the Holy Spirit be with you all. |
| **Et cum spiritu tuo.** | **And with your spirit.** |
| [B] Gratia vobis et pax a Deo Patre nostro et Domino Iesu Christo. | [B] Grace and peace to you from God our Father and the Lord Jesus Christ. |
| **Benedictus Deus et Pater Domini nostri Iesu Christi.** | **Blessed be the God and Father of our Lord Jesus Christ.** |
| *or:* | *or:* |
| **Et cum spiritu tuo.** | **And with your spirit.** |

---

Not all options are shown; for example, the Rite of Blessing and Sprinkling of Holy Water (which may take the place of the Penitential Rite on Sundays), the additional Eucharistic Prayers, solemn blessings, and so on. The people's responses, as well as prayers said/sung by the priest and people together, are printed in **bold** type. This English translation, for study purposes only, was prepared by the St. Gregory Foundation for Latin Liturgy (1992).

[C] Dominus vobiscum.
**Et cum spiritu tuo.**

Fratres, agnoscamus peccata
nostra, ut apti simus ad sacra
mysteria celebranda.

**[A] Confiteor Deo omni-
potenti et vobis, fratres,
quia peccavi nimis cogi-
tatione, verbo, opere, et
omissione, mea culpa, mea
culpa, mea maxima culpa.
Ideo precor beatam
Mariam semper Virginem,
omnes angelos et sanctos,
et vos, fratres, orare pro
me ad Dominum Deum
nostrum.**

[B] Miserere nostri, Domine.
**Quia peccavimus tibi.**
Ostende nobis, Domine,
misericordiam tuam.
**Et salutare tuum da nobis.**

[C] Qui missus es sanare
contritos corde: Kyrie eleison.
**Kyrie eleison.**
Qui peccatores vocare venisti:
Christe eleison.
**Christe eleison.**
Qui ad dexteram Patris sedes,
ad interpellandum pro nobis:
Kyrie eleison.
**Kyrie eleison.**

*Concluding all three penitential
forms:*

[C] The Lord be with you.
**And with your spirit.**

Brethren, let us acknowledge our
sins, that we may fittingly
celebrate the sacred mysteries.

**[A] I confess to almighty
God and to you, brethren,
that I have sinned
exceedingly in thought, word,
deed and omission, through
my fault, through my fault,
through my most grievous
fault. Therefore, I beseech
blessed Mary ever Virgin, all
the angels and saints, and you,
my brothers and sisters, to pray
for me to the Lord our God.**

[B] Have mercy on us, O Lord.
**For we have sinned against you.**
Lord, show us your merciful
love.
**And grant us your salvation.**

[C] You were sent to heal the
contrite: Lord, have mercy.
**Lord, have mercy.**
You came to call sinners: Christ,
have mercy.
**Christ, have mercy.**
You sit at the right hand of the
Father to make intercession for
us: Lord, have mercy.
**Lord, have mercy.**

*Concluding all three penitential
forms:*

Misereatur nostri omnipotens Deus, et dimissis peccatis nostris, perducat nos ad vitam æternam.

**Amen.**

*Then, unless form [C] was used:*

Kyrie eleison.
**Kyrie eleison.**
Christe eleison.
**Christe eleison.**
Kyrie eleison.
**Kyrie eleison.**

**Gloria in excelsis Deo et in terra pax hominibus bonæ voluntatis. Laudamus te, benedicimus te, adoramus te, glorificamus te, gratias agimus tibi propter magnam gloriam tuam, Domine Deus, Rex cælestis, Deus Pater omnipotens. Domine Fili unigenite, Iesu Christe, Domine Deus, Agnus Dei, Filius Patris, qui tollis peccata mundi, miserere nobis; qui tollis peccata mundi, suscipe deprecationem nostram. Qui sedes ad dexteram Patris, miserere nobis. Quoniam tu solus Sanctus, tu solus Dominus, tu solus Altissimus, Iesu Christe, cum Sancto Spiritu: in gloria Dei Patris. Amen.**

May almighty God have mercy on us, forgive us our sins, and bring us to life everlasting.

**Amen.**

*Then, unless form [C] was used:*

Lord, have mercy.
**Lord, have mercy.**
Christ, have mercy.
**Christ, have mercy.**
Lord, have mercy.
**Lord, have mercy.**

**Glory to God in the highest and on earth peace to men of good will. We praise you, we bless you, we adore you, we glorify you, we give you thanks for your great glory. O Lord God, heavenly King, God the Father almighty. Lord Jesus Christ, the only-begotten Son, Lord God, Lamb of God, Son of the Father, who take away the sins of the world, have mercy on us; who take away the sins of the world, receive our prayer. Who sit at the right hand of the Father, have mercy on us. For you alone are the Holy One, you alone are the Lord, you alone are the Most High, Jesus Christ, with the Holy Spirit, in the glory of God the Father. Amen.**

Oremus.
[Collect or Opening Prayer]
**Amen.**

Let us pray.
[Collect or Opening Prayer]
**Amen.**

*Liturgia verbi*

*Following the first (and second) reading (s):*

Verbum Domini.
**Deo gratias.**

[Gradual or Responsorial Psalm]

[Alleluia/Tract]

Munda cor meum ac labia mea, omnipotens Deus, ut sanctum Evangelium tuum digne valeam nuntiare.

Dominus vobiscum.
**Et cum spiritu tuo.**

✠ Lectio (Initium) Sancti Evangelii secundum N.
**Gloria tibi Domine.**

*Following the Gospel:*
Verbum Domini.
**Laus tibi, Christe.**

Per evangelica dicta deleantur nostra delicta.

**Credo in unum Deum, Patrem omnipotentem, factorem cæli et terræ, visibilium omnium et invisibilium.**

*Liturgy of the Word*

*Following the first (and second) reading (s):*

The Word of the Lord.
**Thanks be to God.**

[Gradual or Responsorial Psalm]

[Alleluia/Tract]

Almighty God, cleanse my heart and my lips, that I may ably and worthily proclaim your holy Gospel.

The Lord be with you.
**And with your spirit.**

✠ A reading (the beginning) of the holy Gospel according to N.
**Glory to you, O Lord.**

*Following the Gospel:*
The Word of the Lord.
**Praise to you, O Christ.**

Through the words of the Gospel may our offenses be blotted out.

**I believe in one God, the Father almighty, maker of heaven and earth, of all things visible and invisible.**

Et in unum Dominum, Iesum Christum, Filium Dei unigenitum, et ex Patre natum ante omnia sæcula. Deum de Deo, lumen de lumine, Deum verum de Deo vero, genitum, non factum, consubstantialem Patri: per quem omnia facta sunt. Qui propter nos homines et propter nostram salutem descendit de cælis. Et incarnatus est de Spiritu Sancto ex Maria virgine, et homo factus est. Crucifixus etiam pro nobis sub Pontio Pilato, passus et sepultus est. Et resurrexit tertia die, secundum Scripturas, et ascendit in cælum, sedet ad dexteram Patris. Et iterum venturus est cum gloria, iudicare vivos et mortuos, cuius regni non erit finis.

Et in Spiritum Sanctum, Dominum et vivificantem: qui ex Patre Filioque procedit: qui cum Patre et Filio simul adoratur et conglorificatur: qui locutus est per prophetas.

Et unam sanctam, catholicam, et apostolicam Ecclesiam. Confiteor unum baptisma in remissionem

And in one Lord, Jesus Christ, the only-begotten Son of God, born of the Father before all ages. God from God, light from light, true God from true God, begotten not made, consubstantial with the Father: through whom all things were made. Who for us men and for our salvation came down from heaven. By the power of the Holy Spirit, he became incarnate of the Virgin Mary, and was made man. He was also crucified for us under Pontius Pilate, suffered unto death and was buried. On the third day he rose again, in accordance with the Scriptures, ascended into heaven, and sits at the right hand of the Father. He will come again in glory to judge the living and the dead, and of his kingdom there will be no end.

And in the Holy Spirit, the Lord and Giver of life, who proceeds from the Father and the Son, who together with the Father and the Son is adored and glorified: who has spoken through the prophets.

And one, holy, catholic and apostolic Church. I confess one baptism for the remission of sins. And I await the

peccatorum. Et exspecto
resurrectionem mortuo-
rum, et vitam venturi
sæculi. Amen.

[*General Intercessions*]

*Liturgia eucharistica*
[*Offertory Antiphon*]

Benedictus es, Domine, Deus
universi, quia de tua largitate
accepimus panem, quem tibi
offerimus, fructum terræ et
operis manuum hominum: ex
quo nobis fiet panis vitæ.
**Benedictus Deus in sæcula.**

Per huius aquæ et vini
mysterium eius efficiamur
divinitatis consortes, qui
humanitatis nostræ fieri
dignatus est particeps.

Benedictus es, Domine, Deus
universi, quia de tua largitate
accepimus vinum, quod tibi
offerimus, fructum vitis et
operis manuum hominum, ex
quo nobis fiet potus spiritalis.

**Benedictus Deus in sæcula.**

In spiritu humilitatis et in
animo contrito suscipiamur a
te, Domine; et sic fiat
sacrificium nostrum in
conspectu tuo hodie, ut
placeat tibi, Domine Deus.

resurrection of the dead, and
the life of the world to
come. Amen.

[*General Intercessions*]

*Liturgy of the Eucharist*
[*Offertory Antiphon*]

Blessed are you, Lord God of the
universe, for from your bounty
we have received the bread we
offer you: fruit of the earth and
work of human hands, which will
become for us the bread of life.
**Blessed be God forever.**

Through the mystery of this
water and wine, may we become
sharers in the divinity of him,
who deigned to become a
partaker of our humanity.

Blessed are you, Lord, God of
the universe, for from your
bounty we have received the
wine we offer you, fruit of the
vine and work of human hands,
which will become for us a
spiritual drink.
**Blessed be God forever.**

In a spirit of humility and with a
contrite heart may we be
received by you, O Lord, and
may our sacrifice today be so
rendered in your sight, that it
may please you, O Lord God.

| | |
|---|---|
| Lava me, Domine, ab iniquitate mea, et a peccato meo munda me. | Wash me, O Lord, from my iniquity, and cleanse me from my sin. |
| Orate, fratres, ut meum ac vestrum sacrificium acceptabile fiat apud Deum Patrem omnipotentem. | Pray, brethren, that my sacrifice and yours may be acceptable to God the Father almighty. |
| **Suscipiat Dominus sacrificium de manibus tuis ad laudem et gloriam nominis sui, ad utilitatem quoque nostram totiusque Ecclesiæ suæ sanctæ.** | **May the Lord receive the sacrifice from your hands, to the praise and glory of his name, for our welfare and that of all his holy Church.** |
| [*Prayer over the Gifts*] **Amen.** | [*Prayer over the Gifts*] **Amen.** |
| Dominus vobiscum. **Et cum spiritu tuo.** Sursum corda. **Habemus ad Dominum.** Gratias agamus Domino Deo nostro. **Dignum et iustum est.** | The Lord be with you. **And with your spirit.** Lift up your hearts. **We have lifted them up to the Lord.** Let us give thanks to the Lord our God. **It is right and just.** |
| [*Preface*] | [*Preface*] |
| **Sanctus, Sanctus, Sanctus, Dominus Deus Sabaoth. Pleni sunt cæli et terra gloria tua. Hosanna in excelsis. Benedictus qui venit in nomine Domini. Hosanna in excelsis.** | **Holy, Holy, Holy, Lord God of hosts. Heaven and earth are full of your glory: Hosanna in the highest. Blessed is he who comes in the name of the Lord: Hosanna in the highest.** |

Eucharistic Prayer I (Roman Canon)

Eucharistic Prayer I (Roman Canon)

Te igitur, clementissime Pater, per Iesum Christum, Filium tuum, Dominum nostrum, supplices rogamus ac petimus, uti accepta habeas et benedicas ✠ hæc dona, hæc munera, hæc sancta sacrificia illibata, in primis, quae tibi offerimus pro Ecclesia tua sancta catholica: quam pacificare, custodire, adunare et regere digneris toto orbe terrarum: una cum famulo tuo Papa nostro N. et Antistite nostro N. et omnibus orthodoxis atque catholicæ et apostolicæ fidei cultoribus.

Memento, Domine, famulorum famularumque tuarum N. et N. et omnium circumstantium, quorum tibi fides cognita est et nota devotio, pro quibus tibi offerimus: vel qui tibi offerunt hoc sacrificium laudis, pro se suisque omnibus: pro redemptione animarum suarum, pro spe salutis et incolumitatis suæ: tibique reddunt vota sua æterno Deo, vivo et vero.

Communicantes, et memoriam venerantes, in primis gloriosæ semper Virginis Mariæ, genetricis Dei et Domini nostri Iesu Christi: sed et beati Ioseph, eiusdem

Therefore, most merciful Father, we humbly pray and beseech you, through Jesus Christ your Son, our Lord, to accept and bless ✠ these gifts, these offerings, these holy, unspotted sacrifices, which we offer unto you, first, for your holy Catholic Church, which may it please you to keep in peace, unite, and govern throughout the world; along with your servant our Pope N., and our Bishop N., and for all true confessors of the catholic and apostolic faith.

Be mindful, O Lord, of your servants and handmaids, N. and N., of all here present, whose faith you know and whose devotion you behold, for whom we offer, or who themselves offer unto you this sacrifice of praise, for themselves and for all in their care, for the redemption of their souls, for the hope of their safety and salvation; and who render their homage unto you, the eternal God, living and true.

Joining in communion with, and venerating the memory, first of the glorious and ever-Virgin Mary, Mother of God and our Lord Jesus Christ; and also of blessed Joseph, the spouse of the

Virginis Sponsi, et beatorum
Apostolorum ac Martyrum
tuorum, Petri et Pauli, Andreæ,
(Iacobi, Ioannis, Thomæ,
Iacobi, Philippi, Bartholomæi,
Matthæi, Simonis et Thaddei:
Lini, Cleti, Clementis, Xysti,
Cornelii, Cypriani, Laurentii,
Chrysogoni, Ioannis et Pauli,
Cosmæ et Damiani) et om-
nium Sanctorum tuorum;
quorum meritis precibusque
concedas, ut in omnibus pro-
tectionis tuæ muniamur aux-
ilio. (Per Christum Dominum
nostrum. Amen.)

Hanc igitur oblationem
servitutis nostræ, sed et
cunctæ familiæ tuæ,
quæsumus, Domine, ut
placatus accipias: diesque
nostros in tua pace disponas,
atque ab æterna damnatione
nos eripi et in electorum
tuorum iubeas grege
numerari. (Per Christum
Dominum nostrum. Amen.)

Quam oblationem tu,
Deus, in omnibus quæsumus,
benedictam, adscriptam,
ratam, rationabilem, acceptabilemque facere digneris: ut
nobis Corpus et Sanguis fiat
dilectissimi Filii tui, Domini
nostri Iesu Christi.

Qui, pridie quam pateretur,
accepit panem in sanctas ac
venerabiles manus suas, et
elevatis oculis in cælum ad te

Virgin, and your blessed Apostles
and Martyrs, Peter and Paul,
Andrew, (James, John, Thomas,
James, Philip, Bartholomew,
Matthew, Simon and Thaddeus;
Linus, Cletus, Clement, Sixtus,
Cornelius, Cyprian, Lawrence,
Chrysogonus, John and Paul,
Cosmas and Damian) and of all
your saints; through whose
merits and prayers grant that
in all things we may be
strengthened by the help of your
protection. (Through Christ our
Lord. Amen.)

We, therefore, beseech you, O
Lord, graciously to accept this
oblation of our service and of
your whole family; order our
days in your peace, deliver us
from eternal damnation, and
direct that we be numbered
among the flock of your elect
(Through Christ our Lord.
Amen.)

This oblation, O God, we
beseech you, vouchsafe in every
way to make blessed, approved,
ratified, reasonable, and
acceptable; that it may become
for us the Body and Blood of
your most dearly beloved Son,
Jesus Christ our Lord.

Who, on the day before he
suffered, took bread into his holy
and venerable hands, and lifting
up his eyes to heaven, to you,

Deum Patrem suum omnipo-
tentem, tibi gratias agens
benedixit, fregit, deditque
discipulis suis, dicens:
ACCIPITE ET MANDUCATE
EX HOC OMNES: HOC EST
ENIM CORPUS MEUM, QUOD
PRO VOBIS TRADETUR.
Simili modo, postquam
cenatum est, accipiens et hunc
præclarum calicem in sanctas
ac venerabiles manus suas,
item tibi gratias agens bene-
dixit, deditque discipulis suis,
dicens:
ACCIPITE ET BIBITE EX EO
OMNES: HIC EST ENIM CALIX
SANGUINIS MEI NOVI ET
ÆTERNI TESTAMENTI, QUI
PRO VOBIS ET PRO MULTIS
EFFUNDETUR IN
REMISSIONEM PECCATORUM.
HOC FACITE IN MEAM
COMMEMORATIONEM.

O God, his Father almighty,
giving thanks he blessed it, and
broke it, and gave it to his
disciples, saying:
TAKE THIS, ALL OF YOU, AND
EAT OF IT; FOR THIS IS MY
BODY, WHICH WILL BE GIVEN
UP FOR YOU.
In the same way, when supper
was ended, he took this precious
cup into his holy and venerable
hands, and when he had given
you thanks, he blessed it and
gave it to his disciples, saying:

TAKE THIS, ALL OF YOU, AND
DRINK OF IT; FOR THIS IS THE
CUP OF MY BLOOD OF THE NEW
AND EVERLASTING COVENANT;
WHICH SHALL BE POURED OUT
FOR YOU AND FOR THE MANY
UNTO THE REMISSION OF SINS.
DO THIS IN REMEMBERANCE
OF ME.

Mysterium fidei:
[*Memorial acclamation*]
Unde et memores, Domine,
nos servi tui, sed et plebs tua
sancta, eiusdem Christi, Filii
tui, Domini nostri, tam beatæ
passionis, necnon et ab inferis
resurrectionis, sed et in cælos
gloriosæ ascensionis: offerimus
præclaræ maiestati tuæ de tuis
donis ac datis hostiam puram,
hostiam sanctam, hostiam
immaculatam, Panem sanctum

The mystery of faith:
[*Memorial acclamation*]
Therefore, O Lord, we your
servants and your holy people,
mindful of the ever-blessed
passion of the same Christ your
Son our Lord, his resurrection
from the dead, and his glorious
ascension into heaven, offer unto
your most glorious majesty, from
your own gracious gifts, a pure
offering, a holy offering, a
spotless offering, the holy Bread

vitæ æternæ et Calicem
salutis perpetuæ.

Supra quæ propitio ac sereno
vultu respicere digneris: et
accepta habere, sicuti accepta
habere dignatus es munera
pueri tui iusti Abel, et sacrificium Patriarchæ nostri Abrahæ,
et quot tibi obtulit summus
sacerdos tuus Melchisedech,
sanctum sacrificium, immaculatam hostiam.

Supplices te rogamus,
omnipotens Deus: iube hæc
perferri per manus sancti
Angeli tui in sublime altare
tuum, in conspectu divinæ
maiestatis tuæ; ut, quotquot
ex hac altaris participatione
sacrosanctum Filii tui Corpus
et Sanguinem sumpserimus, ✠
omni benedictione cælesti et
gratia repleamur. (Per Christum
Dominum nostrum. Amen.)

Memento etiam, Domine,
famulorum famularumque
tuarum N. et N., qui nos
præcesserunt cum signo fidei,
et dormiunt in somno pacis.
Ipsis, Domine, et omnibus in
Christo quiescentibus, locum
refrigerii, lucis et pacis, ut
indulgeas, deprecamur. (Per
Christum Dominum
nostrum. Amen.)

Nobis quoque peccatoribus
famulis tuis, de multitudine
miserationum tuarum
sperantibus, partem aliquam

of eternal life, and the Cup of
everlasting salvation.

Deign to look upon these gifts
with a gracious and kindly
countenance, and to accept
them, as it pleased you to accept
the gifts of your righteous
servant Abel, and the sacrifice of
our Patriarch Abraham, and the
holy sacrifice, the spotless
offering which your high priest
Melchisedech offered unto you.

We humbly beseech you,
Almighty God, to bid that these
gifts be carried by the hands of
your holy angel to your altar on
high, in the sight of your divine
majesty, that those of us who
share in them at this altar and
receive the most sacred Body and
Blood of your Son may be filled
with ✠ every heavenly grace and
blessing. (Through Christ our
Lord. Amen.)

Be mindful also, O Lord, of
your servants and handmaids, N.
and N., who have gone before us
marked with the sign of faith, and
who rest in the sleep of peace.
To them, O Lord, and to all that
rest in Christ, grant, we beseech
you, a place of refreshment, light
and peace. (Through Christ our
Lord. Amen.)

To us also your sinful servants,
trusting in your boundless
mercies, vouchsafe to grant some
share and fellowship with your

et societatem donare digneris
cum tuis sanctis Apostolis et
Martyribus: cum Ioanne,
Stephano, Matthia, Barnaba,
(Ignatio, Alexandro, Marcellino, Petro, Felicitate, Perpetua,
Agatha, Lucia, Agnete, Cecilia,
Anastasia) et omnibus Sanctis
tuis: intra quorum nos
consortium, non æstimator
meriti, sed veniæ, quæsumus,
largitor admitte. Per Christum
Dominum nostrum.

Per quem hæc omnia,
Domine, semper bona creas,
sanctificas, vivificas, benedicis,
et præstas nobis.

Per ipsum, et cum ipso, et in
ipso, est tibi Deo Patri
omnipotenti, in unitate Spiritus
Sancti, omnis honor et gloria
per omnia sæcula sæculorum.
**Amen.**

*Ritus Communionis*
Præceptis salutaribus moniti,
et divina institutione formati,
audemus dicere:
**Pater noster** . . .

Libera nos, quæsumus,
Domine, ab omnibus malis,
da propitius pacem in diebus
nostris, ut, ope misericordiæ
tuæ adiuti, et a peccato simus
semper liberi et ab omni perturbatione securi: exspectantes
beatam spem et adventum
Salvatoris nostri Iesu Christi.

holy Apostles and Martyrs; with
John, Stephen, Matthias,
Barnabas, (Ignatius, Alexander,
Marcellinus, Peter, Felicity,
Perpetua, Agatha, Lucy, Agnes,
Cecilia, Anastasia) and all your
saints; into whose company we
beseech you to admit us, not
weighing our merits, but
pardoning our offenses. Through
Christ our Lord.

Through whom, O Lord, you
ever create, sanctify, endow with
life, bless, and bestow upon us all
these good things.

Through him, and with him,
and in him, in the unity of the
Holy Spirit, to you, God the
Father almighty, all honor and
glory for ever and ever.
**Amen.**

*Communion Rite*
Taught by our Savior's
commands, and formed by the
word of God, we dare to say:
**Our Father** . . .

Deliver us, we beseech you, O
Lord, from all evil, graciously
grant peace in our days, that,
assisted by the power of your
merciful love, we may always be
both free from sin and safe from
all distress: as we await the
blessed hope and the coming of
our Savior Jesus Christ.

Quia tuum est regnum, et potestas, et gloria in sæcula.

Domine Iesu Christe, qui dixisti Apostolis tuis: Pacem relinquo vobis, pacem meam do vobis: ne respicias peccata nostra, sed fidem Ecclesiæ tuæ; eamque secundum voluntatem tuam pacificare et coadunare digneris. Qui vivis et regnas in sæcula sæculorum. Amen.

(Offerte vobis pacem.)

Hæc commixtio Corporis et Sanguinis Domini nostri Iesu Christi fiat accipientibus nobis in vitam æternam.

Agnus Dei, qui tollis peccata mundi: miserere nobis.
Agnus Dei, qui tollis peccata mundi: miserere nobis.
Agnus Dei, qui tollis peccata mundi: dona nobis pacem.

[A] Domine Iesu Christe, Fili Dei vivi, qui ex voluntate Patris, cooperante Spiritu Sancto, per mortem tuam mundum vivificasti: libera me per hoc sancrosanctum Corpus et Sanguinem tuum

For yours is the kingdom, and the power, and the glory forever.

Lord Jesus Christ, who said to your Apostles: Peace I leave you, my peace I give you: Look not on our sins, but on the faith of your Church; and deign to grant her peace and unity in accordance with your will. Who live and reign forever and ever. Amen.

(Offer each other the peace of the Lord.)

May this mingling of the Body and Blood of our Lord Jesus Christ bring eternal life to us who receive it.

Lamb of God, who take away the sins of the world: have mercy on us.
Lamb of God, who take away the sins of the world: have mercy on us.
Lamb of God, who take away the sins of the world: grant us peace.

[A] Lord Jesus Christ, Son of the living God, who by the will of the Father and the cooperation of the Holy Spirit, brought life to the world by your death: through this, your most holy Body and Blood, deliver me

ab omnibus iniquitatibus meis
et universis malis: et fac me
tuis semper inhærere
mandatis, et a te numquam
separari permittas.

[B] Perceptio Corporis et
Sanguinis tui, Domine Iesu
Christe, non mihi proveniat
in iudicium et condemna-
tionem: sed pro tua pietate
prosit mihi ad tutamentum
mentis et corporis, et ad
medelam percipiendam.

Ecce Agnus Dei, ecce qui tollit
peccata mundi. Beati qui ad
cenam Agni vocati sunt.

**Domine, non sum dignus,
ut intres sub tectum meum:
sed tantum dic verbo et
sanabitur anima mea.**

Corpus Christi custodiat me
in vitam æternam.

Sanguis Christi custodiat me
in vitam æternam.

[*Communion Antiphon*]

Quod ore sumpsimus,
Domine, pura mente
capiamus, et de munere
temporali fiat nobis remedium
sempiternum.

from all my sins and from every
evil: make me always hold fast to
your commandments, and never
permit me to be parted from
you.

[B] O Lord Jesus Christ, may the
reception of your Body and
Blood not bring me judgment
and condemnation, but by your
kindness may it be for me a
protection of mind and body and
an effective source of healing.

Behold the Lamb of God, behold
him who takes away the sins of
the world. Blessed are those who
are called to the supper of the
Lamb.

**Lord, I am not worthy that
you should come under my
roof: but only say the word
and my soul shall be healed.**

May the Body of Christ preserve
me unto everlasting life.

May the Blood of Christ
preserve me unto everlasting life.

[*Communion Antiphon*]

What we have received with our
mouths, O Lord, may we take
with pure minds, and from a
temporal gift, may it become for
us an eternal remedy.

| | |
|---|---|
| *Ritus conclusionis* | *Concluding Rite* |
| Oremus. | Let us pray. |
| [*Post-communion Prayer*] | [*Post-communion Prayer*] |
| **Amen.** | **Amen.** |
| Dominus vobiscum. | The Lord be with you. |
| **Et cum spiritu tuo.** | **And with your spirit.** |
| Benedicat vos omnipotens Deus, Pater, ✠ et Filius, et Spiritus Sanctus. | May almighty God, the Father, ✠ the Son, and the Holy Spirit, bless you. |
| **Amen.** | **Amen.** |
| Ite, missa est. | Go, the Mass is ended. |
| **Deo gratias.** | **Thanks be to God.** |

# APPENDIX III

## THE POSTCONCILIAR EUCHARISTIC LITURGY: PLANNING A "REFORM OF THE REFORM"

*Brian W. Harrison, O.S.*

### I. *The Current Crisis in Eucharistic Faith and Practice*

The postconciliar era has scarcely been a period of undisturbed harmony and tranquillity in regard to the way Catholics worship. On the contrary: it seems probable that the last thirty years have been the most liturgically troubled period since at least the era of the Reformation—now nearly half a millennium ago. Indeed, the recent

Address to the St. Thomas Aquinas Society Eucharistic Conference, Colorado Springs, March 26, 1995. This address was serially printed in *Adoremus Bulletin*, November through January 1996.

Father Brian W. Harrison, O.S. is an Australian priest of the Society of the Oblates of Wisdom. Raised a Presbyterian, he converted to Catholicism in 1972, and was ordained to the priesthood in St. Peter's Basilica by Pope John Paul II in 1985. Fr. Harrison's theological qualifications include a licentiate from the Angelicum University and a doctorate from the Pontifical University of the Holy Cross. He is the author of two books and many articles, including an essay on a "Reform of the Reform" (published for the first time in full in this volume). This essay has won praise from Cardinal Joseph Ratzinger and others. Fr. Harrison currently holds the position of Associate Professor of Theology in the Pontifical Catholic University of Puerto Rico.

discord could well be judged more serious than that of the sixteenth century, because at that time the controversial liturgical changes were introduced by those outside the Catholic Church—Protestants who openly rejected any kind of allegiance to the pope. Now we find similar disturbances within the heart of the Catholic Church herself.

We are talking here, not about mere differences of opinion or points of academic debate, but about deep divisions and at times a sense of profound alienation within the Mystical Body of Christ, whether the dissatisfied Catholics concerned see themselves as "progressive", "traditionalist", "liberal", "middle-of-the-road", "conservative", or whatever. Not only does every Catholic seem to have his or her definite preference for one or other style of worship in the pluralistic liturgical supermarket represented by the dozens (or hundreds) of very diversified parish Masses now offered in each of our cities; we go farther than mere preferences and quickly reach the point of either hating or loving this or that style of eucharistic celebration. We now have feminist women who feel insulted and outraged at being excluded by virtue of their sex from being able to preside at the Eucharist; we also have non-feminist women—and plenty of men!—who feel outraged at the Vatican's decision last year to allow female altar servers (never mind female *priests!*). For some Catholics any liturgy seems cold, mechanical, and dreary unless the priest ad libs and jokes his way through the Mass, insisting on mutual introductions in the pews at the beginning, everyone holding hands at the Our Father, and about five minutes of hugging and kissing at the Sign of Peace. But many other Catholics find the artificial intimacy of such aberrations so annoying and out of place as to make Mass attendance unbearable—or at least, enough to turn it into a severe weekly penance.

At a still deeper level, we have seen liturgical dissension become a major factor in formal ruptures in the Church: the popes have been openly defied; anathemas have been hurled from Rome; grave mutual recriminations of heresy and schism have been exchanged; several antipopes have arisen among fringe groups who claim that the new Mass is invalid and that there has not been any true pope living in Rome since before Vatican II. All in all, an estimated million "traditionalist" believers around the world (sometimes just as opposed to each other as they are to Pope John Paul) now worship regularly in a state of total or virtual separation from the Catholic Church under Peter's successor.

At the opposite extreme, we have an "establishment" of liturgical experts among whom the very mention of the traditional (Tridentine) Latin Mass can be guaranteed infallibly to produce the same effect as that of the proverbial red flag waved in front of a wounded bull. I was studying in Rome in 1984 when the Holy Father issued the indult permitting the renewed (although very limited) use of the 1962 Latin Missal and will never forget the anger and frustration this decision provoked among "progressives" in and around the Vatican. For instance, an international liturgical conference was under way in Rome at the time, and one enraged Irish liturgist was reported to me by an eyewitness as branding the Pope's indult "the worst betrayal since Judas".[1]

In short, what we have witnessed in these thirty years has been a tragic polarization and fragmentation among Catholics, in regard to the liturgy. But while so many have been drawing swords either to defend or attack the post-conciliar changes in the rite of Mass, not many seem to have noticed that the very existence of such tension, bitterness, and division is about the most eloquent possible evidence that the liturgical reform introduced in the name of Vatican Council II has been seriously defective. What both liberals and conservatives often forget is the fact that, in the words of Saint Thomas Aquinas, "The Eucharist is the sacrament of the Church's *unity*."[2] When Saint Thomas said that, he was commenting on the words of an authority far higher even than his: those of the Holy Spirit, who inspired Saint Paul to write, "Because there is one bread, we who are many are one body, for we all partake of the one bread."[3]

The *Catechism of the Catholic Church* explains this revealed mystery as follows: "The Eucharist is the efficacious sign and sublime cause of that communion in the divine life and that unity of the People of God by which

---

[1] Shortly after that, a priest friend of mine visiting Rome told me how a nun serving in the official Vatican bookshop reacted indignantly when he was naïve enough to ask if they stocked the old Missal, now that the Pope had permitted its use once again. "Certainly not!" she snapped, "Nothing here from before Vatican II!"

[2] *Summa Theologiæ*, IIIa, q. 73, a. 2 (emphasis added).

[3] 1 Cor 10:17.

the Church is kept in being." [4] A little farther on, in treating of "the fruits of Holy Communion", the *Catechism* first sets out this sacrament's effects of grace in the individual believer [5] and then sums up its communal effect—"The unity of the Mystical Body"—with the strikingly bold and sweeping affirmation that

> *The Eucharist makes the Church.* Those who receive the Eucharist are united more closely to Christ. Through it Christ unites them to all the faithful in one body—the Church. Communion renews, strengthens, and deepens this incorporation into the Church, already achieved by Baptism. In Baptism we have been called to form but one body. [6]

The implications of this profound truth for the post-Vatican II liturgical reform seem to me very serious. If one of the main purposes of the eucharistic liturgy is to "renew, strengthen, and deepen" the *unity* of all Catholics in the one Mystical Body, then what are we to think of a reform that, whatever its positive results may have been, has also managed to provoke more discord, mutual alienation, and disunity than any officially introduced liturgical innovation in the entire history of the Church? Let us listen to the very first paragraph of the very first Vatican II document—the Constitution on the Liturgy—and ask

---

[4] CCC 1325, quoting the Congregation of Rites, Instruction *Eucharisticum mysterium* (May 25, 1967), no. 6.

[5] CCC 1391–95.

[6] CCC 1396 (emphasis in original); cf. 1 Cor 12:13.

ourselves honestly how well these optimistic expectations
of the Council Fathers have been fulfilled:

> The sacred Council has set out to impart an ever-
> increasing vigor to the Christian life of the faithful;
> to adapt more closely to the needs of our age those
> institutions which are subject to change; to foster
> whatever can promote union among all who believe
> in Christ; to strengthen whatever can help to call all
> mankind into the Church's fold. Accordingly it sees
> particularly cogent reasons for undertaking the re-
> form and promotion of the liturgy.[7]

Now, can the new rites be said to have promoted "unity"
among believers, when we see more strife and *disunity* than
ever in connection with the liturgy? It may be true that
Catholics and Protestants now feel less divided than before, but not in the way the Council Fathers expected.
They hoped that liturgical reform would help Protestants
to become more Catholic in their thinking; but all that
has happened is that Catholics have demonstrably become
more Protestant in their thinking! The Vatican II Fathers,
as we have just heard, hoped that a revised liturgy would
be a means of "help[ing] to call all mankind into the
Church's fold". But how could anyone claim that this hope
has been even partially fulfilled when in most countries
rates of conversion to Catholicism have plummeted to an
all-time low, priests and religious have abandoned their
holy vocations in tens of thousands, innumerable other
Catholics have given up the faith altogether, and of those

---

[7] SC, no. 1.

who do still profess it, fewer than ever now attend Mass regularly?

Finally, can anyone seriously claim that the postconciliar liturgy has managed to "impart an ever-increasing vigor to the Christian life of the faithful" (as the Council Fathers hoped) when reliable surveys show that fewer Catholics than ever believe in the central and fundamental mystery of the Mass: that is, the true change of the bread and wine into the living Body and Blood of our crucified and risen Savior? According to a 1994 New York Times/CBS poll cited by Germain Grisez and Russell Shaw in last month's *Homiletic & Pastoral Review*, a good 45 percent—nearly half—of even the oldest age group among American Catholics (those aged sixty-five years or more) now hold a more or less Protestant view of the Eucharist, thinking that the consecrated Host is a mere "symbolic reminder" of Jesus. Among those a little younger (aged forty-five to sixty-four) this "protestantized" group increases to 58 percent; and among the youngest age group (eighteen to forty-four years)—that is, those Catholics who were still children or not yet born when the liturgical changes began—the proportion holding this heretical view shoots up to 70 percent.[8]

In other words, *disbelief in the Real Presence among professing Catholics in the United States increases in direct proportion to the proportion of their own lifetime in which the Eucharist has been celebrated with the new postconciliar Missal.* According to the same survey, we have reached the point where

---

[8] G. Grisez and R. Shaw, "The Crisis in Eucharistic Faith", *Homiletic & Pastoral Review*, February 1995, p. 17.

even the majority (51 percent) of the most regularly practicing Catholics—those who say they attend Mass every Sunday—expressed the protestantized "symbolic-reminder" view of this most holy Mystery.[9]

Now, I am not suggesting, of course, that the recent liturgical changes should bear *all* the blame for this decadence. A number of factors have undoubtedly contributed to this deplorable situation, which is in turn only one part—although a very major one—of the more generalized crisis of faith, morals, and discipline that has afflicted Catholicism in the last thirty years, especially in the affluent and secularized West. But I do submit that the experience of the last quarter-century should be sufficient for us to recognize in retrospect, with all due respect to the memory of Pope Paul VI, that the way in which the liturgical reform was handled after Vatican II has been one significant cause of the present decline in eucharistic faith and practice. After all, if the alarming facts and statistics we have surveyed do *not* convince us that the reform was badly done, what conceivable evidence *would* convince us?

Not only is it clear that the new rite of Mass has failed to achieve the principal objectives that were clearly set out at the beginning of the Council's document on the liturgy; it seems to me highly debatable whether even the secondary objectives have really been achieved. For instance, it is often said that the laity now participate more actively in the Mass instead of being mere passive spectators. In a sense this may be true. But if so, this victory must be judged an extremely hollow one for at least two

---

[9] Ibid.

reasons. In the first place, it must be remembered that in most countries a much smaller percentage of the laity even attend Church *at all* than was the case previously; and those millions of nominal Catholics who have now completely given up going to Mass can scarcely be said to participate more actively in it.

Secondly, of the minority who still *do* attend Mass, their "more active participation" has often consisted in doing things that only the clergy could previously do: handling the sacred vessels, touching the Sacred Host itself through Communion in the hand, standing instead of kneeling to receive it, proclaiming the Scriptures, passing freely in and out of the sanctuary, distributing Holy Communion as extraordinary ministers, and so on. But this kind of "clericalization" of the laity is not what the Council Fathers had in mind when they called for more "active participation": *Sacrosanctum Concilium* does not say one word about opening up an ever-increasing number of "ministries" to the laity. This tendency toward a certain "liturgical egalitarianism" has, I believe, become part of the very problem we have already outlined. It has often fomented division among the faithful (since conservative lay people dislike the trend, while liberals applaud it); and by emphasizing the common, human, and "fraternal sharing" aspects of the liturgy at the expense of the divine, mysterious, and sacred aspects, it has contributed to loss of faith in the Real Presence of Christ in the eucharistic species.

For an excellent presentation of how this secularizing process has worked psychologically, I would refer you to another recent article in the *Homiletic & Pastoral Review*, entitled "Restoration of the Priesthood", by Frederick

Heuser of the Milwaukee Archdiocese.[10] Father Heuser argues that by over-reacting to the alleged clericalism of preconciliar times, and by minimizing as far as possible the distinction between priests and laity, we have robbed the priesthood of much of its special mystique. (We priests, of course, have also been partly to blame for that by so often dressing and living very much like laymen.) But this "demystification" of the priesthood has in turn contributed not only to a drastic decline in priestly vocations but to a corresponding demystification of the priest's most sublime responsibility—the Most Holy Eucharist.

## II. *Some Inadequate Solutions to the Crisis*

The great question, therefore, is: What can we *do* about the present state of emergency regarding the central act of Christian worship? Certainly, a large part of the solution will have to consist in more solid and orthodox preaching and teaching about Eucharist and liturgy at all levels, from seminaries and universities right down to children's First Communion classes. A renewal of eucharistic devotions, more dignified and reverent Church music, and so on, will also be important factors. But all such measures will only have limited success, I believe, if we do not also take a long and hard look at the actual prayers, texts, and rubrics of the postconciliar Mass itself. These, after all, are the very *substance* of the liturgical rites, and so their im-

---

[10] *Homiletic & Pastoral Review*, January 1995, pp. 7–14.

pact on Catholic ideas and attitudes can hardly have been a merely accidental or superficial one. In this context, before explaining the plan of action that seems to me to have the best long-term chances of success, I wish to criticize two other suggested plans of action that one hears put forward by many good and faithful Catholics but that I think will probably prove to be inadequate.

### a. The Ultramontane Proposal

The first of these could perhaps be termed the Ultramontane Proposal,[11] and I believe it is too legalistic and superficial. This is the solution offered by those who tell us that all liturgical decisions emanating from the Holy See should automatically be accepted with cheerfulness and docility and should never be the object of any kind of criticism, letter-writing campaigns, and so on, on the part of loyal Catholics. Such brethren tend to equate any disagreement in such matters with *disobedience* and insist that the present situation of eucharistic disunity and loss of faith is caused principally by the "disobedience" of both "right" and "left" wings in the Church. Ultramontane Catholics believe that everything could soon be straightened out if only both these extremes would dutifully return to the

---

[11] The term "ultramontane" means, literally, "beyond the mountains" (referring to the Alps separating Italy from northern Europe). It arose in France several centuries ago at a time of tension between important sectors of the French Church and the Holy See and has come to refer to those Catholics who take delight in the strong and direct exercise of papal authority throughout the universal Church and insist on the strictest possible conformity to the decisions and policies of the pontiff reigning at any given time.

center, stop telling the Vatican how to do its job, and just snap to attention, as it were, with full and grateful acquiescence in whatever official liturgical norms happen to be established, now or in the future, by papal authority.

This is, I suppose, a very natural way of thinking for those loyal Catholics who were brought up in the very centralized, tightly disciplined, and apparently peaceful and unified Church of Popes Pius XI and XII and John XXIII, when it often seemed that practically any ecclesial problem could be solved simply by the strong exercise of authority on the part of the pope, accompanied by a passive and unquestioning acquiescence in his decisions on the part of all other Catholics—even administrative and policy decisions of the Holy Father that afford no occasion for either obedience or disobedience, and much less require internal assent from all the faithful.

Now, the main reason I do not think the Ultramontane Proposal will solve our current liturgical crisis is that the official norms themselves now laid down by the Holy See are already so broadly defined, and allow for so many varied and local options, that they leave too much room for precisely that kind of celebration which in effect overstresses the human, communitarian aspect of the Mass at the expense of the sacrificial, the divine, the mysterious, and the supernatural. By choosing certain legitimate options, and without violating a single official liturgical rule or rubric, for instance, it is quite easy—and, indeed, all too common!—for a priest and his congregation to carry out a liturgical celebration in which the general atmosphere and overall psychological effect approximate quite closely that of a Protestant communion service. In fact, one of Pope Paul VI's closest friends, his intimate confidant the French philosopher Jean Guitton, declared in a nationally transmitted French radio program in December 1993 that this was one of the Pope's deliberate aims: an ecumenical step that he hoped would contribute to the reunification of the separated Churches. Guitton was most emphatic about this and said it several times: "I can only repeat that Paul VI did all that he could to bring the Catholic Mass away from the tradition of the Council of Trent towards the Protestant Lord's Supper." [12]

Even without Guitton's testimony, the most cursory glance at the new Mass of Paul VI, in comparison with the traditional Latin rite standardized by Saint Pius V, suffices to reveal the far greater similarities that exist between the new rite and a typical Protestant service. Indeed, the most ardent defenders of the new rite of Mass, far from denying these similarities, are usually the first to proclaim them triumphantly, trumpeting them as a mark of ecumenical progress. But it is very plain, after a quarter-century, that this ecumenical aspect of the liturgical reform has not succeeded in drawing significant numbers of separated brethren into the Catholic Church, as the Fathers of Vatican II hoped. On the contrary, what we have

---

[12] These remarks were made by Prof. Guitton on December 13, 1993, during the broadcasting of "Ici lumière 101", a religious program hosted by a Lutheran, François-Georges Dreyfus. Dreyfus, although a non-Catholic, was expressing his disappointment at the secularization of the Catholic liturgy since Vatican II, its abandonment of Latin, Gregorian chant, etc. Guitton, in turn, made the remarks cited above in the context of expressing his astonishment that a Protestant, of all people, should react negatively to such changes in the Catholic Mass. After all, he assured Dreyfus, they were introduced by Pope Paul VI precisely in order to *attract* Protestants toward the Catholic Church, not to alienate them still further! An English translation of the transcript of this broadcast has been published in *The Latin Mass*, vol. 4, no. 1 (winter 1995), pp. 10–11.

seen—as those recent opinion polls demonstrate with devastating clarity!—is a massive protestantization of Catholic attitudes and opinions about what the Blessed Eucharist really is.

Moreover, those who think that returning to the "center" will solve our problems often seem to forget that the "center" itself keeps on moving—and usually toward the left. There does not yet appear to be any end in sight to the officially authorized liturgical changes. Defiant feminist pressure for more change has if anything been stimulated rather than discouraged by the Pope's solemn declaration last year that women can never be priests; and the Vatican's recent concession to that pressure in the matter of female altar servers, by appearing to reward disobedience to the previous norm (which began with the apostles!), will only encourage more disobedience and increase the expectation of still more radical change.

Last month's issue of the respected and well-informed Roman magazine *Inside the Vatican* carries an editorial commenting on the instability and confusion caused by constant changes in authorized English translations of liturgical texts and cites the head of the International Commission for English in the Liturgy (ICEL), Dr. John Page, as assuring us that change will indeed be permanently ongoing! After the present revision is complete, Dr. Page expects "a further revision of the Church's prayers and creeds in perhaps 35 years, and changes every few decades thereafter, 'perhaps more frequently, perhaps less.' " [13]

---

[13] *Inside the Vatican*, February 1995, p. 7.

Meanwhile, among many liturgists and theologians in Asia, Africa, and the Pacific, the demand for still more "inculturation" is growing increasingly strident. For many of these experts, expressions of national pride and rejection of alleged "Western cultural impositions" often seem to be much higher liturgical priorities than safeguarding reverence and belief in the Real Presence. Such trends among "Third World" Church leaders (which go *against* the wishes of many ordinary indigenous believers) are now being viewed more sympathetically than ever by the Holy See.

This was brought home to me several days ago when I received from a friend in Australia a report of the Holy Father's recent Mass in Sydney for the beatification of our country's first candidate for canonization, Mother Mary McKillop. The title of the report in Sydney's *Catholic Weekly* is all too significant: "The Mass of Many Firsts".[14] The "progressive" priest-liturgist who wrote the report, Father John McSweeney, seems almost lost for words in his breathless enthusiasm for this "liturgical breakthrough" and "milestone" for "the world-wide Church", not just Australia. He describes lovingly the "rhythmical movement of hands, feet and head, together with the swaying of the body" of those who regaled the Holy Father with their liturgical dance; he rejoices that a group of women, having accompanied the procession to the sanctuary, stood "on the podium with the Pope during the Mass [and then] actually ministered to him as acolytes and servers"; he expresses his "happiness" that the Nicene Creed was

---

[14] Fr. John McSweeney, "The Mass of Many Firsts", *Catholic Weekly* [official newspaper of the Archdiocese of Sydney], March 5, 1995, p. 21.

replaced by what he calls an "interesting question/answer format"; and enthuses over the "inculturation" displayed in the substitution of a pagan Australian aboriginal "smoke and fire" ritual instead of the Penitential Rite. " 'The smoking ceremony' became part of the Mass—another first!" exclaims Father McSweeney triumphantly. Most significantly of all, he stresses over and over again that all this "radical new ground" (as well as still another innovation that I will describe below) "has been broken with the full permission of the Vatican".

For all these reasons, I do not see as a realistic solution to our present crisis in eucharistic faith and worship the approach that I have called the Ultramontane Proposal: that is, the naïve belief that even in administrative and disciplinary matters no pope can ever make a seriously false move, so that an unquestioning acquiescence in whatever may come out of the Holy See will be enough to restore the Church's worship to what it should be. Please do not mistake my meaning here. I am not saying we should be *disobedient* to the Holy See. My point is not that obedience in liturgical matters is unnecessary; but rather, it is insufficient—and that in any case it need not necessarily be passive and uncritical.


*b. The Traditionalist Proposal*

The second alternative I believe to be inadequate is what can be called the Traditionalist Proposal. This is the view that the solution to our crisis in Catholic worship is simply a return to the traditional Latin Mass as it was before Vatican Council II. Once again, I wish to avoid any misunderstanding here. I am by no means opposed to the traditional rite of Mass. In fact, I have permission from the Holy See to celebrate that rite in private in accordance with the Pope's Apostolic Letter *Ecclesia Dei*; and I frequently use this permission, since, given the choice between the old and the present new rite, I definitely prefer the former. However, I do not consider myself a traditional*ist* Catholic. Traditional, yes; traditional*ist*, no. The difference is that the term "traditionalist" is normally used to designate those who more or less reject the distinctive teachings of Vatican Council II, and that is not my position—particularly not in regard to the liturgy.

Why do I suggest that the proposal of a simple return to the preconciliar liturgy is *not* the best option? Basically, because I think it is a case of settling for second-best—in two distinct senses. And second-best is not good enough for the sacred liturgy.

In the first place it means settling for a kind of second-class citizenship in the Church on the part of those who love the traditional Latin liturgy. Traditionalists themselves are by and large very dissatisfied with the present degree of official recognition of the Mass they love. The use of the 1962 Missal is hedged about with many restrictions, and whether it can be lawfully used at all depends entirely on the personal preference of each diocesan bishop. Most bishops do not in fact permit it, and when they do, the permission is often granted under conditions that worshippers find irksome and even humiliating.

What all traditionalists really want, of course, is complete equality of status for the old rite of Mass, alongside the new rite. But this, I submit, is simply a pipe dream.

It just is not going to happen. Already the head of the Vatican's *Ecclesia Dei* Commission, Cardinal Innocenti, has made it clear that in his view the present arrangements permitting the old Mass should be seen as temporary and that the final end in view is the "integration" of traditionalist Catholics into the mainstream worship of the Latin rite—that is, full acceptance of the Mass of Paul VI. Not one of the cardinals with any chance of being elected as the next pope has given any reason to think that he would grant full equality to the preconciliar rite of Mass, and, indeed, any such decision would probably be unenforceable: it would provoke uproar among most of the world's bishops, in an age when the predominance of "collegiality" has for practical purposes put an end to the era when popes could impose their will against a solid bloc of episcopal resistance right round the globe.

Moreover, such resistance would be entirely understandable, because any papal decision to establish full parity between the old and new rites of Mass would in effect be the rejection of a solemn Constitution promulgated by the most recent ecumenical council of the Catholic Church, after receiving a nearly unanimous positive vote from the conciliar Fathers and the approval of the Supreme Pontiff. Such a decision would be saying that the Vatican II Constitution on the Liturgy, *Sacrosanctum Concilium*, is purely optional and so can simply be shredded or thrown out the window, as it were, by those who consider it a disastrous mistake. I have made this point to various traditionalists and have sometimes encountered the answer that there are a number of precedents in Church history for the eventual abandonment or reversal of merely disciplinary—as distinct from doctrinal—decisions of ecumenical councils. But a constitution as long and as weighty as *Sacrosanctum Concilium*, dealing, moreover, with those most sacred actions that constitute the very heart of the Church's life, is in a very different category from brief disciplinary canons regulating this or that point of Church order, often in response to situations that by their very nature were temporary and transient.

In short, the full restoration of the Latin Mass according to the 1962 Missal is simply not on the Church's agenda, and those who cling to that hope, I believe, will be doomed to frustration. Even that "second-class citizenship" which they now enjoy by virtue of the 1984 indult and the Apostolic Letter *Ecclesia Dei* may well prove increasingly difficult to maintain.

But there is another and more fundamental sense in which I believe the Traditionalist Proposal is settling for second-best. It is not simply a question of the legal authority of the Vatican II Liturgy Constitution, or of the current state of Church politics, but of the liturgical rites *in themselves*. I believe that even if it were possible to restore the preconciliar rite to full parity with the new, that would not be the most desirable solution. In my view, the conciliar Constitution on the Liturgy was not only binding and authoritative; it was also *right!* I personally agree with the more than two thousand bishops, including Archbishop Marcel Lefebvre, who voted in favor of that document, which was the fruit of more than a century of profound, prayerful, and erudite studies, led by some of the great European monasteries, which had come to be known as the "liturgical movement".

The great problem since Vatican II, it seems to me, has not been simply that we have changed the preconciliar rite, but that we have introduced the *wrong sorts* of changes—changes that went far beyond those the great majority of Council Fathers had in mind when they approved and signed *Sacrosanctum Concilium*.

## III. *A Long-Term Solution: The Gamber Proposal*

This brings me, finally, to the plan of action that I think has the best long-term chances of restoring the eucharistic liturgy to what it should be. We may call it the Gamber Proposal.

Many of you may be familiar already with the name of the German scholar Msgr. Klaus Gamber, one of the most erudite historians of liturgy of the present century, who died in 1989 after more than thirty years as founder and director of the Liturgical Institute in Regensburg. Cardinal Joseph Ratzinger has described Gamber as "the one scholar who, among the army of pseudo-liturgists, truly represents the liturgical thinking of the center of the Church".[15] In recent years Gamber's last and probably most important work, published in English as *The Reform of the Roman Liturgy*, has aroused great interest and great controversy, not least because of the public endorsement given

---

[15] Quoted by Msgr. Wilhelm Nyssen in his "Testimonial" at the beginning of the English translation of Gamber's work *Die Reform der Römischen Liturgie: The Reform of the Roman Liturgy: Its Problems and Background* (San Juan Capistrano: Una Voce Press, and Harrison, N.Y.: Foundation for Catholic Reform, 1993), p. xiii.

to his work by no less than three cardinals of the Roman curia: Cardinal Ratzinger, Cardinal Silvio Oddi, former Prefect of the Congregation for the Clergy, and Cardinal Alphonse Stickler, former Prefect of the Vatican Library. All three of them wrote highly commendatory prefaces to the French edition of the book, which was published in 1992,[16] even though it is severely critical, not just of recent unauthorized abuses in the celebration of Mass, but also of many of the officially introduced changes themselves.[17]

Gamber's central thesis can be summed up by the following citation from his book. Referring to the context of spiritual crisis within which the postconciliar changes took place, Gamber writes:

We are dealing with ... the satiated state of mind of modern man who, living in our consumer society, approaches anything that is holy with a complete lack of understanding and has no appreciation of the concept of religion, let alone of his own sinful state. For them, God, if they believe in him at all, exists only as their "friend."

At this critical juncture, the traditional Roman rite, more than one thousand years old and until now the heart of the Church, was destroyed. A closer

---

[16] Msgr. Klaus Gamber, *La Réforme Liturgique en Question*, trans. Simone Wallon (Éditions Sainte-Madeleine, 1992). Cardinal Oddi's preface (no page number) is followed by those of Cardinals Ratzinger and Stickler on pp. 6–10.

[17] See also the reviews of Gamber's book by the present writer and three other priests (Fr. Kenneth Baker, S.J., Msgr. Richard J. Schuler, and Fr. Gerald E. Murray) in *The Latin Mass*, vol. 3, no. 2 (March–April 1994), pp. 38–43.

examination reveals that the Roman rite was not perfect, and that some elements of value had atrophied over the centuries. Yet, through all the periods of unrest that again and again shook the Church to her foundations, the Roman rite always remained the rock, the secure home of faith and piety. . . .

Obviously, the reformers wanted a completely new liturgy, a liturgy that differed from the traditional one in spirit as well as in form; and in no way a liturgy that represented what the Council Fathers had envisioned, i.e., a liturgy that would meet the pastoral needs of the faithful. Liturgy and faith are interdependent. That is why a new rite was created, a rite that in many ways reflects the bias of the new (modernist) theology. The traditional liturgy simply could not be allowed to exist in its established form because it was permeated with the truths of the traditional faith and the ancient forms of piety.[18]

What Gamber recommends, therefore, is a "reform of the reform": that is, a true implementation of what the Vatican II Fathers really called for in *Sacrosanctum Concilium*. Cardinal Ratzinger, in his preface to Gamber's book, takes up this invitation, noting that there are young Catholics, not merely old and "nostalgic" ones, who see the need for something much better:

A young priest said to me recently, "What we need today is a new liturgical movement." It was the expression of a wish that could be brushed aside in our

---

[18] Gamber, *Reform*, pp. 99–100.

times only by deliberately superficial minds. What
mattered to that priest was not the conquest of new
and audacious freedoms.... He sensed the need for a
new beginning, springing from deep within the liturgy itself, as had been the intention of the [earlier]
liturgical movement when it was at its true peak; that
is, when liturgists were not concerned with fabricat-
ing texts and inventing actions and forms, but rather,
with rediscovering the living center, of penetrating
what is in reality the liturgical tissue, in order that
renewal of the liturgy should issue forth from its own
very substance. The liturgical reform in its concrete
application, has increasingly alienated itself from this
origin. The result has not been a reanimation but a
devastation.[19]

I believe that we must take up the call of Gamber and
Ratzinger for a new liturgical movement—one that will
work toward an alternative proposal for implementing the
Vatican II Constitution on the Liturgy, in the light of what
Ratzinger calls the "heart" of the traditional Roman rite
itself. This will not be the work of one month or one year
or even ten years. Time will be needed to reflect carefully,
to organize international liturgical gatherings, to publish
studies and exchange ideas, taking into account not only
the Vatican II decrees but also the rich and authoritative
liturgical teaching now enshrined in the *Catechism of the
Catholic Church*. The long-term aim will be threefold. First,

---

[19] Gamber, *La Réforme*, p. 6 (present writer's translation from the French
original).

it will be necessary to build up a consensus among those very large numbers of Latin-rite Catholics throughout the world, including bishops and cardinals, who are far from satisfied with the way the liturgical reform has been carried out up till now but who do not see the Mass in its preconciliar form as being the most perfect possible liturgical expression. Secondly, this consensus should be given concrete expression in the form of a proposed missal and lectionary. Finally, after this has been published, circulated, and possibly revised, it could be presented to the Holy See, possibly some time during the next pontificate, with the request that it be approved for use throughout the Church—perhaps after a period of local use *ad experimentum*—as an alternative implementation of Vatican Council II, having *equal status and recognition* with the rite introduced by Paul VI.

Just what kind of liturgy might this be in specific terms? Let us now review briefly the fundamental principles laid down by Vatican II. Above all, it will be necessary to keep in the forefront of our minds as an overall guiding principle the conciliar Constitution's words in article 7:

> The liturgy, then, is rightly seen as an exercise of the priestly office of Jesus Christ.... From this it follows that every liturgical celebration, because it is an action of Christ the Priest and of his Body, which is the Church, is a sacred action surpassing all others.[20]

---

[20] Unless otherwise stated, quotations from Vatican Council II in this article are taken from the English version edited by Austin Flannery, O.P. rev. ed. (Boston: St. Paul Editions, 1988).

That is, the liturgy is first and foremost the action of our Lord himself, not simply *our* action and *our* invention. It is a sacred mystery that we receive and enter into, rather than something we create for ourselves. It could even be said that neglect of this great truth is the basic source of all the postconciliar liturgical confusion, in which the human community and its activity and "creativity" have come to predominate over the divine presence and the divine activity.

In keeping with this overall guiding principle, *Sacrosanctum Concilium* lays down several "general norms"[21] that are to be observed in all liturgical revision, including the following, which has unfortunately been very much neglected:

> Innovations are to be admitted only when necessary in order to bring some true and certain benefit to the Church (*nisi vera et certa utilitas Ecclesiæ id exigat*), and care must be taken that any new forms adopted should in some way grow organically from forms already existing.[22]

After this, there are just nine articles of the Constitution (nos. 50–58) decreeing specific areas in which the eucharistic liturgy is to be revised. I would like now to survey each of these in turn, suggesting ways in which each of them could be implemented without in any way harming

---

[21] SC, nos. 22–25.

[22] SC, no. 23 (present writer's translation of the expression cited above in the original Latin).

the integrity of the traditional Roman rite or opening the way for the abuses with which we are all too familiar.

### SC, no. 50: Changes to the Order of Mass

Article 50 is the most important of this group of nine, since it has to do with changes to the "Order" in the sense of the Ordinary of the Mass—the central structural parts that remain more or less the same in every eucharistic celebration. It is worth quoting in full:

> The rite of the Mass is to be revised in such a way that the intrinsic nature and purpose of its several parts, as well as the connection between them, may be more clearly manifested, and that devout and active participation by the faithful may be more easily achieved.
>
> For this purpose the rites are to be simplified, due care being taken to preserve their substance. Parts which with the passage of time came to be duplicated, or were added with little advantage, are to be omitted. Other parts which suffered loss through accidents of history are to be restored to the vigor they had in the days of the holy Fathers, as may seem useful or necessary.

This instruction is in turn to be seen in the light of another more all-encompassing norm laid down earlier (in article 34) for all the sacramental liturgies: "The rites should be distinguished by a noble simplicity. They should be clear by virtue of their brevity, and free from useless rep-

etitions." [23] Keeping in mind that other general norm that
no innovation is to be admitted unless the good of the
Church genuinely and certainly requires it, and taking as
our point of departure the last preconciliar edition of the
Roman Missal (that of 1962), how might we envisage an
alternate implementation of this particular decree?

With regard to manifesting more clearly the intrinsic
nature and purpose of the distinct parts of the Mass, and
the connection between them, we can take a lead from
the new *Catechism*, which affirms the now-familiar distinction between Liturgy of the Word and Liturgy of the
Eucharist as *the* fundamental dichotomy.[24]

It seems to me that the Vatican II decree could be fulfilled in this regard perfectly well without changing a single word of the old Missal. It would be sufficient for the
celebrant, after entering and kissing the altar with the appropriate prayers at the beginning of Mass, always to carry
out the Liturgy of the Word from the chair and lectern.
This practice, with which of course we are now familiar
in the new liturgy, was already standard in more solemn
and Pontifical Masses of the traditional rite. It highlights
clearly the privileged and central location of the altar as
the place of sacrifice, to which our attention is directed
*after* our hearts and minds have been duly prepared by hearing and reflecting on God's Word. It was only at the old
Low Mass that this distinction between Liturgy of the Word

---

[23] This is a more accurate rendition of the Latin (*sint brevitate perspicui*) than
Flannery's translation: "They should be short, clear, and free from useless rep-
etitions" (p. 12). The original places brevity at the service of clarity, whereas
Flannery's translation makes it seem an end in itself.

[24] CCC 1346.

and Liturgy of the Eucharist was somewhat blurred by the fact that the priest recited everything in both these parts at the altar, never facing the people except during the homily. This, however, was the staple fare Sunday after Sunday for the vast majority of Catholics before Vatican II.

With regard to "simplifying" the rites (while carefully preserving their substance), it seems to me that this would apply mainly to the celebration of Solemn High Mass or a Pontifical Mass, wherein some of the traditional rubrics do indeed seem a little over-meticulous and complex. In regard to the Low Mass, which was by far the most common form of celebrating the traditional rite, there are only half a dozen slight changes that suggest themselves to me, as one who has personally celebrated that rite for several years now.

First, I think the double *Confiteor* recited at the foot of the altar first by the priest and then by the servers is a little tedious and could perhaps be classed as a "useless repetition". Having just the one *Confiteor* recited together by priest, servers, and people, as in the new rite, would I think be an improvement.

Another rather inessential duplication comes just before the Gospel, when the priest recites two prayers, the second of which really adds nothing substantial to the very beautiful and longer one that precedes it and could well be omitted.

Likewise, the recitation of seven verses of Psalm 25 at the *Lavabo* during the Offertory (also in silence) takes longer than is necessary to accompany the action of washing the hands, and, since the last three verses (in which the psalmist proclaims his own innocence and denounces the wicked who accept bribes) are not in any case clearly linked to that liturgical action, they could well be omitted.

Also, there are several occasions in the Canon of the Mass where the old rubrics call for three signs of the cross in rapid succession over the eucharistic elements. This obliges the celebrant either to slow down the natural pace of the words artificially or else speed up artificially the three signs of the cross in a way that is scarcely reverent. If the three were replaced by just one sign of the cross on each of those occasions, the result would be more flowing and dignified.

Another way in which the old Roman Canon could be perfected is by giving it a more integrally trinitarian emphasis. One of the authentic fruits of the liturgical movement has been a deeper appreciation of the role of the Holy Spirit in the liturgy, as the One by whose power the bread and wine are changed into the Body and Blood of Christ. This is something stressed in the great and ancient Eastern rite liturgies; but the Roman Canon, while it is directly addressed to the Father and is deeply christological, contains only one mention of the Holy Spirit (right at the end, in the doxology). As the Australian liturgical scholar Father Clement Hill has recently pointed out,[25] the new *Catechism* gives more emphasis to the Holy Spirit's action in the liturgy than did the Vatican II Constitution itself.[26]

---

[25] Clement Hill, " 'Power that Goes out of Him': Perspectives on the Liturgy", in Andrew Murray, ed., *The New Catechism: Analysis and Commentary* (Catholic Institute of Sydney, 1994), pp. 49–53.

[26] Cf. for instance CCC 1073 and the long and beautiful section 1091–1109, entitled "The Holy Spirit and the Church in the Liturgy".

Accordingly, I would suggest two changes to emphasize the role of the Holy Spirit at those key moments of the Eucharistic Prayer, the *epiclesis*, or invocation of the Spirit over the gifts, and the doxology. First, the words *Spiritus Sancti virtute* ("by the power of the Holy Spirit") could well be inserted into the *epiclesis* prayer that begins *Quam oblationem* after the word *quaesumus*; and secondly, the entire doxology (which begins, "Through him, with him, in him, in the unity of the Holy Spirit") could be given greater emphasis by saying or singing it aloud, as in the new rite, while elevating the chalice and paten, as an invitation for the people to respond with the final "Amen." The contrast between this moment and the preceding silence of the rest of the Canon would provide a beautiful and dramatic consummation to the majesty of the Eucharistic Prayer.

The recitation from the altar of the so-called Last Gospel (the prologue of Saint John's Gospel) at the end of every single Mass, after the final blessing, did seem somewhat excessive and liturgically misplaced. I suspect this sublime reading would be appreciated better if it were heard less frequently, for instance, only during Advent, Christmastide, and on the Feast of the Annunciation, when the liturgical emphasis is precisely on the mystery of the Incarnation. At the end of Mass on those occasions it could be recited in the vernacular by the priest at the foot of the altar, as a brief meditation, together with the other extraliturgical prayers that were added a century ago by Pope Leo XIII.

Finally, article 50 also calls for revisions that further encourage the "devout and active participation by the faithful". It seems to me that the well-known practice of having "dialogue Masses", which was introduced in some countries even before Vatican II, would be quite adequate to comply with the Council's expectations in this regard: the people would for the most part join in reciting or singing the same parts of the Mass as they do now in the new rite. In this context we could also insert into the old rite, straight after the Creed, the ancient and laudable practice of the Offertory procession, in which the faithful participate by bringing the gifts to the foot of the altar. This would be one of the main points the Council Fathers had in mind in calling for the restoration of parts of the Mass that "suffered loss through accidents of history".

## SC, no. 51: More Extensive Use of Scripture

This article calls for "the treasures of the Bible ... to be opened up more lavishly" in the eucharistic liturgy. As we all know, this has been implemented by the two-year cycle for weekday readings and the three-year cycle for Sunday Mass. The scriptural selections in the old Missal were certainly very limited, but in the pastoral experience of many priests—myself included—we have gone from one extreme to the other in regard to the Sunday readings: two in the old rite and now four (first reading, Responsorial Psalm, second reading and Gospel). This is really too much for the vast majority of ordinary parishioners to assimilate in one sitting, and I am afraid most of it tends to go in one ear and out the other. It is very difficult for the preacher to explain adequately such a large selection of readings, especially since the second reading—normally a

New Testament Epistle—is seldom related thematically to the other readings. The usual result is that it tends to be ignored in the homily.

Furthermore, as Gamber points out, the old order of Sunday readings was abruptly abolished in the reform. It was not even taken into account, even though it had remained unchanged for nearly thirteen hundred years and had thus come to be, in effect, an integral part of the Roman rite.[27]

I would suggest that the alternate implementation of Vatican II that we are contemplating might well omit one of the four readings on Sundays, retaining just the first reading, Responsorial Psalm (which is an ancient Roman liturgical custom),[28] and Gospel. Within such a scheme, all the traditional Sunday readings (Epistle and Gospel) could be retained as those for Year A of a different three-year cycle, for the sake of maintaining the complete integrity of the ancient Roman rite in both Liturgy of the Word and Liturgy of the Eucharist. Then, for Years B and C, the most pastorally and catechetically valuable readings from the new rite could be selected and appropriately redistributed, omitting the more obscure texts, such as some of the lesser Old Testament ones whose only real value in a liturgical context lies in some sort of parallel or foreshadowing of the Gospel, which is of course what the preacher will concentrate on anyway. This kind of revision, I believe, would contribute toward a more effective

---

[27] Gamber, *Reform*, p. 70.

[28] Cf. Josef Jungmann, S.J., *The Mass* (Collegeville, Minn., Liturgical Press, 1976), p. 176.

scriptural formation for the faithful, by emphasizing the quality rather than just the quantity of the Sunday selections.

## SC, no. 52: The Homily

This article needs little or no comment because it simply emphasizes the importance of preaching and insists that the homily not be omitted on Sundays and Holy Days of obligation. Nobody, I suspect, would disagree with that.

## SC, no. 53: The "Prayer of the Faithful"

Here the Council mandates the restoration of these "common prayers" on Sundays and Holy Days. This was an ancient part of the Roman rite that fell into disuse, and, provided it is done well, I do not see why any reasonable Catholic should object to this reform.[29]

## SC, no. 54: Use of the Vernacular

This article must be read in the light of the earlier general norm applying to all the liturgical rites (not just the Mass), which states that "The use of the Latin language ... is to be preserved in the Latin rites." [30] This is now rather famous for having become, in pastoral practice, the most

---

[29] Some traditionalist authors apparently bent on finding fault with the new Mass at all costs have objected that the Prayer of the Faithful was rightly dropped centuries ago because it was "tedious" or "boring". This objection scarcely seems to show much appreciation for the power of intercessory prayer for the needs of the Church—surely more necessary than ever in these times of crisis!

[30] SC, no. 36.

flagrantly neglected—or even violated!—instruction in the entire Constitution on the Liturgy. Article 54 applies that general norm to the proposed revision of the eucharistic liturgy by stating that "a suitable place may be allotted to the vernacular . . . especially in the readings and the 'common prayer,' and also, as local conditions may warrant, in those parts [of the Mass] which pertain to the people." (The "parts" referred to here would, I think, be the *Confiteor* and Creed in particular.) There is clearly not one word here to justify the translation of the *whole* Mass into the vernacular.

An alternate reform, I suggest, might well use the following criterion: Latin could be retained for all those parts that are recited in a low voice by the priest—that is, the whole of the Offertory and the Canon—and also for most of the *unchanging* (or relatively unchanging) parts of the Mass that are recited or sung out loud: that is, the various common invocations and the final blessing, the *Kyrie*, *Gloria*, Preface, *Pater Noster*, *Sanctus*, and *Agnus Dei*. (Article 54 actually specifies that the faithful should be able to sing or recite many of those parts in Latin.)[31] This would leave for translation into the vernacular those publicly audible parts of the Mass that, because they change every day, would be most unfamiliar and unintelligible to the faithful if they remained in Latin: the opening Introit, antiphon, and Collect; the Scripture readings, Prayer of the Faithful, the

---

[31] An exception could be made for the *Confiteor* if, as I am suggesting, it is to be recited just once at the beginning of Mass by both priest and people. Since there is no tradition of singing this prayer, and since the Latin contains several passages that are awkward in pronunciation, recitation in the vernacular would probably be more appropriate here.

Offertory and Communion antiphons, and the postcommunion prayer. I suggest that such a distribution of languages would provide very much the kind of balance that most Council Fathers probably had in mind.

## SC, no. 55: Reception of Holy Communion

This article makes the uncontroversial point that it is preferable to distribute Hosts consecrated during the current celebration of the Eucharistic Sacrifice rather than those previously reserved in the tabernacle. It also states that in particular cases decided by the Apostolic See, Communion under both species may be given to the faithful, provided the Council of Trent's teaching on that matter is duly respected. Again, this is not likely to prove very controversial if, indeed, Communion under both species is restricted to particular cases and does not become the norm.

## SC, no. 56: Early Arrival at Mass

Only very lazy Catholics could object to this article! It simply emphasizes the importance of the Liturgy of the Word, which forms one unified act of worship together with the Liturgy of the Eucharist. The Council here instructs pastors to urge the faithful to take part in the *entire* celebration, from start to finish.

## SC, nos. 57–58: Concelebration

These last two decrees concerning changes in the rite of Mass simply extend the conditions under which the ancient

Eastern and Western practice of concelebrating Mass is to be permitted and stipulate that a rite for concelebration is to be drawn up and inserted into the liturgical books. Since the right of each priest to celebrate individually if he so desires is also reasserted here,[32] these decrees should not disturb anyone except the most intransigent traditionalists.

* * * * * * *

This completes our survey of the Vatican II decrees specifically dedicated to changes in the eucharistic liturgy. There remain only certain points that apply to the sacred liturgy in general: that is, including the Divine Office and other sacraments as well as the Mass.

Several of these concern a revision of the liturgical year or calendar. Chapter 5 of *Sacrosanctum Concilium* calls for an adjustment to modern conditions of the "traditional customs and discipline of the sacred seasons",[33] so as to emphasize more clearly their specific character. This is to be done particularly in regard to Lent, wherein the ancient emphasis on penance and preparation for baptism is to be restored more fully.[34]

If anything, the existing postconciliar reform has given *less* emphasis than ever to penance during Lent by its unnecessary changes in the prayers and by reducing the minimum time of the eucharistic fast practically to the vanishing point. The proper implementation of these conciliar dis-

---

[32] SC, no. 57: 2.
[33] SC, no. 107.
[34] SC, nos. 107, 109–10.

positions would not require any great changes in the rites and would consist mainly in different emphases in preaching and catechesis, which article 109 itself mentions.

This chapter of the Liturgy Constitution also calls for greater attention to the feasts of the Lord, and the Proper of the Time in each season, so that feasts of the saints do not detract from those great mysteries of salvation that are being emphasized. With that end in view, it also calls for the removal from the universal calendar of some minor saints whose feasts would be better celebrated only in those local areas or religious communities for whom they are more important.[35] These instructions have of course been implemented vigorously in the postconciliar reform— some would say rather too vigorously. But it is undeniable that the preconciliar calendar did contain many minor feasts of very obscure saints. An alternate and somewhat less drastic implementation of what the Council calls for should not be too problematical.

Finally, chapter 6 of *Sacrosanctum Concilium* concerns sacred music and, as is well known, calls for great care in preserving and cultivating the existing "treasury of sacred music", insisting that, other things being equal, Gregorian chant should be given "pride of place" in liturgical celebrations, with the participation of the people, where possible.[36] These decrees have of course been notoriously neglected, and, indeed, even before Vatican II it seems that a neglect of this sublime and uplifting music was quite common at the grass-roots level: the majority of Catholics

---

[35] SC, nos. 108, 111.
[36] SC, nos. 114–18.

apparently had little opportunity to hear it on a regular basis at their local parish church.

Having said that, we have now outlined virtually all the changes mandated by Vatican II for the eucharistic liturgy and have suggested an alternate implementation. The point I would now like to stress is that such an alternate reform would contain none of those features of the present post-conciliar rite that have disturbed and even scandalized tradition-conscious Catholics, even provoking schism among the more extreme traditionalists. For instance:

1 Latin has not been abandoned and is retained for almost the entire Ordinary of the Mass.

2 Only the Roman Canon (the first Eucharistic Prayer) is used. Vatican II never even hinted at the composition of new Eucharistic Prayers, not even as options. Even if the newly composed ones were in themselves of equal quality with the old—which is questionable, especially with no. 2, which now seems to be the most frequently used—they represent in effect the creation of a new rite, not the revision of the old. Gamber insists that to change anything so central as the 1500-year-old Canon—the very heart of the Roman rite and the fundamental defining point of its very identity in comparison with other rites—"is synonymous with the destruction of the rite in its entirety".[37] And the Council certainly never dreamed of any such abolition of the old rite in order to replace it with a newly invented one.

3 In our alternate revision, none of those existing Offertory prayers has been removed that clearly expressed the sacrifi-

---

[37] Gamber, *Reform*, p. 31.

cial character of the Mass. Their abolition has been a major source of scandal for many Catholics, and with the widespread decline in belief that we noted earlier, the experience of the last quarter-century surely enables us to conclude with more certainty than ever that the removal of these prayers definitely did *not* meet with the Council's requirement, namely, that any innovation must be "genuinely and certainly required by the good of the Church".[38]

4 Our alternate reform would also leave unchanged, and merely translated into the vernacular, the vast majority of the *proper* prayers in the traditional Missal, that is, those that change from day to day. The Council never suggested any substantial revision of these prayers; and yet, as Father Anthony Cekada's scholarly study has pointed out, nearly two-thirds of all the Opening Prayers (the Collects or "orations") were simply abolished, and only 17 percent of them have been retained untouched in the Missal of Pope Paul VI.[39]

What is worse, the motivation for most of the changes has been markedly ideological: in an astonishing contrast with what the Council actually called for in article 109 (b) of the Liturgy Constitution,[40] there has been such a drastic reduction or mutilation of the traditional prayers mentioning such themes as human weakness, guilt and repentance on the part of sinners, the wrath of God, hell, the souls in Purgatory, the Church's need for protection from her spiritual and temporal

---

[38] SC, no. 23.

[39] Anthony Cekada, *The Problems with the Prayers of the Modern Mass* (Rockford, Ill., TAN Books, 1991), p. 9.

[40] SC, no. 109 (b) stresses that in Lent, especially, it is important to "impress on the minds of the faithful the distinctive character of penance as a detestation of sin because it is an offense against God. The role of the Church in penitential practices is not to be passed over, and the need to pray for sinners should be emphasized."

enemies, and other topics that were evidently considered too "negative" for the needs of "modern man",[41] that in effect the whole spirit of the eucharistic liturgy has been seriously altered. Instead of these timeless and essential aspects of Catholic doctrine and spirituality, we have been given a liturgy that to an alarming extent reflects the naïve and transient optimism of the 1960s: consciousness of sin, guilt, enemies, and judgment had to yield to that "insight" of popular modern psychology that reassures us all: "I'm O.K., you're O.K."

5 Also in our proposed reform, the sacred silence—so important as an aid to true recollection, adoration, and an appreciation of the Real Presence—is preserved throughout the Offertory and Canon, which would be recited by the priest in the traditional reverent whisper. A great many Catholics have found that in the new Mass the constant patter of words (now trumpeted through microphones and amplifiers) brings our liturgy uncomfortably close in spirit to the more rationalistic atmosphere of Protestant services, devoid of mystery, in which the edification of the faithful by preaching and instruction in the Word is of primary importance.

6 Equally conducive to true adoration were the many gestures of reverence to the altar, signs of the cross, and genuflections, Communion received kneeling and on the tongue, all of which characterized the traditional Roman rite. So it

---

[41] One of the reforming liturgists, Fr. Matias Augé, C.M.F., stated openly in the official Vatican liturgical publication the reason for getting rid of these traditional prayers: "Some of these collects, in fact, spoke of, among other things, the punishments, anger, or divine wrath for our sins, of a Christian assembly oppressed with guilt, continually afflicted due to its disorders, threatened with condemnation to eternal punishment, etc." ("Le Collete del Proprio del Tempo nel Nuovo Messale", *Ephemerides Liturgicæ* 84 [1970]: 275–76). Quoted in Cekada, *Problems*, p. 11.

should be stressed that nearly all of these rubrics would be preserved in the alternate reform I have suggested, following the lead of Msgr. Klaus Gamber. At a time when their abolition, or reduction on a sweeping scale, has been accompanied by a terrible decline in belief in the Real Presence, it would seem that the retention of such gestures and postures is more urgent than ever.

7 I have already remarked that the "clericalization" of the laity by giving them more and more liturgical roles that were once reserved for those in Holy Orders was not at all what the Council had in mind by "more active participation" on the part of the laity. Literally not one word in *Sacrosanctum Concilium* calls for the introduction of new "lay ministries". But now, no end appears in sight to this trend. In the recent papal Mass in Sydney that I have already described, yet another "breakthrough" for the laity was announced gleefully by the priest-reporter of this event: for the first time ever, lay ministers—three hundred of them, male and female!—each held a ciborium full of altar breads while "the Pope at the altar some distance away" consecrated them. Thus, as the writer commented in triumphant and aggressive tones,

> laymen and women were involved in the central mystery of the Eucharist more closely than they've ever been before.... Randwick [the Sydney racecourse where the papal Mass was celebrated] has changed the benchmark of liturgical correctness; the ante has been pushed up; individuals and groups are now challenged to adjust. The Vatican liturgical watchdog has turned out to be more liberal and progressive than was thought.[42]

---

[42] McSweeney, "Mass", p. 21.

If we are to have ever-increasing "egalitarianism" of this sort in the new rite of Mass, this only underlines the need for an alternate and more faithful application of the Council that more clearly manifests the special dignity of the ordained male priest in his unique relationship to the sublime eucharistic mystery. I would suggest that extraordinary ministers not participate at all in this parallel reform and that only priests, deacons, and male altar servers be present in the sanctuary, together, perhaps, with men who are duly instituted to the ministries of lector and acolyte, which have now replaced the old liturgical roles of the subdeacons.

8  Finally, our alternate reform will once again have the priest in front of the altar, facing the same way as the people, throughout the Offertory and Canon. Mass "facing the people" is regarded by Gamber as the most harmful single innovation of the entire liturgical reform—one that, as he demonstrates with convincing scholarship and at great length, has no precedent in any ancient liturgical tradition.[43] Again, Vatican II never remotely suggested this change, which is more radically Protestant in spirit even than the Lutheran custom and traces its origin to the Calvinist "Lord's Supper".[44]

More than any other single innovation, this one focuses attention on the "community meal" aspect of the Eucharist instead of its sacrificial character and highlights the human personality of the priest (his voice, facial expressions, and gestures) instead of downplaying those features in the interests of the person of Christ, the true High Priest whom he

---

[43] Gamber, *Reform*, part 2, "Facing the Lord", pp. 115–84.

[44] Lutheran pastors celebrate the Eucharist with their "back to the people", as I remember from my Protestant days working with the Lutheran Mission in New Guinea and as the Lutheran F.-G. Dreyfus reminded Prof. Jean Guitton in the radio interview already referred to (cf. n. 12 above).

unworthily represents. (It will be noted that I spoke of the priest "facing the same way as the people", not "with his back to the people". Once we even use the latter expression, we are already defining this ancient position of the priest in very negative-sounding terms and thus playing straight into the hands of those who want to abolish that tradition. For of course, we only speak of "turning one's back" on someone in a pejorative context, rebuking his rudeness in turning away from someone he should be speaking to. But the whole point is that during the Offertory and Eucharistic Prayer the celebrant is *not* in dialogue with the people, but in supplication before Almighty God in the name of the people.)

In concluding this talk, I would stress that the specific proposals for a "reform of the reform" that I have suggested here make no pretense of being definitive. They could be seen as offering a mere "working draft", so to speak, to begin the quest for a broad consensus in the years ahead. I am under no illusions that either die-hard traditionalists or die-hard ultramontanists will find this proposal attractive (and much less the "progressive" liturgical establishment!). Even many of those who might in principle sympathize with the call of Msgr. Gamber and Cardinal Ratzinger for "a new liturgical movement" will doubtless find all sorts of immediate reasons, based on the current state of ecclesiastical politics, for shelving this project indefinitely as an impractical dream.

But even very farfetched dreams have more than once ended up becoming a reality. And if this one turns out to be not only farfetched but also farsighted, then the Holy Spirit himself will in due course bring it to fruition, so that once again the Divine Sacrifice may be celebrated in the perennial and restored Roman rite with the beauty and perfection it deserves and with the full and unreserved approbation of Holy Mother Church.

# APPENDIX IV

## SALUTARY DISSATISFACTION:

## AN ENGLISH VIEW OF "REFORMING THE REFORM"

*Aidan Nichols, O.P.*

### Some Generalities

*Is* there a liturgical crisis in Western Catholicism? Many would deny that there is—and deny that they are "entering into denial" in so doing. The overwhelming majority of practicing Catholics, it is affirmed, are perfectly content with the liturgical forms in which they worship Sunday by Sunday, and even day by day. Leaving aside those on the far-flung margins to right and to left (and the suggestion may be made that these are in any case over-represented in letters to the Catholic press), we have a Church of, liturgically speaking, satisfied customers.

In the first part of this essay, I concede that it may be so, but I add that it is far from certainly so. I go on to argue that, *if* it is so, it definitely ought not to be so. And I end by saying how a situation both ambiguous and regrettable has arisen and what positively may be done to correct it. And this will lead by a natural progression into a consideration of Father Brian Harrison's recent proposal.

I

Is the Church in the West composed of a liturgically happy clientèle? The decline in Mass attendance, whether in traditionally Catholic countries or in lands such as my own, where commentators frequently remarked in the past on the cohesiveness of a community whose sense of confessional identity was strong to the point of overpowering, may have a variety of causes. Those who have ceased to practice sacramentally *may* not have fallen away because the ethos of Catholic worship ceased to hold them. But anthropologists strongly suggest that modern simplified rites placing a premium on verbal intelligibility and group interaction are likely to alienate those portions of the population who are either less articulate or seek more subtle forms of ritual participation. An honest answer to the question, Have we lost people because of the liturgy? can only be: Quite possibly, yes.

But in addition to the Catholics who are absent because they have ceased to practice, we must add that other group of absentees—those who are not with us because they have not heard that here, in ordinary Catholic parish churches up and down the land, there lies enchantment. The Mass should be evangelical, a means of conversion, and this it cannot be unless it conveys a supernatural impression. In a justly famous passage from the *Russian Primary Chronicle* when the (still pagan) envoys of Vladimir, prince of Kiev, returned from the Divine Liturgy they had attended in the great church of the Holy Wisdom at Constantinople, they reported:

We knew not whether we were in heaven or on earth,
for surely there is no such splendour or beauty anywhere on earth. We cannot describe it to you: only
this we know, that God dwells there among men,
and that their service surpasses the worship of all other
places. For we cannot forget that beauty.[1]

This is not aestheticism. It is what we should expect naturally to be the case if the liturgy of the Church really is
the glorification of the God of glory, the God in whom
there coincide absolute holiness (and so, from our side,
awe), love (and so, from our side, devotion), and beauty
(and so, from our side, wonder). There was not always
beauty in the older liturgy, and doubtless there was not
universally to be found awe and devotion. But by the
strangeness of its language, the submission of the liturgical
actors to an objective rite celebrated facing the Beyond,
and not the immediate participants, and gestures that
were clearly intended to be a choreography of reverence
even if very imperfectly executed by this or that individual, it communicated effortlessly a sense of the difference
and the seriousness of what was being carried out. It had
that power of enchantment, difficult to analyze (though I
have done my best), which draws non-Catholics because—
precisely—it is not, like so much of the rest of existence,
banal. So can we say that it is owing to the present state of

---

[1] Cited in: T. Ware, *The Orthodox Church* (Harmondsworth, 1963; 1967),
p. 269.

the liturgy that more people—above all, as this decade of evangelization approaches its end—are not asking to enter our communion? We must answer: We cannot say that it is *not* owing to it.

Then in addition to these two crowds of shadows at the feast—those who have left us and those who have failed to join us—there are those who are actually present, on the benches. Can we safely assume that they are satisfied with what they find? Here we must recall the heavy emphasis laid on the virtue of obedience to the Church's pastors by the restored Catholicism of the later nineteenth and early twentieth century, reaching its apogee in the 1870 definition of the pope's universal, ordinary, and immediate jurisdiction. The habit of obedience makes good Catholics slow to criticize. But absence of critical comment cannot be taken without further ado to imply approval of the manners of celebrants at the altar, the quality of church music, or the casual atmosphere that too frequently reigns in our churches. The new pastoral orthodoxy whereby priests, cantors, and readers are encouraged to establish immediate rapport with congregations, not altogether unfairly compared to that customary with live television audiences, is, it must be remembered, a novelty for which Church history provides no precedent and Church discourse, therefore, no agreed language. It may well be, therefore, that many Catholics who would not dream of abandoning their attendance at Mass nonetheless feel, if not habitually, then at least occasionally and sufficiently often to be a matter of concern, a sense of incongruity and discomfort. "It shouldn't be like this" may be the reaction of more people than is generally thought simply because they are hard put to find the language to say how it *should* be.

Now if the liturgical reform has significantly contributed to the lapsation of Catholics, if it has largely failed to attract new converts, and if much of its apparent acceptance depends on the sheer obedience of those habituated, with whatever perhaps inarticulate misgivings, not to reason why, then we can, I think, properly speak of a crisis in the Roman liturgy today. If, if, and if: I grant the conjectural nature of the considerations I have put forward, though I also maintain they are not without plausibility.

## II

Even were it the case, however, that the Church public is by and large adequately satisfied with the form of worship customarily offered to them in the modern Roman rite, it is still possible to assert that they should *not* be. The Church is not a business, whose management can rest content if its customers express consumer satisfaction. To "feel comfortable with a worship situation" is an infallible sign that we have missed the real meaning of the liturgy in its sacrality, its difference, its supernatural power. If we are to use commercial analogies here, then we must say of the Church that she is in the business of making people realize they have needs they have barely dreamed of. Because we are made in the image of God, made to tend to our divine archetype when he appears to us in the suffering and glorified God-man Jesus Christ, we have a need precisely *not* to be confirmed in our ordinary everyday personas by the easy uplift of a worship that consists in quickly appropriated words and sounds. By an apparent paradox, we need the liturgy *not* to be intrusively relevant to the secular roles that the society of a fallen world constructs for us. We need the liturgy to *estrange* us from our ordinary workaday selves by enabling us to find a new identity in those voices that speak there of adoration, purification, and the endless transcendence of the peace beyond all understanding of the City of God.[2]

These are the most important tasks that the historic liturgies of Christendom have performed, and from them flow their power to affect us at the deepest level of our being—to bring us not only consolation in the face of unnegotiable evils but also courage to change the world. The power of the Mass to unsettle us and to give us a vocation that takes us beyond our secular identity and the duties we share with others as fellow citizens derives from the identity of the Mass, at its heart, with the Sacrifice of Calvary, considered as the saving revelation of the Holy Trinity, with whom we commune in eucharistic reception, thus anticipating our share in that suffering turned to everlasting joy which is, please God, our destiny in heaven. At every Mass we are to see the Crucified in his glory; and when we communicate, we are to receive him in his own person as he gives us by anticipation a share in the life of blessed sacrifice that is the Holy Trinity, and which will be ours in fullness—if only we cooperate with it—at the end of time.

---

[2] These themes have been highlighted in a recent work of great difficulty yet offering much reward: C. Pickstock, *After Writing: The Liturgical Consummation of Philosophy* (Oxford, 1998).

It follows that three doctrines of the Church about the Holy Eucharist constitute a series of indispensable litmus tests for the right functioning of the liturgical organism that is the Church. The liturgy must make us aware of the identity of the Mass with Calvary. It must make us appreciate the Real Presence of the Savior in his full Humanity and Divinity in the consecrated Gifts. And it must be for us, as Saint Thomas' antiphon puts it, *pignus futurae gloriae*, a pledge of future glory, an anticipation of heaven. It is a matter of increasingly common knowledge among Protestants—whether they welcome it or regret it—that the present eucharistic practice of Western Catholics generally fails to pass the standards set by these doctrines. To cite but one example: a recent number of the journal *Lutheran Forum*, and here we must recall that classical Lutherans hold to the Real Presence as strongly as we do ourselves, records what it calls the "stunning results" of a recent and much-publicized poll about eucharistic beliefs among Catholics in America. In an essay entitled "Will the Real Catholics Please Kneel for Communion?", A. G. Roeber, who is professor of early modern history and religious studies at Pennsylvania State University, writes:

> If the survey is to be believed, American members of that communion are as Zwinglian as protestants, regarding the Mass only as a "remembrance" of Christ and a vague celebration of "community". Despite a teaching magisterium and its claims for "apostolic succession", the Roman Catholic Church in the United States has its hands full demonstrating that a genuine community of belief, and not just nominal

adherents, has received official church teaching on
*the* central mystery of the faith.[3]

It would be comforting, but, I fear, wholly delusory, to
suppose that all this is an American disease from which
other parts of the Western patriarchate are shielded, its
symptoms unknown. And here we must take candidly into
account the way modern liturgical style has contributed
to the weakening of the "sense of the faithful" in this realm
over large areas of the Latin Church.

How did it happen? I can give a bald and unadorned
explanation by summarizing in briefest possible form the
argument of my small book, *Looking at the Liturgy*, which
has three chapters.[4]

In the first, I suggest how certain presuppositions of
the Catholic Enlightenment of the eighteenth century—
the age in which most of the liturgical reforms enacted
by the Second Vatican Council were first presented as
*desiderata*—survived to skew liturgical revision in the direction of an excessive emphasis on the liturgy as preaching, as moral stimulus, and as an exercise in community
building—at the expense of its primarily latreutic or God-
centered character, in which, in fact, its deepest instructive, ethical, and Church-upbuilding power actually
consists. Then, secondly, I show how the liturgical reform
came just too late to take advantage of the insights into
the nature of ritual of an inherited and complex kind ar-

[3] A. G. Roeber, "Will the Real Catholics Please Kneel for Communion?",
*Lutheran Forum* 32, 1 (1998): 17.

[4] A. Nichols, O.P., *Looking at the Liturgy: A Critical View of Its Contemporary
Form* (San Francisco, 1996).

rived at by social anthropologists—especially, as it happens, in England. Had their voices been heard, it would have been realized that such goals of the liturgical reformers as enhanced community sense and more engaged participation are not necessarily best achieved by thrusting them into people's faces. Thirdly, the translation, adaptation, and pastoral application of the revised rites and their associated documents took place in a phase of Western culture that was profoundly inimical to the same project conceived by the Council Fathers. At a time when our culture was more "horizontal", less open to the transcendent, than at any previous time in its history, and when the gap between high culture and popular was singularly difficult to bridge, it is hardly surprising that we were landed with a liturgy that seems both anthropocentric and Philistine.[5]

And where do we go from here? I believe that the answer lies in the convergence of the two rites, the classical and the modern. The historic Roman rite can only be enriched by the incorporation of the best aspects of the reform—a fuller cycle of readings, the wonderful Prefaces of the new rite, and the possibility, where opportune, of concelebration and the administration of the chalice to the laity—and these are the only terms on which Rome will be able to convince the episcopate that general access to the classical rite and the training of ordinands in its celebration are desirable. At the same time, the new rite, in other respects impoverished and a poor vehicle— especially as commonly performed—for doctrines we hold

---

[5] A. Nichols, O.P., "Zion and Philistia: The Liturgy and Theological Aesthetics Today", *Downside Review* 115, 398 (1997): 53–73.

dear can only profit by a movement to celebrate it in the spirit of the old rite and with the reverence, dignity, and craftsmanship that the historic liturgy has such power to call forth from its servants. Then one day, though doubtless I shall not be alive to see it, the unity of our ritual Church, both in herself and with her past, can be reconstituted as, gradually, the two become one. At the same time, the kind of general orientation for "reform of the reform" I have suggested will realign the Roman rite, in the overall spirit of its celebration, with the liturgies of the Eastern Catholic Churches, so that we shall be able once again to appeal to the "ethos of the liturgy" as expressing the essence of Catholicism without in so doing appearing to fall into self-contradiction of an egregious kind.

## A Specific Proposal

But Father Brian Harrison, of the Oblates of Wisdom, has outlined a possible shape for a re-reformed liturgy with much greater specificity than this. His is a coherent and cogent proposal, which I was not at all surprised to see, having been exposed to his acute intellect during my time as a teacher at the Roman College of the Dominicans (the Angelicum). It is also a brave initiative—for there is something faintly absurd about a lone presbyter offering to re-design the Roman rite, especially when he has criticized the inorganic character of previous reform! On the other hand, *someone* has to set the ball rolling—and it should be, I believe, precisely by "Harrison's Move", namely, to take as departure point the Missal of Saint Pius V, but seen in the light (in different respects flattering and unflattering) of the Mass of Paul VI and the liturgical experience of Western Catholicism over the last thirty and more years. If, then, I dissent from some of the measures he would have Church authority take, disagreeing as I do not only with details but even with the occasional basic norm, this should not be ascribed to any lack of sympathy for the basic nature of his project.

So much survives of the classical rite of Low Mass, *more romano*, in the Harrison scheme that one can hardly accuse him of a rationalist construal of the Second Vatican Council's call for "noble simplicity". He does, however, use the same language of "misplacement", "unnecessary duplication", and "excessiveness" that is generally the hallmark of the liturgist of an Enlightenment stamp. A reading of the commentary on the Tridentine Low Mass that occupies the final chapters of Catherine Pickstock's study of the relation of doxology and ontology—worship and the sense of reality—in Western culture might disabuse him (as it disabused me). What she shows is that it is just those features of the rite most severely criticized by self-consciously modern liturgists (and echoed by Harrison) that render the form of classical liturgy most useful to us.[6] Anticipations and reprises, reiteration and excess, these convey to us (once the prejudice against them is removed)

---

[6] See note 2 above. For those who cannot face the whole work, there is an incisive summary of the book by the distinguished theologian of the Eucharist Father Robert Sokolowski in "Theology and Deconstruction", *Telos* 110 (winter 1998): 155–66.

the distinctive rhythm of true worship. For in the Mass
we have already arrived at the goal of our pilgrimage and
yet are always rebeginning it; in the liturgy there are many
voices even for the single agent of the priest, for here no
one is to be straightforwardly the center of his world; and
at worship a certain dislocated "stammering" before the
"excess" of the divine mystery and its saving generosity is
far from out of place. I think one must frankly say that,
while the doctrinal sections of *Sacrosanctum Concilium* ought
to be regarded, along with all teaching on faith and morals by general councils, as sacrosanct (no pun intended!),
the bishops enjoyed no assistance of the Holy Spirit—
even negatively—in matters of the aesthetics of ritual. In
that realm they had only human prudence to guide them,
a prudence that, sadly, lacked access to resources of an-
thropological understanding more fully available to us now.
One can indeed argue that the main doctrinal advance
achieved by the Council Fathers in the Liturgy Constitution—the much fuller awareness of the eschatological
bearings of worship when compared, for instance, with
Pius XII's *Mediator Dei*, was (and is) threatened by a prudential commitment to the "noble simplicity" notions of
Enlightenment and Neo-Enlightenment advisers, for it is
precisely the "stammering" quality of traditional liturgy
that opens the worshipper to the divine transcendence, to
God as End.

This difference of principle with Father Harrison naturally gives me pause when I mull over some of his specific suggestions. The double *Confiteor*, for example: to
my mind, turning the confession of sin into a *conversation*,
where the priest not only prays for the absolution of the

people but accepts their prayer for his absolving likewise, is a beautiful expression of the sacramental fraternity of lay and ordained. Again, the Last Gospel, as I see it, is a coda that sums up the whole meaning of the eucharistic action that has preceded it—at any rate when what we are talking about is, as mostly in the historic rite, the Prologue to Saint John's Gospel. In an age of often deplorably low Christology, can the faithful ever hear those words too often?

I note, however, that the Dominican use (which, with permission, I celebrate on a number of occasions in the year) contains neither the twofold prayer before the Gospel in the Liturgy of the Word nor the more extended citation from Psalm 25 in the Liturgy of the Sacrifice—so I would hardly be well situated to criticize a desire for abbreviation of *these* texts!

The other major point on which I should be more "conservative"—in the sense of anxious to preserve the structure of the classical rite—than Father Harrison concerns his provisions for the lectionary. The laudable desire of the Council for a fuller feasting of the people on the banquet of the Bible does not necessitate a triennial, or even biennial, cycle of readings. Such cycles have as their inevitable result (except when, as on some major festivals, three Gospels furnish quasi-identical readings) the obscuring of the properly integrated character of a liturgical day. Thus, for instance on the Lenten Sundays, any "pastoral" or "catechetical" advantage to be gained by offering alternative readings is surely outweighed by the building up of a culture of association for the "Sunday of the Samaritan Woman" or "the Sunday of the Raising of Lazarus", these mighty moments, with meditative meat to sustain one for a lifetime, in the ministry of the Savior en route to his Passion. As this example suggests, it is not that the reformers of the 1960s were wrong to think one could sometimes go back beyond the inherited choice of readings, but that they did wrong in sweeping away the latter wholesale. In order to offer an ampler selection from the Word of God, would it not suffice to enrich the weekday readings of the old lectionary from the new—without recourse, then, to the unpoetic Years A, B, and C? (And while on offenses against lyricism, may we have back Sundays "after Pentecost", or, at least, "after Trinity", in place of the uninspired "of the Year"—never mind that ICEL monstrosity "Ordinary Time", *monstrosity* because no saving time is ever "ordinary".)

I find no difficulty with the modest emendation of the Roman Canon (fewer syllables than John XXIII's addition of a reference to Saint Joseph) by which Father Harrison would render the Great Prayer more pneumatologically explicit. We should notice, however, that the prayer *Supplices te rogamus*, which asks the Father to identify our earthly altar with the heavenly, may betoken a more ancient theology of the Eucharistic Sacrifice than that represented by a more developed pneumatology. The latter is, in the liturgical context, a gift of the Christian East to Catholicity—but why not indeed acknowledge that gift, as so often in the history of Western worship, by a discreet adaptation of the Canon?

On the bidding prayers: I understand that a number of the liturgical scholars who in the 1950s recommended their restoration had it in mind that they would take a form closer to that of the litanies in the Liturgy of Saint John Chrysostom: recited *versus altarem* and more by way of a sustained supplication than a shopping list. On Offertory processions: I imagine Father Harrison would not insist on these at *every* Mass (where two or three are gathered together?), but at the principal parochial or conventual Mass of a Sunday or greater festival they are highly appropriate. On concelebration, I should like to see some requirement that would limit the acceptable sum total of concelebrants: both so as to avoid the impression of a sacerdotal rally and also (and this is the spiritually weightier point) to prevent a concelebrant being so physically distanced from the altar, and from the manual acts of the chief celebrant, that his impression of really acting at Mass *in persona Christi* becomes attenuated.

Finally, it surprises me that Father Harrison has not included on his blueprint the one piece of "hybridization" of Old and New that, in my limited experience, even those intransigently wedded to the Mass of Saint Pius V can accept, and that is the incorporation of most if not all of the wonderful Prefaces in the Missal of Paul VI.

## Conclusion

Father Harrison's scheme warrants wider study and reflection—as, apparently, exalted figures at Rome have already insinuated. With the reservations I have entered, I support it myself. We should note, however, the extreme likelihood that it will meet with rejection from protagonists of the two versions of the Western liturgy that it proposes to supplant. There is a danger that it will become the ritual equivalent of the "third pope", elected, vainly, in the Great Schism of the West in the fond hope that to him all would rally from either side.

Should a version of what he suggests, close in every way to the rite abrogated by Paul VI, be adopted, I think it would be fair, after a transitional period, to expect the "traditional" to treat it as the legitimate—and, on our hypothesis, universally available—successor of the rite of Saint Pius. That it could ever manage to replace the rite promulgated by Paul VI—especially outside the (culturally defined) West, many will surely doubt. Any attempt to re-impose the Latin language—albeit for the unchanging parts of the Mass alone—would surely engender new versions of the "Chinese Rites" controversies of the past. And yet, the texts of a *re*-reformed Roman rite could still be enacted in a suitably dignified vernacular, and analogues sought—as currently now in India—for its sacred gestures.

# A REFORM OF THE REFORM?

## *The Reverend J. P. Parsons*

Reform of the liturgical reform introduced into the Western Church during the 1950s and 1960s was the subject of a paper delivered by my friend Father Brian Harrison at Colorado Springs in 1995. It was that paper which moved Father Joseph Fessio, S.J., to launch the *Adoremus* movement to work toward such a reform.

Having been asked by Father Harrison to respond to his paper, the first question that presents itself is "How realistic should one be?" It is always possible to indulge personal preferences about an "ideal" liturgy, but, apart from the unlikelihood of these preferences being put into practice, any such scheme would constitute an arbitrary and eclectic exercise of the very sort that Archbishop Bugnini's Consilium permitted itself when producing the existing set of liturgical options. If that conception of liturgical "reform" is in large part a source of the problems we face,

---

Fr. John Parsons was born in Australia and was raised as a Protestant. He entered the Catholic Church in 1975, and he studied for the priesthood in Rome at the English College and in the Pontifical Gregorian University, from which he holds a licentiate in Theology. Fr. Parsons' priestly ministry has been mainly in Australia's capital city, Canberra, where he has been the pastor of a Traditional (Tridentine) Mass congregation under the terms of the *Ecclesia Dei* papal indult. His articles have appeared in *Catholic World Report* and other journals. At present he is ministering to Arab Catholic refugees in the Middle East.

more of the same theorizing is not only futile in practice but objectionable in principle.

At the other end of the pragmatic spectrum, there stands the possibility of suggesting a few modest improvements to the 1969 Roman Missal. These would be so small and piecemeal as to present no unified vision and would be equally open to the charge of subjectivism and eclecticism, which must somehow be avoided if any "reform of the reform" is to be intellectually coherent or to gain acceptance on a wide scale.

I think the most appropriate way into the subject is to attempt to identify the fundamental problem or *mentality* that has created the present liturgical malaise. To do that, one must begin historically by attempting to trace the motor forces in liturgical change.

## I. *The "Modern" Mentality and the Search for an Ideal Liturgy*

The received histories of the liturgical movement sometimes deal with the neo-Gallican experiments of the eighteenth century but more generally begin the story with Dom Guéranger and the Abbey of Solesmes from the 1830s, continue to Dom Lambert Beauduin at the Abbey of Mont César prior to the Great War, and conclude with Odo Casel, Pius Parsch, and the other names familiar in liturgically conscious circles during the 1950s.

While not attempting a history of the liturgical movement, one could perhaps summarize the movement's course by saying that prior to Vatican II, it passed through three "moments" or phases. The first, typified by Guéranger, stemmed from the realization that the liturgy was no longer being celebrated perfectly anywhere and was devoted to creating ideal conditions in which it could be lived out. The second, typified by Beauduin, stemmed from the realization that the liturgy was not being celebrated perfectly by the mass of the faithful and was devoted to promoting the liturgical life as far as possible in the setting of a parish. The third, in the period after the Second World War, with increased experimentation in France and elsewhere and the annual International Liturgical Congresses from 1950, stemmed from the realization that it was impossible to involve the mass of the faithful in the existing liturgy in a full and equal way. Attention was therefore devoted to changing that liturgy in the hope of procuring the perfect participation of everyone. We note here the beginnings of a Copernican revolution: initially the idea is to make modern life revolve around the liturgy, but as the movement develops, there is an increasing tendency to make the liturgy revolve around modern life. After the Second Vatican Council, the latter tendency clearly had the upper hand, and the postconciliar Missal and Office marked a definite break with historic forms in an attempt to make the Church's worship simpler, easier, and more immediately comprehensible to *homo modernus*, be he an uninformed Catholic, a non-Catholic, or a non-Christian.

If the liturgical standard of the immediate preconciliar period was no worse and, in fact, thanks to the liturgical movement, a good deal better than it had been for much of the Church's history, why was a change felt to be desirable in the second half of the twentieth century? Increasing

popular education and the democratic or egalitarian spirit
of the age may be part of the answer, as these would give
rise to an expectation of a heightened degree of universal
and equal "involvement" in the liturgy. I think, however,
that a more fundamental factor was the increasing awareness in Western society of the relativities of human culture across time.

If a wrestling with historical relativity is the root of the
matter, then the spirit of the recent liturgical revolution
may be grasped by beginning, not with the revivalist ultramontane traditionalism of Dom Guéranger, but with
the revolution, part antiquarian, part rationalist, part historicist, that was attempted at the beginning of the contemporary period by the Jansenist party. The most formal
move in this direction occurred at the diocesan Synod of
Pistoia in Tuscany, convened by Scipio de Ricci, bishop
of Pistoia and Prato, in 1786 and condemned by the Holy
See for the first time in 1794 and for the last in 1947.
With the benefit of hindsight, Pistoia can be seen as the
beginning of the current Catholic debate on the cultural
adaptation of the liturgical *lex orandi* and on its subtle but
profound connection with the *lex credendi*. The Holy See's
*volte face* in its response to the kind of adaptation the Synod
of Pistoia proposed also serves to demonstrate how far the
papacy has been prepared to reverse its historico-cultural
judgments on liturgical matters in the past. This in turn
should provide supporters of the traditional liturgy with a
helpful precedent to cite when the time comes for the
Holy See to reform its own recent reform.

It can hardly be denied that the spirit that hovered over
Archbishop Bugnini's Consilium following Vatican II was

more akin to the spirit of Scipio de Ricci and his synod than to that of Prosper Guéranger and his abbey. In the bull *Auctorem Fidei* of 1794, Pius VI censured as "heretical" the Synod of Pistoia's assertion that "in recent centuries a general obscuring has occurred regarding truths of great importance relating to religion." It is true that the doctrinal assertions of the synod that contradict the Church's *lex credendi* were the principal object of this condemnation; but the synod's implicit assertion that the Church's *lex orandi* had also been defective and contrary to the will of God for many centuries would certainly have been held by Pius VI to be, if not heretical, then at least close to it; *haeresi proxima*, as the traditional phrase has it.

The age of rationalism, standing as it does between a pre-Modern Christendom and the post-Modern present, was an inadequate first attempt to respond to the awakening of the historical sense. With the intensification of historical scholarship from the end of the seventeenth century (one thinks of the efforts of Jean Mabillon and the Benedictine Maurists, the Jesuit Bollandists, the great Theatine liturgist Saint Giuseppe Maria Tommasi, and a philosopher of law and literature such as Gianbattista Vico), the consciousness of change across time, both in the Church and in the general culture, was borne in upon the thinking of the educated classes. (A telltale sign of this shift is the end of the artistic practice of depicting historical characters in contemporary dress.) This growing awareness of historical change poses a crisis of confidence in existing practice, whether secular or sacred. What had been predominantly perceived as necessary and timeless comes to be predominantly perceived as contingent and the product of shifting fashion.

In the "post-Modern" or the "radically orthodox" perspective, we may be inclined to overcome such a crisis of sensibility by frankly acknowledging the historical relativity of much of human culture and continuing nonetheless to use traditional forms for good reasons of our own, which are impervious to historicist attack. The "Modern" or rationalist mentality, on the other hand, does not react in that way. Its first response to the crisis of historical relativity is an attempt to "dig deeper" beneath existing practice and to "expose" an ideal order that really is as "true" and "timeless" as the older forms had been spontaneously assumed to be by precritical minds. Deism in religion and "enlightened" revolution of the French kind were both, at the intellectual level, attempts to carry out this enterprise. Belief in a self-evident order that has been overlaid by historical accretions, but which will satisfy and convince everyone except the culpably perverse, if only it can be "restored", is the foundation of the Modern approach.

Although the Jansenist programs of reform in Austria, Italy, and elsewhere were ostensibly Christian and patristic in inspiration, the eighteenth-century dawn of the Modern spirit definitely influenced the Pistoian call for a change that would be not only the revival of an ideal patristic past, but also the production of a more logical, simple, and rational Church. The Pistoians' rejection of postpatristic developments in the forms of Catholic life was predicated upon the belief that the Christianity of the patristic era was the original, true, and normative Christianity—we

might almost say the "rational form" of Christianity—
and that it had a prescriptive right to overturn subsequent
developments deemed to represent a declension from the
primitive ideal. This is really a kind of "patristical rationalism", less radical than the "scriptural rationalism" of
the sixteenth-century reformers, but based, like it, on the
assumption that the Church has been in error for centuries past.

The tendencies inherent in this desire to "restore" a
lost rational archetype by means of a sweeping "reform"
are analogous whether the instinct be applied in civil leg-
islation (like that of the Enlightened despots and the French
revolutionaries) or in matters ecclesiastical or liturgical (as
in the case of Scipio de Ricci or Archbishop Bugnini's
Consilium).

First, the reform is implicitly totalitarian. If there is one
and only one rational or authentic way of doing things,
then there is no room for tolerance of any other way of
behaving. Tradition, whether in Church or State, will have
to submit to sharp and compulsory correction. In liturgical matters, this means that if one can deduce from first
principles a "correct" way to celebrate Mass, as the tone
of the *General Instruction of the Roman Missal* of 1969 implies, then there is logically no room in the Church for a
family of different Mass rites. The Eastern rites, as well as
any of the "unreformed" Western rites, must be viewed
as at best superfluous or at worst an obstacle to truth. Rights
to worship based on long-standing custom are abolished
by this rationalist totalitarianism. This is the direct antith-
esis to the reform of 1570, which aimed to abolish recent
innovations and to leave long-standing custom untouched.

Second, the reform minimizes or denies the worth of historical developments. If one is "digging deeper" to reach the bedrock of first principles, then the most primitive form of all is closest to nature and is thus the most desirable. Historical development can only be seen as the corrupting or overlaying of a pristine original. This mentality rejects the actual course of the development of the liturgy, as Protestantism rejects the actual course of the development of doctrine. Both indulge in an anachronistic and logically incoherent rifling of the resources of the historic mainstream of Christianity, upon which they are parasitic.

Since precise and detailed texts of the liturgy in the Ante-Nicene period are rare, it is to the fourth and following centuries that the more pronouncedly antiquarian kind of reformer must look for his primitive model. So far as the detail of the Roman rite is concerned, the form recorded in the earliest *Ordines Romani*, giving the practice of the seventh and eighth centuries, before the Carolingian Empire adopted and adapted the Roman rite, must serve as the antiquarian's guide. The more distinctly rationalist reformer, on the other hand, will go even farther back and base himself on Saint Justin Martyr's description of the Eucharist in the second century, the earliest we have. From this he will create an "ideal Mass" that has never actually existed but that will simultaneously derive from and prescind from all the traditional historic rites of Christendom. The Neo-Roman Missal of 1969 is the joint product of these two mentalities, antiquarian and rationalist, with the rationalist greatly predominating.

The extrinsic difference between the Catholic liturgy in the Greco-Roman period, on one hand, and in the postclassical period, on the other, is that even in the Latin part of Europe, the liturgy ceases to be celebrated in the vernacular speech, since the daily language of the people has developed. Thus the antiquarian possibly, and the rationalist certainly, will conclude, like the Pistoians, that the restoration of a vernacular liturgy is one essential element in a reestablishment of a lost authentic relation between worshippers and the cultic forms in which their worship is expressed.

The rationalist also values the conveying of information above the symbolic, ritual expression that is so fundamental to worship of the Divine Mystery. He will therefore tend to shift the balance in the liturgy and to move it toward a didacticism in which a relentless stream of informative words takes precedence over sacramental action, ritual singing, silence, or ceremonial movement. The making present of a saving mystery, at a variety of levels and in diverse ways, will tend to be replaced by the monolinear delivery of a lecture. To someone imbued with this mentality, a nonvernacular ritual language is simply an absurdity.

Let us then briefly recall the mixed rationalism and antiquarianism of the Pistoian project, noting the similarities between the changes in theology and practice that that synod wished to make and those that have occurred de facto since Vatican II.

These include the notions:

— that the Church is wholly ministerial and that therefore the clergy act as delegates of the laity and derive their authority from them;
— that the pope is likewise a representative of the Church deriving authority from her and not from Christ via Saint Peter;

— that the Church should not be governed by binding laws but by moral suasion only;

— that bishops need not obey the pope but can govern their particular Churches and alter traditional discipline as they like;

— that priests have equal doctrinal authority with bishops;

— that local synods can sit in judgment on Roman decrees;

— that the doctrinal decisions made in the past by Rome are not binding on local Churches;

— that Masses said by a priest with only a server in attendance are somehow defective;

— that the doctrine of transubstantiation should not be insisted upon;

— that Masses cannot be offered for particular intentions;

— that side altars should be removed;

— that the liturgy should be celebrated aloud and in the vernacular;

— that frequent use of the sacrament of penance should be done away with and that venial sins should not be confessed;

— that indulgences are of no benefit to us upon arrival in the next world and that, in addition, they cannot be offered up for the dead;

— that the minor orders should be abolished and that lay people should take part in conducting public worship as readers, acolytes, and so forth;

— that the Church should not regulate marriage law but should accept whatever civil society decrees on the matter;

— that devotion to the Sacred Heart should be done away with;

— that conventional popular devotions should be discouraged;

— that books condemned by the Holy Office should nonetheless be publicized by parish priests;

— that the use of devotional statues and icons should be downplayed;

— that Holy Days of obligation ought to be reduced or transferred to Sundays;

— and finally that all the traditional forms of religious life ought to be abolished except for the occasional monastery of which the inmates would all be laymen except for a few priests who would concelebrate at a single daily Mass.

Are these the proposals of the 1780s or the 1980s? They are both.

Striking as these parallels are, it is even more important to note that the synod was praised by its supporters as being "perhaps the most regular that has been held for ten or twelve centuries", that is, since the age of Saint Gregory the Great. Taking the patristic Church as normative, the Pistoians, carried along by a spirit of revolutionary pedanticism, outlined an impossible scheme for recreating her. It was a hankering to create a modern analogue of that same patristic Church that haunted the imagination of many in the reform party in the mid-twentieth century and that inspired them with the same revolutionary zeal.

## II. *The Change in Curial Policy*

The Pistoian line of argument was solemnly rejected by the Holy See. From Pius VI, in the bull *Auctorem Fidei* of 1794, to Pius XII, in the encyclical *Mediator Dei* of 1947, the papacy explicitly condemned the synod by name and also its contemporary emulators as promoting a false "liturgical antiquarianism". The synod had asserted it to be "against apostolic practice and the counsels of God unless easier ways are provided for the people to join their voice with the voice of the whole Church". Article 66 of the *Auctorem Fidei* condemns this proposition, understood as proposing the introduction of the vernacular into the liturgy, as "false, temerarious, disruptive of the order laid down for the celebration of the mysteries, and easily productive of numerous evils". It is the unhappy privilege of those living in the late twentieth century to see how prescient that condemnation was! *Mediator Dei* reiterated "the serious reasons the Church has for firmly maintaining the unconditional obligation on the celebrant to use the Latin tongue". In 1956, at the International Liturgical Conference held at Assisi, the Holy See maintained its warnings against a vernacular liturgy, though the rites for the sacraments were being vernacularized with Roman authority by that time in countries where the more advanced liturgical thinking prevailed. Even as late as 1962, in the encyclical *Veterum Sapientia*, John XXIII said "let no innovator dare to write against the use of Latin in the sacred rites... nor let them in their folly attempt to minimize the will of the Apostolic See in this matter."

From 1948, however, the year after *Mediator Dei* appeared, the Roman line had begun to change. In that year a commission for liturgical reform was established in the Roman Curia, of which the most influential members seem to have been Augustin Bea, S.J., confessor to Pius XII, and Annibale Bugnini, the secretary of the commission, who was to remain the central bureaucratic figure in Roman liturgical reform until his dismissal by Paul VI in 1975. The sentiments of *Auctorem Fidei* are not those of this extremely influential figure, for Bugnini shared Scipio de Ricci's conviction that Catholic worship had been in need of reform for many centuries and shared also in the complacent conviction that he was just the man needed to reform it.

When in 1969 Hubert Jedin, the distinguished historian of the Council of Trent, criticized the effects of the postconciliar liturgical changes in an article in *L'Osservatore Romano*, and in particular the introduction of the vernacular as sacrificing an important bond of unity in the Western Church, Archbishop Bugnini replied, saying:

> As a good historian who knows how to weigh both sides and reach a balanced judgment, why did you not mention the millions and hundreds of millions of the faithful who have *at last achieved worship in spirit and in truth?* [my italics]. Who can at last pray to God in their own languages and not in meaningless sounds, and are happy that henceforth they know what they are saying? Are they not "the Church"?
>
> As for the "bond of unity": Do you believe the Church has no other ways of securing unity? Do you believe there is a deep and heartfelt unity amid lack of understanding, ignorance, and the "dark night" of a worship that lacks a face and light, at least for those out in the nave? Do you not think that a priestly pastor must seek and foster the unity of his flock—and thereby of the universal flock—through a living faith

that is fed by the rites and finds expression in song, in communion of minds, in love that animates the Eucharist, in conscious participation, and in entrance into the mystery? Unity of language is superficial and fictitious; the other kind of unity is vital and profound.... Here in the Consilium we are not working for museums and archives, but for the spiritual life of the people of God.... The present renewal of the Church is serious, solid, thoroughgoing, and *safe* [Bugnini's italics] even if it also brings suffering and opposition.... Do you not think, Professor, that historians too ought to search historical events and discover signs of God in them?

The "ignorance and 'dark night' of worship" to which the archbishop refers is reminiscent of the Synod of Pistoia's belief in a centuries-old "general obscuring of truths of great moment relating to religion". Since Archbishop Bugnini's argument is based on the existence of a non-vernacular liturgy, we must assume that his dark night has reigned from at least the eighth century, if not the sixth; just the same point identified by the Synod of Pistoia's supporters as the beginning of the decadence of the Church.

In his invaluable work *La Riforma Liturgica 1948–1975*, published in 1983,[1] Archbishop Bugnini repeatedly makes it plain that his words to Professor Jedin are not a misrepresentation of his habitual state of mind. A very negative

---

[1] English trans.: Annibale Bugnini, *The Reform of the Liturgy, 1948–1975*, trans. Matthew J. O'Connell (Collegeville, Minn.: Liturgical Press, 1990).

and dismissive evaluation of the liturgical practice of the
Catholic Church, at least in the Latin rites, ever since the
Carolingian period is a strikingly persistent part of his mentality. The assumption underlying the work of the Consilium over which Archbishop Bugnini presided is distinctly
parallel to that of the Pistoian reformers. The assumption
is that the Church has been off course for centuries, since
the end of the patristic age, and that it is now the task of
the Consilium to sweep away whatever it deems appropriate from the "accretions" of the past, in order to implement its own ideas as to what Catholic worship should be.
Antiquity can be appealed to where possible, but rationalist clarity or "pastoral need" must be invoked whenever
antiquity stands in the way; thus, on one ground or the
other, the will of the Consilium must always prevail, since
no fixed and objective criterion can be invoked against it.

The two flaws of the rationalist mentality noted earlier,
namely, its totalitarian and its anti-traditional tendencies,
were much in evidence in the Consilium's "reform". First,
the implication was drawn that all other Catholic rites,
from Milanese to Malabarese, were to undergo a rational-
ization based on the neo-Roman model. This has consequently been done, with results that Rome has regretted,
at least in the South Indian case. Second, no tolerance was
shown to those who believed in the merits of the liturgical development that had occurred down the centuries.
Such people were seen rather as obscurantists who failed
to appreciate what the revolution was trying to achieve. It
was entirely in keeping with this spirit that the historic
Roman rite of Mass was put under a de facto if not a de
jure ban between 1974 and 1984 and that some people

were even driven out of full communion with the Church in pursuance of the Consilium's policies.

We should note in passing that like all revolutions, this one has its unconsciously humorous side. As the poet Robert Burns puts it, "O wad some Pow'r the giftie gie us, To see oursels as others see us." On July 3, 1999, Cardinal Medina Estévez, Prefect of the Congregation for Divine Worship, signed a protocol beginning with the splendid assertion that "After the Liturgical Restoration mandated by the Second Vatican Council, a certain group of the Catholic faithful *appeared*, [who were] strongly attached to preceding forms of the Roman Liturgical tradition". This is like saying that "After England turned Protestant, a group of Englishmen *appeared* who were strongly attached to the Old Religion". In both cases, it is not the *appearance* of the group in question that is the novelty calling for comment, but rather the disappearance of traditional loyalties on the part of everyone else!

A policy of an *aggiornamento*, or updating, of the Church, undertaken in the modern context, logically implies that the secularized culture of a decayed Western Christendom shall provide the standard by which the Church is to be updated. It was in this context that the reconstruction of the historic liturgy rapidly became a *damnatio memoriae* of the Church's practice, at least since the time of Charlemagne, when the definitive liturgical forms of that same Western Christendom emerged.

The symbolic repudiation of the tradition of Christendom, as Cardinal Ratzinger has stated, has contributed very greatly to an undermining of confidence in the Church in general. While it may be possible *logically* to believe in a

Church that is an infallible guide in doctrines of faith and morals but that, for most of the time since her foundation, has promoted, in Archbishop Bugnini's striking phrase, "lack of understanding, ignorance, and dark night" in the worship of God, it is not possible *psychologically* to carry out a mental juggling act of this sort for very long or on a scale that involves any great number of people. If the *lex orandi* could be so profoundly misguided for so many centuries, what confidence can be placed in the *lex credendi* upheld through these long centuries by the same misguided papacy and ecclesiastical authorities? Here again the adage *lex orandi, lex credendi* rules, but with a new and destructive twist. Either the *damnatio memoriae* of the traditional liturgy must be clearly and publicly revoked, or confidence in the Church's authority will never be recovered.

If this is indeed how matters stand, what is to be done?

### III. *Restoring Respect for the Church's Traditional Practice*

If the crisis is one of confidence in the Church and her tradition, then the only way out of the crisis is via a clear, modern reaffirmation of tradition, vindicating the historic Roman *lex orandi* as the *Catechism of the Catholic Church* has vindicated the historic *lex credendi*. We must attempt a modern presentation of the historic Roman rite, analogous to the *Catechism's* modern presentation of the historic Catholic faith. We must negate the negations and overcome the discontinuities of the postconciliar period, always remembering, however, that the faith is one, while liturgies are diverse. The *Catechism* is for Coptic and Greek

Catholics as much as for Westerners, while the liturgical families of the Catholic Church are available at choice to any Catholic who feels particularly drawn to them.

Does such a reaffirmation mean an immobile traditionalism? Are we to press for the abolition of the 1969 regime and a universal return to the state of liturgical affairs as they stood in 1962? Not at all. The very idea that the Holy See would, or even effectively could, abolish the postconciliar changes is absurd. In that sense, a "reform of the reform" is impossible. One cannot in fact expect *any* of the permissions, variations, exceptions, delegations, or modifications made to the historic Roman rite in order to transform it into the new set of liturgical options, or any of the ceremonial developments that have accompanied these changes, such as the introduction of Communion in the hand and of female altar servers, to be reversed. If one *were* attempting this impossible task of compulsorily changing the existing official *Novus Ordo*, I would support a reform of the kind I have already outlined elsewhere.[2]

In fact, however, I believe Father Harrison is right when he envisages the real way forward as entailing a new *parallel* implementation of *Sacrosanctum Concilium* that would be available to all who wished to use it. His proposal is that "an alternative ... for implementing the Vatican II Constitution on the Liturgy" should be gradually elaborated and then "presented to the Holy See, possibly some time during the next pontificate, with the request that it be approved for use throughout the Church—perhaps after a

---

[2] See "Towards Re-creation of a Unified Roman Rite", in *Adoremus Bulletin*, May 1997.

period of local use *ad experimentum*—as an alternative implementation of Vatican Council II, having *equal status and recognition* (his italics) with the rite introduced by Paul VI." If, therefore, any "reform of the reform" can entail only the establishment of yet another parallel rite for the celebration of the Eucharist, is the task worth undertaking? To such a proceeding there are many objections. The Holy See and the bishops are unlikely to be favorable. Will not confusion be compounded? Can the eclectic and subjective character of the 1969 reforms be avoided the second time around?

Despite the obstacles and difficulties, I believe the attempt is worth making, provided that the new reform is founded upon a careful respect for the historic Roman rite.

When they voted for the conciliar decree on the liturgy, the Fathers of the Second Vatican Council never imagined that they were launching a process whereby the Mass rite that most of them had known all their lives would disappear. They thought, as they declared in their decree on the Oriental Churches, that the various rites were of equal dignity and that "the Catholic Church wishes the traditions of each particular church or rite to remain whole and entire". In decreeing a reform of the Roman rite, the Council Fathers did not authorize the introduction of alternatives to the Roman Canon as the sole Eucharistic Prayer; yet many have been introduced. The Council Fathers did not authorize the destruction of the immemorial Roman lectionary; yet it was destroyed. The Council Fathers did not authorize a recasting of the annual cycle of Sundays or any change to the very ancient Sunday Collects; yet both these changes were made. The Council

Fathers did not authorize a redistribution of saints' days; yet that is what was undertaken. The Council Fathers did not authorize the abandonment or tendentious alteration of over 80 percent of the orations (Collects, Secrets, and Postcommunions) throughout the Missal; yet this momentous step was taken. The truth is that the Fathers of the Second Vatican Council assumed that the great Roman rite as known to history would be maintained in all its essentials and would continue to be the principal form for the celebration of the Catholic Eucharist. In this they were deceived. The historic Roman rite was suppressed de facto. The reform as implemented is not the reform the Council authorized. *Adoremus* is therefore attempting to be genuinely loyal to the Fathers' intentions when it takes their document, *Sacrosanctum Concilium*, as the fundamental reference point for any scheme of reform.

*Sacrosanctum Concilium* presupposes that the Missal of 1962 is the benchmark from which any change in the Roman rite will commence. After all, the Latin majority of the bishops at the Council, and of Catholics around the world, were using the ancient rite in its 1962 edition to celebrate Mass each morning during the years in which the Council met. Proposals based on *Sacrosanctum Concilium* must therefore be proposals to make variations in that Missal, with everything in it remaining in force unless otherwise specified. I presuppose that the reader is familiar with the traditional Missal, and hence I do not attempt to explain its structure or terminology in the course of this article. My aim is merely to take up the discussion begun by Father Harrison and to present what I suggest is a legitimate implementation of the conciliar decree of 1963.

There are three principal elements in the Council's proposal regarding the rite of Mass. They are given in articles 50, 51, and 54, which deal respectively with the Ordinary, the lectionary, and the use of the vernacular. Let us deal with them in turn.

## IV. *The Ordinary*

Article 50, in Flannery's translation, reads:

> The rite of Mass is to be revised in such a way that the intrinsic nature and purpose of its several parts, as well as the connection between them, may be more clearly manifested, and that devout and active participation by the faithful may be more easily achieved.
>
> For this purpose the rites are to be simplified, due care being taken to preserve their substance. Parts which with the passage of time came to be duplicated, or were added with little advantage, are to be omitted. Other parts which suffered loss through the accidents of history are to be restored to the vigor they had in the days of the Holy Fathers, as may seem useful or necessary.

Speaking as a priest who has celebrated Mass in a parish church almost daily in the traditional Roman rite since 1989, and the ceremonies of Holy Week since 1993, much of this paragraph seems coy and vague in meaning. First, the "intrinsic nature and purpose" of the parts of the rite become apparent to worshippers insofar as the latter have osmotically absorbed Catholic tradition or insofar as somebody now takes the trouble to instruct them. Conversely, without instruction, the rites' "intrinsic nature and purpose" can never be made clearly manifest, no matter how much one tinkers with the traditional forms. An uninstructed stranger wandering into a Latin Mass according to the Missal of 1969 is no more spontaneously aware of the meaning of the parts of the Mass than the same uninstructed stranger would be on wandering into a celebration according to the Missal of 1962.

Second, the meaning of a desire to make "the connection between" the several parts of the Mass more manifest is, I am afraid, so unmanifest to me that I cannot see its connection with the historic Roman rite. Has the connection been insufficiently clear for centuries? Why so, to whom, and in what respect? And how is this connection more clear in a Latin celebration of the rite of 1969? What can the article mean? What did the Council Fathers think it meant? Was it ever explained to them, or is the expression "the connection between them" just a piece of woolly drafting that, intentionally or not, invites post-conciliar committees to indulge in indefinite and unlimited experimentation?

Third, as for "devout and active participation by the faithful" in a wholly Latin liturgy (for it is a revision of the *rite* not the *language* that is under discussion in this article, as distinct from article 54), it seems that such participation had already been encouraged as fully as possible, at least from 1903 on. Saint Pius X in his motu proprio of that year had officially encouraged the movement toward the singing of the appropriate parts of the Ordinary by the whole congregation. The Instruction on Sacred

Music and Sacred Liturgy of September 3, 1958, issued one would assume with the approval of Pius XII, forms part of the rubrics of the 1962 Missal (see *no. 272*). It encourages and regulates both the fullest possible congregational participation in sung Masses and also the dialogue Low Mass in its various forms. Once again, it is hard to see how the laity participate more fully in a wholly Latin celebration in the new rite of 1969 than they do when celebrating the historic rite of the City, in the ways encouraged by the instruction of 1958.

It is interesting to note that the 1958 instruction also provides (perhaps unwisely) for the simultaneous public proclamation, at Low Mass, of the Epistle and Gospel in the vernacular by a cleric or layman, while the celebrant is reading these texts quietly at the altar. In fact the instruction even provides (quite unwisely, I think) for that debatable creature the "liturgical commentator", who gives a commentary on events as Mass progresses. He can even talk during the first half of the Canon and is only obliged to hold his tongue from the Consecration to Our Father!

This being the situation from 1958 onward, one is forced to ask how *Sacrosanctum Concilium* and the new rite in Latin improve on such a state of affairs. What fuller manifestation of the "nature and purpose" of the rites, what fuller manifestation of the "connection between" them, what more "devout and active participation" now takes place in celebrations of the modern Roman rite in Latin as distinct from the historic Roman rite in the same language? Has the first half of article 50 actually been implemented by the official postconciliar changes? Is it at all clear how it *could* ever have been implemented?

It has been suggested that article 50's meaning would be sufficiently grasped and expressed by celebrating the Mass of the Catechumens, or Liturgy of the Word, from the chair and from a lectern or place of reading distant from the altar, as has always happened in pontifical and abbatial Masses, and indeed in High Masses celebrated by a priest, so far as the Epistle and Gospel are concerned. This practice was in fact adopted from January 1965, in accordance with a revision of the rubrics. In Masses with a large congregation, as on Sundays or great feasts, there would be no harm in optionally extending this practice from High Mass to Low Mass. Even so, there seems little point in the change, unless the parts of the Mass in question are also put into the vernacular. At Low Mass on a weekday morning, on the other hand, when the style of celebration is more likely to be quiet and meditative, and a dialogue Mass is perhaps not being used, there seems no point in disturbing the unity and tranquility of the ritual by turning to read texts that the people can follow in their bilingual Missals if they want to and that most of them cannot understand in Latin anyway, irrespective of where the reader is standing. At Masses with only a server in attendance, reading the Scriptures from a lectern would be even more redundant. It is suggested that the privileged and central location of the altar as the place of sacrifice would be highlighted by proclaiming the readings at a distance from it, but the traditional rite congregations of which I have experience already possess a strong sense of the altar as the place of sacrifice, which would not be heightened in their minds if the first part of the Mass were read at the chair. Their sensibility does not operate in such narrowly spatial terms.

The second part of article 50 says, "the rites are to be simplified, due care being taken to preserve their substance", and that things that have been "duplicated" or "added with little advantage" are to be omitted. If one is to avoid subjectivism and eclecticism at this point, one must not attempt to produce a personal list of elements one would like to retain or to change. Everybody will have his own personal preferences, and these afford no common or reliable basis for a reform. A new reform should, as I have said above, be "founded upon a careful respect for the historic Roman rite", and therefore any simplification of the Roman rite of Mass must respect the clear distinction between what I will call First Order and Second Order elements in it.

Speaking globally and not altogether precisely, one can say that the First Order elements are Greco-Roman in origin, classical in period, public in nature, primary in structural importance, and (excepting the Canon and *Libera nos*) sung at High Mass, while the Second Order elements are the reverse of all these qualities: Frankish in origin, mediaeval in period, private in nature, secondary in structural importance, and said in a low voice. This distinction is perfectly clear and quite fundamental to any legitimate attempt at reforming the Roman rite, as distinct from destroying it.

Applying these distinctions to a sung Sunday Mass celebrated by a priest will clarify the matter:

| First Order Elements | Second Order Elements |
|---|---|
| The words and chant (of the propers) of the | The words of the: |
| Introit | Prayers prior to Introit |
| *Kyrie* | |
| *Gloria* | |
| Collect | |
| Epistle | |
| Gradual Psalm | |
| Alleluia | Prayers with the incense |
| Gospel | Prayers before and after the Gospel |
| Creed | |
| *Oremus* | |
| Offertory Antiphon | Prayers with the Offertory, |
| Secret | Incensation, and Washing of Hands |
| Preface and Sanctus | |
| Canon | |
| Our Father | |
| *Libera Nos* | |
| *Pax* | Prayers at the Commingling |
| *Agnus Dei* | Prayers before Communion |
| Communion Antiphon | Prayers at Communion |
| Postcommunion | Prayers at Purifications |
| *Ite Missa est* | *Placeat tibi* and Last Gospel |

Of course this listing leaves out some subtleties; as, for example, that the *Gloria* was primitively sung, we are told, at a bishop's Mass but not in Mass celebrated by a priest and that the Creed was not used at Mass in Rome until the eleventh century, and other points of that sort. Nonetheless, anyone at all familiar with the history of the liturgy will immediately accept the validity of the distinction between the First Order elements, which from one source or another give us substantially the ancient rite of the City of Rome as it developed up to the seventh century, and the Second Order elements, which constitute the northern European mediaeval embroideries upon the ancient rite, which substantially originated between the eighth and twelfth centuries and which are all said privately because they represent the personal devotion of the clergy celebrating the Mass. For my part, I welcome these mediaeval additions and see them as an enrichment.

Nonetheless, if simplification and the removal of duplication and of elements added over time with supposedly little advantage are to be the order of the day as the Council decreed, it is from these Second Order texts that the excisions must come. If a reform is to respect the integrity of the Roman rite, it will have to leave the First Order elements intact. Proceeding thus, one would "simplify while taking due care to preserve the substance". "Substance" here must be taken as meaning the substance of the *Roman rite*, not merely the substantial shape of the eucharistic liturgy, as described by Justin Martyr in the second century and prescinding from all the historic rites of Christendom. To interpret "substance" in the latter, broader sense would be to open the way to a melting down of all the liturgical families, to an eclectic rifling of material from Oriental and other non-Roman sources, and to the limitless substitution of newly composed material for the genuine texts of the Roman tradition.

These, alas, are the precise faults into which the Consilium's "reform" fell. The result was not really a "reform" at all. It was the creation of a new rite, loosely derived from the historic Roman rite, but differing from it as much as do some of the historic non-Roman rites, and a great deal more than, for instance, the rites of the Carthusians, Cistercians, and Dominicans. Monsignor Gamber's terminology of a "Roman rite", describing the ancient tradition still maintained in the Missal of 1962, and a "modern rite", describing the Missal and lectionary of 1969, is scientifically accurate and just.

The last part of article 50 specifies the restoration of "other parts which suffered loss through the accidents of history". The *Preces*, intercessions, or Prayer of the Faithful spring to mind at this point, but they are dealt with as a distinct question in article 53. What other element is therefore intended here? The Introit psalm perhaps, or the responsorial form of the Gradual psalm? The congregational reading of the Responsorial Psalm at a Low Mass was part of no ancient liturgy and therefore did not "suffer loss through the accidents of history", but its bathetic and ragged character might lead us to conclude that if it had been part of any ancient rite, its loss would have been far from accidental.

Father Harrison suggests, I suspect correctly, that an Offertory procession of the type with which we are now familiar in the new rite is one of the parts the drafters of the decree wished to "restore". It seems, however, that the notion of a vanished procession during the celebration of the Eucharist, in which the laity carried up from the nave of the church the bread and wine to be consecrated at that Mass, is a romantic fantasy. The idea of such a vanished rite is assiduously promoted by Jungmann in his book *Missarum Solemnia*. A close inspection of every piece of evidence Jungmann gives relating to offertories and processions reveals, however, that his argument is an argument from silence. Not one example of a procession of that particular kind in any rite, Latin or Greek, is produced, and it certainly would have been if Jungmann had known of any. Such silence is eloquent. This is not the place to engage in a detailed discussion of the point, but liturgical scholars have assured me that the notion of a vanished people's Offertory procession in the Roman rite, of the type introduced in 1969, lacks any shred of evidence in the sources. Such a procession cannot therefore now be introduced on the ground that it is being "restored".

In the light of these observations and criticisms, how would one implement article 50 of *Sacrosanctum Concilium*? The call for simplification and the removal of reduplications and of elements added with arguably little advantage seems to be the most coherent and intelligible part of the paragraph. It would be possible to achieve those ends, while respecting the complete integrity of the historic core of the Roman rite, by optionalizing *en bloc* the Second Order elements identified above. In any one celebration of Mass, all would have to be omitted or all retained, since a piecemeal omission or retention of individual elements would be eclectic intellectually and would also create a jumbled confusion in liturgical practice. An *en bloc* optionalization of this sort would remove "accretions" that had occurred over time, but would remove them without doing violence to the historic core of the rite. This would provide a simplified, streamlined, rationalized, and in that sense "modern" Roman rite of Mass, which would paradoxically be at the same time wholly traditional.

Nevertheless, the optional character of this change is very important. It was high-handed, unprecedentedly disrespectful to sacred tradition, and pastorally insensitive to attempt to *prevent* priests and people from continuing to worship using the Ordinary they and their ancestors had used from time immemorial. It is simply not possible to show, as required by article 23, that the "true and certain benefit of the Church...demanded" the *mandatory* abandonment of texts that had been in daily and devout use for a thousand years. It seems appropriate to record here what an Australian bishop said to me when I told him I thought it was reasonable to create a new rite of Mass, if desired, but unreasonable to forbid the celebration of the traditional form. His words were "Oh, but if they hadn't banned the old rite, nobody would have gone to the new!"

Article 23 of the Council's own decree, in addition to the dictates of equity and common sense, forbade the binding suppression of any part of the historic Ordinary of the Mass. It is precisely that kind of violent attack on tradition that constitutes a *damnatio memoriae*, and it is therefore that kind of change that must be "clearly and publicly revoked", as I noted above, if confidence in the Church is to be restored.

The two main objections to what I have just proposed regarding the Ordinary will be that the Penitential Rite at the foot of the altar and the Offertory prayers over the gifts would no longer be obligatory.

It should be remembered in reply that from the time of the apostles right up until the present century, the celebration of the Mass of the Roman rite *never* began with a public and corporate act of confession and repentance by the congregation. One should have done one's penance before coming to join in the essentially post-penitential celebration of the Eucharist. Of course even the just man sins seven times a day, and a personal spirit of repentance is always in place, but the *apologiae* of the priests and ministers have never traditionally been said by the congregation, or been said so loudly as to be heard throughout the Church. Again, there is objection to beginning this practice in the dialogue Mass. I regularly celebrate Mass in a dialogue form with a Sunday congregation and can see a value in this novel communal way of reciting these ancient private prayers, but it is not possible to argue on the grounds of preserving or restoring ancient tradition that such communal recitation is an essential practice proper to any rite of Mass or to the Roman rite in particular. Monsignor Gamber records that it dates in his view from the German youth Masses of the 1920s. It is in any case no more ancient than Dom Lambert Beauduin's phase of the liturgical movement in the first quarter of the twentieth century.

As to the mediaeval Offertory prayers, some people have called for their retention as an assertion of the sacrificial character of the Mass, but their desire to retain them is largely motivated by the elision of the idea of sacrifice in many of the variants possible under the new liturgical regime. Since in the version of the reform here proposed, the Roman Canon, with its very explicit sacrificial language, is retained as the sole Eucharistic Prayer, there is no danger of the notion of sacrifice being played down, and it would be quite safe, though not my own preference, to revert to the practice of the pre-Carolingian period and to perform the action of the Offertory with only a silent personal prayer of the celebrant accompanying it.

## V. *The Lectionary*

Let us proceed to article 51. It reads "The treasures of the Bible are to be opened up more lavishly so that a richer fare may be provided for the faithful at the table of God's word. In this way a more representative part of the sacred scriptures will be read to the people in . . . a prescribed number of years."

We should note that upon being opened up, the Scriptures proved to contain such "rich fare" that parts of the banquet were removed at once from the "table of God's word", lest they should prove indigestible to liberal stomachs. In twenty-two places the new lectionary expunges whole verses from the text of the Gospels used at Mass in order to remove references to the Last Judgment, the condemnation of the world, and sin.[3] A reform of this particular reform would obviously be in order.

The idea of reading "representative parts" of the whole of Scripture at Mass is untraditional. The hour of Matins is the proper liturgical vehicle for reading the Scriptures through in the course of a year. Remember the Cluniac monks getting through the whole of Isaiah in one week of Advent: sixty-six chapters chanted in an icy church during the small hours of a winter's night in Burgundy; rich fare indeed! The readings at Mass, on the other hand, have

---

[3] See R. Kashewsky, in *Una Voce Korrespondenz*, 1982, nos. 2/3.

always been chosen to illustrate the doctrine or sentiment appropriate to the liturgical day. Even in the time after Pentecost, which has the least pronounced character, a course of moral instruction flowing as a kind of postbaptismal catechesis is discernable in the historic Roman lectionary. As the event has shown, the attempt to impose representative parts of the whole of Scripture upon the rite of Mass simply leads to incongruous Old Testament readings being proclaimed to a bemused congregation.

It has been alleged that the discrepancy in the conjunction of Sunday Epistles and Gospels in the ancient lectionaries of the Roman rite means that the themes of the readings of each Sunday have been obscured in the traditional Roman Missal. This hypothesis presupposes a very precise, rather than a general, thematic correspondence. To demonstrate that the obvious general thematic correspondence that exists in the traditional lectionary is botched, one would have to reverse the alleged dislocation and show that Epistles and Gospels were manifestly more connected in that "reconstructed" order. I am not aware that anybody has attempted this demonstration, still less succeeded in making it.

The words "in a prescribed number of years" are also ominous. The liturgy, like the natural cycle of spring, summer, autumn, and winter, goes in an annual cycle, not a biennial or triennial one. So far as I am aware, all the liturgical rites of Christendom, both East and West, have always done the same. To break with this instinct and this tradition is to go against the poetry of nature as well as the consent of the ages. Only an insensitive rationalism, an obsessive didacticism, could produce such a proposal.

Even overlooking these objections and accepting a two- or three-year lectionary, the conciliar decree does not in the least require the abandonment of the extremely ancient annual Roman cycle of Sunday Epistles and Gospels, which dates back to an unknown period prior to the seventh century. In his account, Archbishop Bugnini gives no weight at all to the argument from tradition. He tells us, "Some members [of the Consilium] suggested that the lectionary be kept intact and serve as one of the cycles, out of respect for tradition and for ecumenical reasons, since most of the churches issuing from the Reformation use the traditional lectionary. The *ecumenical* argument was given great weight in the discussion, but Father Vagaggini demonstrated, ably and skillfully, that it was in fact weak." Vagaggini, who was one of the key figures in the Consilium and the principal enemy and critic of the Roman Canon, pointed out that most of the Protestants had abandoned or were on the point of abandoning the ancient Roman cycle of readings. On October 8, 1966, it was arranged that the Protestant observers attached to the committee should "read a statement in the public assembly in which they asked the Roman Church not to consider itself obliged for ecumenical reasons to abstain from revising the lectionary". Once it was clear that Protestant support, which was paradoxically deemed to be the only serious reason for saving the ancient Roman cycle, did not exist, the members of the Consilium voted for its extirpation, with only one dissentient voice.[4]

---

[4] See Bugnini, *Reform*, p. 417.

If antiquity had really been the criterion for the reform, that is, in the Council's words, the restoration of "parts which have been lost through the accidents of history", then the Consilium would not only have retained the Sunday cycle, but would have restored the ancient ferial readings for Wednesdays that are found in our earliest detailed sources, the eighth-century manuscripts of Wurzburg and Murbach, which record the Roman practice of the seventh century and earlier. The Friday readings given in one or other of these documents could also have been used with the Wednesday ones to create one of the two new weekday ferial lectionaries. A three-year Sunday cycle could have been formed, as Archbishop Bugnini says was suggested at the time, by declaring the traditional Epistles and Gospels of those of Year A and forming complementary Years B and C from a wider range of Scripture in accordance with the conciliar injunction. As is in fact the case with the Sundays of Lent in the 1969 Missal, a rubric should have been inserted stating that the readings of Year A could be used in any year. This would allow those who were perfectly happy with the historic one-year cycle to retain it.

As regards the Old Testament, we are repeatedly assured that there was an Old Testament reading each Sunday morning at Mass but that quite mysteriously these all vanished by the seventh century, and vanished leaving no memory that they had ever existed: no homilies on them by Leo or Gregory, no inadvertent cross-references to them in any surviving source, not one palimpsest listing one pericope and the Sunday to which it was assigned, no tradition as to what pope suppressed them or why; just an

a priori assertion that there is a reading missing between
the Gradual and the Alleluia, which would, incidentally,
place the Old Testament reading after the New, contrary
to practice elsewhere in the traditional Missal. This argument from silence is wildly improbable. There are indeed
Old Testament lessons on penitential days in the traditional Roman lectionary, but these are quite a different
matter. The alleged set of vanished Old Testament readings is, I fear, a romantic fantasy like the vanished people's
Offertory procession. They are only a theory on the lips
of a liturgist, like the smile on the face of the Cheshire cat
that is not really there. If it is now thought desirable to
introduce Old Testament readings, let a new three-year
cycle of them be drawn up and introduced, but on an
optional basis and not on the specious ground that some
element due in the liturgy had disappeared.

After a decade or so of celebrating the traditional Roman rite, I can see that a broadened choice of readings for
the Commons might be desirable and that a wider section
of Prefaces could be introduced without damage to the
integrity of the historic rite. We note in passing that a still
unpublished report on the Roman rite made by a committee of eight cardinals in 1986 at the request of the Pope
encouraged adaptations of this kind. We note, too, that
the cardinals also found, by a majority of seven to one,
that in law the Roman rite had never been suppressed and
that every priest of the Latin rite is, and has always been,
entitled to use the historic liturgy. In the now flowing
spate of papal apologies and admissions of truths supposedly long denied, might not the current Roman authorities admit the truth about the legal status of the Roman

rite and apologize for that truth's confused suppression since 1974 and for its studious suppression since 1986?

## VI. *The Vernacular*

The last of our three paragraphs from *Sacrosanctum Concilium* is no. 54:

> A suitable place may be allotted to the vernacular in Masses which are celebrated with the people, especially in the readings and the 'common prayer', and also, as local conditions may warrant, in those parts which pertain to the people....
>
> Nevertheless care must be taken to ensure that the faithful may also be able to say or sing together in Latin those parts of the Ordinary of the Mass which pertain to them.
>
> Wherever a more extended use of the vernacular in the Mass seems desirable, the regulation laid down in Article 40 of this Constitution is to be observed.

This is the paragraph that sank a thousand missals and more than a thousand years of unity in the Roman rite, which had been one of the principal factors in the emergence of a unified Western civilization.

There is the famous story of how the Dominican Cardinal Browne urged the Council Fathers to beware of allowing the vernacular, lest Latin vanish from the liturgy within ten years or so. He was laughed at by the assembly, but as so often, the pessimistic reactionary proved to be more in touch with the flow of events than the optimistic progressives. The Council Fathers' incredulous laughter at Cardinal Browne helps to remind us that a general council, like a pope, is only infallible in its definitions of faith and morals, and not in its prudential judgments or in matters of pastoral discipline or in acts of state or in supposed liturgical improvements. It is thus false to assert that a Catholic is logically bound to agree with the prudential judgments a council may make on any subject. It is still more illegitimate to extrapolate from the negative immunity from error that a general council enjoys in definitions of faith and morals to belief in a positive inspiration of councils, as if the bishops were organs of revelation like the apostles, and their prudential decrees inerrant like the Scriptures. It is only a false ecclesiology and a false pneumatology that can lead to the exhorbitant assertion that a council is "the voice of the Holy Spirit for our age". Are we really *obliged* to believe that the Holy Spirit demanded the launching of a crusade at the Fourth Lateran Council in 1215? And *must* we hold that in 1311 the Holy Spirit dictated the Council of Vienne's rules regulating the use of torture by the Inquisition? And is it *de fide* that when Alexander IV ordered those suspect of heresy to be tortured to confess their guilt, this was what "the Spirit was saying to the churches" on May 15, 1252? If so, are we to condemn the *Catechism of the Catholic Church* of August 15, 1997, which comes to us on the same papal and episcopal authority and which condemns the use of torture to extract confessions of guilt and openly says that "the pastors of the Church" erred on the matter?

As to the liturgy, is it mandatory to believe that in 1963 the Holy Spirit wanted the abandonment of the principle

of the weekly recitation of all 150 psalms, on which the
Office of the Roman rite has been based from its very
beginnings prior to Saint Benedict? And is it *de fide* that
God wanted the Hour of Prime suppressed from January
1964? No, this doctrine of the Infallibility of the Party
Line simply will not do. It is not Catholic teaching that
the Church is infallible in pastoral or prudential judgments. We are therefore logically free to hold that any
council can be ill-advised when making these kinds of
decision, and thus ill-advised in allowing the conversion
of the liturgy into the vernacular, even if that had taken
the form of a direct translation of the 1962 Missal.

For what are the facts? Historically the liturgy, like the
faith, has been received by cultures as a sacrosanct whole
at the time of conversion and has rarely been put into
another language thereafter. Whether that language was
the vernacular or not seems to be utterly arbitrary and a
matter of historical accident. In Italy, Gaul, and Spain, the
Latin liturgy was initially vernacular but ceased to be so
within five hundred years; the language, however, remained sacrosanct precisely because it was used for sacred
purposes. In Russia, the liturgical language now known
as Old Church Slavonic was used for the vernacular version of the Greek books; it is now *old* Slavonic precisely
because it differs from the current language; but because
it is sacred, it has been left undisturbed. In Ethiopia the
liturgical language is Gheez, which centuries ago was replaced by Amharic as the vernacular; again no change was
made to the liturgy. On the other hand, among the Irish,
English, Dutch, Germans, Basques, Poles, Swedes, Ceylon-
ese, Bantus, Vietnamese, Finns, Norwegians, Lithuanians,

Hungarians, and so many others, the liturgy had never been in the vernacular up until the 1960s. And are we to say that these great peoples and cultures were never Christian, never properly evangelized as a result? In South India the faith had been quietly flourishing for a thousand years prior to the arrival of the Portuguese in the sixteenth century, but the liturgy had never been translated and was still celebrated in the Syriac tongue in which it had arrived. English Catholics from Saint Augustine of Canterbury until the 1960s never used the vernacular for Mass.

In the 1960s, when mass literacy, inexpensive people's missals, and bilingual editions were more in evidence than ever before, and it was thus easier to follow the Mass than ever before, there was less justification than there had ever been for switching to the vernacular. Why, then, did it happen?

To the growing awareness of historical and cultural relativism I mentioned at the outset, and the rationalist temptations to which that gives rise, I think we must add the spirit of an anthropocentric liberalism as a crucial ingredient in the mixture; after all, did not Paul VI proclaim in his speech closing the Council that the Church, too, had now adopted the "Cult of Man"?

The whole aggiornamentist enterprise can, in lengthening retrospect, be seen as the moment when the Church at last gave in to that rising cult of human liberty which has increasingly dominated the Western imagination since the eighteenth century. Liberal Man wants an atomistic freedom to "do his own thing". In this context, a binding, sacral, non-vernacular and theocentric liturgical ethos enshrined in ancient tradition must be replaced by an option-filled, secularizing, vernacular, and anthropocentric approach, reflecting the aspirations and tastes of the human spirit in the present day. The authority of the Roman Church and her historic liturgy had to be taken out of the way as an essential precondition to the installation of the cult of freedom. It is the entry of this *Zeitgeist* into the temple of God, through the window thrown open by John XXIII, that is the fundamental driving force behind the liturgical revolution. The mass desertion of the liturgy among peoples of old Christian culture that began the instant the new anthropocentric rites appeared shows not only that the renewal has been a failure de facto, but that, at the time of the changes, the bulk of the faithful felt no overwhelming attraction to the vernacular.

If it be argued that the needs of mission territories called for the abandonment of Latin, then it should be remembered that all the Christian cultures of northern Europe were once as barbaric as Rwanda and that in the passage of centuries a Black Latin Christendom could have proved no more absurd or unattainable than a Teutonic Latin Christendom must have seemed in the age of Augustine and Boniface. The pressure for change did not in fact come from the missions but from European liturgical scholars and European liberal Catholics who were losing confidence in their own traditions. I will never forget one Corpus Christi at Bolsena, when a sanctuary full of white priests could barely stumble through the *Pange Lingua* while the only black priest among us sang it perfectly from memory!

Now that the vernacular has triumphed, for the time being at least, it seems to me that one way toward to the recovery of the doctrinal, ritual, and other values of the

Roman rite would be a careful translation of the 1962 Missal into the vernacular, *sicut jacet*, with all its rubrics unchanged. This would be a legitimate reform of the reform, since it would, paradoxically, be closer to what the Council Fathers *thought* they were voting for in 1963 than is the neo-Roman Missal produced by the Consilium in 1969. It would obviously be closer to the Fathers' wishes than the current de facto regime of evolving options and permutations, which, by polite misnomer, is still called a *Rite* of Mass.

## VII. *Some Other Possible Reforms*

Having concluded our consideration of articles 50, 51, and 54 of the conciliar decree (and setting aside a host of other issues, such as the Bugninian committee's unauthorized suppression or modification of the Sunday Collects, which action constitutes an alteration of the *lex credendi* through a manipulation of the *lex orandi*), let me end by mentioning two areas in which the 1962 typical edition of the Missal does seem to stand in need of reform.

The sanctoral cycle contains some interesting personages, such as Saint Venantius of Camerino, Saint Martina, and Saint Catherine of Alexandria, of whom Saint Robert Bellarmine remarked that he wished he could be certain she was more than a literary fiction. The martyr status of most of the early popes is in the same dubious category. Common sense would dictate that the worldwide fellowship that follows the Roman rite does not need to devote a whole liturgical day every year to the celebration of persons of whom nothing is certainly known and whose very existence is in some cases unproven. Space also needs to be found for new saints' days as the sanctoral cycle goes through its inevitable growth toward congestion. The changes of 1955 and 1960 had done much in this regard, and there is a simple way of going one step farther.

A rubric in the 1962 Missal allows any commemoration to be celebrated *ad libitum* as a third-class feast; a parallel rubric should be added allowing any third-class feast to be reduced *ad libitum* to a commemoration. Perhaps, going farther, the historically unknown saints could be left in the Martyrology on their traditional dates, with the option of celebrating a votive Mass in their honor on the day in question. These proposals are not new. The elimination of unhistorical feasts and the reduction of those below the rank of double major (that is, the vast majority) to the rank of a commemoration was proposed by Benedict XIV's reform commission as long ago as the 1740s.

The second matter unmentioned by the Council, but which the reformers of the 1960s took in hand, this time with some real success, was the readings of the Easter Vigil, which had been reduced to unintelligibility in 1951.

Archbishop Bugnini explains how he reformulated the shape of the very ancient "Mother of all Vigils" and sprang it on the universal Church for the Easter of 1952. Many of the archbishop's characteristic methods were displayed in microcosm in this very first exercise in "reform". The backstairs approaches to the pope while deliberately keeping the hitherto responsible authorities (chiefly the Sacred Congregation of Rites) in the dark, the cavalier disregard for ancient tradition, the calculation that an absurdly centralized and bureaucratic manipulation of the liturgy would be swallowed by the whole Church, out of loyalty to the pope or from sheer indifference, are features of the process that Archbishop Bugnini was often to repeat after the Council.

Having celebrated the Easter Vigil from 1993 to 1997 with the four readings retained in 1951 and reproduced in the typical edition of 1962, I increasingly felt that there was something wrong with the readings; they suffered from an undeniable air of anti-climax and incoherence. When I took the time to study the traditional series of twelve "prophecies", each followed by a collect summing up its meaning in the mind of the Church, and to study the sung responsories mysteriously placed after the fourth, eighth, and eleventh in the series, I realized that they were not twelve readings in a row, but rather three nocturns of four readings each, and that each nocturn had a theme that was summed up in the sung responsory that marked its end. The first four, the Creation, the Flood, the Sacrifice of Isaac, and the Crossing of the Red Sea, are about God's creation of a Chosen People; the second four are about the increasing inadequacy of that people's response to God's call; while the last nocturn is about God's solution of this conundrum through the sending of the Messiah, who is foreshadowed in three readings as respectively Priest, Prophet, and King.

The twelfth reading, mysteriously placed after the final sung responsory and unaccompanied by the penitential gesture of kneeling, is explained by the fact that the Vigil, properly speaking, is over; the reading looks forward to what is immediately at hand. In the crowded baptistery on Easter night, the candidates descend up to their waists into the waters of the enormous font and walk about in them, saved and praising God for their deliverance from the worship of the idol of Caesar that the Roman imperial power had so recently demanded. The *baptizandi* are seen by the Church, through her choice of Old Testament reading, as foreshadowed by the three young Hebrews who walk about in the flames saved and praising God in Nebuchadnezzar's fiery furnace, likewise delivered from the worship of the idol of the Babylonian king and from the dilemma of physical or spiritual death. The fiery furnace is a kind of antitype of the Lateran baptistery.

In retaining only the opening description of the Creation, and the readings that happened to be followed by sung responsories, the changes made in 1951 were an uncomprehending dismantlement of a finely crafted structure, which left behind a correspondingly incomprehensible debris. The new optional seven-reading Vigil of 1969, though retaining only two of the original twelve prophecies, is in itself a great improvement. The fact that the 1969 Missal requires as a minimum only the Red Sea reading and one other has meant, however, that the Easter Vigil has been effectively abolished in many churches. The Vigil deserves the restoration of its triadic structure, reflecting the dialectic of salvation in the themes of its three nocturns, which also correspond to the three watches of the night, just as the twelve prophecies correspond to the twelve nocturnal hours.

Having celebrated the Vigil with its traditional readings for four successive Easters from 1998 on, I can testify that doing so is not only pastorally possible, but also vastly more

satisfying than using only the fragmented readings that survive in the Missal of 1962. Ironically, it is the unrecon-
structed form that, in accordance with the Council's wishes,
"sets before the people a richer fare from the word of
God". I suggest that this return to tradition be publicly
encouraged by Rome. There is no reason why the ancient
set of readings should not be used in the 1969 Vigil ceremonies. If their length is thought to be prohibitive for
*homo modernus*, who is deemed to love the liturgy but not
to love it all *that* much, then the first nocturn, from the
Creation to the Crossing of the Red Sea, could be used,
with the other two nocturns being optional.

To conclude: the aggiornamentist Quest for the Ideal
Liturgy that would solve all problems of popular incom-
prehension and lack of participation has failed, and the
spirit of liberalizing rationalism that inspired it was, like
the spirit of the Synod of Pistoia, never wholly congenial
to historic orthodoxy. No liturgy can be all things to all
men, and therefore the quest for an impossible perfection
has turned out, as so often in human affairs, to be the
enemy of an existing good. As Lord Salisbury observed a
century ago: "It is a characteristic of the Progressive Mind
to believe that all problems admit of a solution. Conservatives, on the other hand, are quite prepared to confess
that the solution to some problems may escape us
altogether."

Yet more profound is Dietrich von Hildebrand's citation of a remark by Hans Urs von Balthasar: "If that myth-
ical entity 'Modern Man' becomes the measure of what
God has or has not to say, then religion is obviously at an
end."

# APPENDIX VI

## A QUESTION OF CEREMONIAL

*Monsignor Peter J. Elliott*

Proposals for a "reform of the reform" often seem to concentrate too much on texts and translations, on the fabric
and structure of the "rite", while overlooking the important question of ceremonial. But a review of the visible
action, the movements or "ritual", of the Roman rite is
essential in preparing a better implementation of the intentions of the Fathers of the Second Vatican Council.

I must first confess that I differ from Father Brian Harrison, not so much over his intent, which is admirable,
but over his starting point. I do not believe we need to go
back to the very beginning of the postconciliar reform
and, as it were, start all over again, taking the preconciliar
rites as our basis. I assume that the given field for proposing a "reform of the reform" is what is happening in
our parishes. In varying degrees, parish worship is derived
from the Roman Missal and other liturgical books published for the postconciliar Roman rite. It seems more realistic to begin here, not that this excludes looking back
to noble elements in the preconciliar rite that may guide
us today.

In terms of prescribed ceremonial actions, the postconciliar reform has to be interpreted carefully. We may
then understand why and how changes were made, always

aware of a specific historical context, the years during and after the Council. Then we should reflect on whether these changes had the effects intended. At the same time the theory behind the development of the postconciliar liturgy becomes clearer through understanding the transition from one style of worship to another. Based on such an understanding, I will make some proposals for improving and enriching the ceremonial dimension in any future revision of official sources.

## The Ceremonial Transition

To understand the transition that has taken place in terms of the ceremonial of the Roman rite, we need to think in terms of sacred space and sacred action. In the preconciliar Mass the space of the celebration was strictly defined by way of a standard plan for the sanctuary and altar, which, with minor variations, became virtually universal. The space set the limits for the movements of the celebrant and other ministers. While the planning of the sanctuary was apparently influenced by the rubrics for Solemn Mass in the papal chapel, in practice what happened at monastic side altars, Low Mass, became the standard for the action that the faithful followed on Sundays at the altar of their parish Church.[1] The ceremonial action of the Low Mass is more

---

[1] It is interesting to observe that those who promote the preconciliar rite regard Low Mass as their "ideal liturgy". Others, aware of the classical tradition and guided by the liturgical movement, envisage Solemn Mass as the norm. Apparently there are tensions between these groups.

restricted in scope, being contained mainly within a series of movements between four or five points at the mensa and predella of the altar itself.

The radical ceremonial change involved in the *Missa normativa* as it emerged in the sixties "opened out" this Low Mass style of liturgical action. When we compare the action of a public parish Low Mass of 1963 to a standard parish Mass in 2003, the transition could be described as *a change from a tableau to an open action*.

Salient moments in the reform process marked the opening out of the ceremonial action. The arrival of the celebrant's presiding chair in the mid-sixties brought the standard parish Mass closer to a simplified version of Pontifical High Mass at the faldstool, where the bishop sat facing the people. The appearance of an ambo or lectern meant that Scripture readings no longer took place at the altar, but away from it, as at a Solemn Mass. It could thus be argued that these changes emerged from what was already there. Elements from solemn forms of celebration, when the celebrant was not restricted to the altar, entered the normative rite that was finally authorized by Pope Paul VI in 1969. At the same time, this process blurred the distinction between solemn and said celebrations, evident in the *General Instruction of the Roman Missal*, 1969.

An even more significant change was the arrival of the freestanding altar with the celebrant facing the people. By the late sixties, the ceremonial role of the priest standing at the altar facing east had vanished in most churches. This completed the move away from a liturgical tableau to an open action, now finding its focus in a face-to-face dialogue between priest and people. The celebrant's hieratic leader-mediator role became a hieratic presiding-mediator role, still sacerdotal but with a new emphasis. The face-to-face style coincided with the transition to the vernacular, full and active participation by the people, and the end of the "silent Canon". Inevitably the celebrant's role became more personal, more dependent on his words than on ritual gestures.

Some have criticized the transition as exchanging the role of a eucharistic celebrant for that of a eucharistic preacher, hence a move toward a Protestant style of worship. Certainly, in not a few churches we now find a rather didactic or homiletic style of celebrating Mass, so that the altar becomes a pulpit. But it would be more accurate to perceive the influence of mass media communication in the transition. A speaker on television seeks to create an impression of intimacy and dialogue. Again, decades of expanding television create a historical context that is an important factor to bear in mind.

The ceremonial role of servers changed as the action of liturgy opened out. From being a fixed part of the visual tableau, kneeling on altar steps and making Latin responses, they became ministers entrusted with actions once reserved for servers at solemn forms of Mass, such as carrying processional cross and candles, incense, book, and so on. Even actions once reserved to the deacon and sub-deacon could now be carried out by servers, for example, unfolding the corporal, setting up vessels, bringing vessels to the altar, and so on. Some priests have still not adjusted to this part of the ceremonial transition and either limit the role of servers or eliminate them altogether.

It is obvious that the role of the people changed from silent participation to active involvement, although this had been pioneered well before the Council in the Latin dialogue Mass. The opening out of the ceremonial action as it affected the laity was more evident in the emerging lay ministries, especially lectors, commentators, and extraordinary ministers of the Eucharist. Communion under both species and Communion in the hand eliminated taboos of the preconciliar era. Lay men and women were no longer forbidden to step into the sanctuary or touch sacred vessels. The Sign of Peace of Solemn Mass was adapted and extended to all the faithful.

I do not criticize this steady transition from the liturgical tableau of Low Mass to the open action of the *Missa normativa*. In fact I endorse it in my own attempts to interpret it in a classical way, that is, within the "continuity of our tradition".[2] Once we perceive how much of the transition emerged from the existing ceremonial of the preconciliar Roman rite, we should recognize that it is rooted in a continuous liturgical tradition. This is why I believe that it is unfair, even ignorant, to parody postconciliar worship as "pseudopatristic" or to allege that it proceeds from radical Reformation traditions. Nor can the reform be dismissed always as a simplification of what preceded it. In various ways, the open ceremonial of a parish Mass today is more elaborate than the simple tableau of the Low Mass of 1962.

---

[2] On the "continuity of our tradition", see Peter J. Elliott, *Ceremonies of the Modern Roman Rite* (San Francisco: Ignatius Press, 1995), nos. 16–24.

## Looking East

Perhaps the best way to see this continuity with tradition is to link the ceremonial transition to the liturgies of the Christian East.

Moving from a tableau to an open action has had the effect of bringing the Western liturgy closer to the liturgies of the East, especially the Byzantine family of rites. Elements in the open ceremonial action of various Eastern rites may now be found in a standard Roman rite Mass: a series of processions (entrance, Gospel, gifts, Communion, recessional), readings at an ambo, intercessions in the form of a litany, music as a normal component of worship, a credence table functioning like the table of prothesis, wider scope for Communion under both species, more frequent use of incense, processional candles, cross, and so on, even at simple celebrations.

The Roman liturgical space is now closer to the plan of a Byzantine sanctuary. While it lacks an iconastasis, the Roman sanctuary now has a freestanding altar, often shorter than previous altars, a presiding chair, often directly behind the altar, an ambo and a credence table placed to the left, like the table of prothesis. As with a Byzantine sanctuary, usually there are fewer steps near the altar, to allow space for concelebration. The postconciliar Roman rite sanctuary is easily adapted for a Byzantine liturgy. This struck me while visiting a new church in Slovakia where a large side chapel, without iconastasis, had been built for Catholics of the Byzantine rite. Apart from an array of icons, it was not much different from the sanctuary in the main church.

However, the major difference with the East is that now the Roman Mass is almost universally celebrated facing the people. This is not envisaged in the Eastern rites, although there have been attempts to "romanize" some Eastern rites in this way. A significant *Instruction for Applying the Liturgical Prescriptions of the Code of Canons of the Eastern Churches* (1996) required eastward celebration in Eastern rites. Regrettably, this *Instruction* is largely ignored in a certain Eastern rite prone to much "romanization" in the past.

If the ceremonial transition represents a demonstrable move toward the East, this should be welcomed but interpreted cautiously. The Roman tradition of simplicity tends to produce ceremonial that lacks much of the mystery and pageantry associated with the actions I have indicated. The East implicitly invites us to enrich our worship now that we have returned to a similar open style of ceremonial.

## Imprecise Rubrics

While the ceremonial transition in the Roman rite can be shown to arise from sound traditions, it was not accompanied by precise rubrics to cover the details that in fact pass on a liturgical tradition. This is a major weakness that we need to understand and remedy.

People often ask why we do not find precise rubrics in the earlier editions of *General Instruction of the Roman Missal* (first published in 1969). The style of the *General Instruction* is best explained in the light of the mood and intent of the reform at that time. The goal was not only to open out the action of the Roman liturgy, but to move beyond the legalism of the rubricians, especially to free priests from the burden of committing a mortal sin by offending against a rubric. Moreover, in the arcane world of the rubricians there were many complexities, subtleties, and fine points of interpretation. Much of this was rightly simplified or swept aside; hence the reaction against liturgical legalism. But it now seems to have been an overreaction.

The underlying weakness of the new approach was a swing from legalism to unrealistic idealism. Here we enter a fantastic realm, let us call it "Liturgyland", where every priest or deacon is a keen creative liturgist, where parish clergy have hours of free time to create beautiful liturgies, where they have only to blink and expert cantors and choirs will break into song. In Liturgyland a few broad indications suffice, and joyful celebrations naturally unfold before our eyes. The mood was "let it all happen naturally", typifying the social currents of the era of "flower power" and "make love not war". In this regard, one also suspects that some of the naïveté came from gentle minds more at home in a monastic choir than a busy parish church.

The other weakness was a naïve assumption about liturgical skills that underlies the *General Instruction*. It could be described as, "There is no need to spell it all out because they know that anyway." Apparently, in Liturgyland traditional skills and practices are passed on by some magical intuitive process. However, the publication of the *Ceremonial of Bishops* in 1984 was a tacit admission that the idealism of the *General Instruction* was somewhat mistaken. While ceremonies were still described in an economical style in the *Ceremonial of Bishops*, more precise guidance was offered, and some interesting footnotes mandated precise instructions given in the preconciliar *Ceremonial of Bishops*, published in 1886.[3]

It is also instructive to note the parallel with developments in religious education in the sixties and seventies. Effective catechetics was virtually destroyed by the same naïve assumption that the details of a tradition can be passed on when they are no longer explicitly taught. This disaster was based on an erroneous intuitive theology of Revelation, also beset with naïveté, and it occurred in the same years as the liturgical reform.

## A Liturgical Revolution?

My observations put a charitable interpretation on the vagueness in the earlier editions of the *General Instruction*. Polemicists have claimed that the *Instruction* was deliberately drafted in a vague way to allow as much latitude as possible for future "development"; in other words, anarchy was contrived to bring about a liturgical revolution without end. That polemic implies base motives in favor of a kind of liturgical Maoism. There is no solid evidence for such a conspiracy, which seems not only ludicrous but besmirches the good name of fine liturgists of the caliber of Josef Jungmann, S.J., and Bernard Botte, O.S.B.[4]

---

[3] See *Ceremonial of Bishops*, no. 90, n. 72–74; no. 91, n. 75, on incensations.

[4] One of the best explanations of the reform is Josef A. Jungmann, *The Mass, an Historical, Theological and Pastoral Survey* (Collegeville, Minn.: Liturgical Press, 1976).

At the same time, a liturgical rationalism was at work in the postconciliar liturgical reform. In retrospect we may now recognize that this was closer to the Enlightenment spirit of the condemned Synod of Pistoia (1786) than the inspired mind of the Second Vatican Council. Liturgical rationalism focused more on texts and the structure of rites, for example the need to avoid repetitions and to help "the people" to comprehend and learn through celebrations. Catholic worship was seen as an expression of human culture, hence to be radically inculturated. Worship was not envisaged as a means of transforming, redeeming, or enriching existing cultures. The rationalism also sought to demystify the Roman rite by pruning back ceremonial and visual splendor, all in the name of eliminating bad taste and sinful "triumphalism". The rationalist spirit was also unsympathetic to popular piety and devotions.

While a healthy reaction against the mood of that era is obvious today, we still face a situation where the ceremonial of the venerable Roman rite often descends to banality and confusion. In not a few places, what is slipshod, chaotic, vulgar, and uninspiring is imagined to be "good liturgy" precisely because it is casual or confused! This is supposed to be creative "spontaneity" or "informality".

The Roman liturgy has thus become prey to predators with their own obsessions. A few proponents of liturgical Maoism are still promoting further simplification of the rubrics, such as the dreary proposals sent to Rome several years ago by some German liturgists describing a crudely abbreviated "weekday Mass".

Liturgical innovators of the dated school also want to "involve" the laity more—by turning them all into concelebrants. They are to stand at the altar, but they must not kneel. They are to elevate chalices (or glass goblets), break Hosts at the fraction rite, and distribute Communion or, better still, receive it like concelebrants. This overemphasis on the collective, on the assembly, is rooted in the agenda of a "lay-centered" Church, which provoked the Vatican's *Instruction on Certain Questions Regarding the Collaboration of the Non-Ordained Faithful in the Sacred Ministry of Priests* (1997).

The continuing assault on the Roman rite by innovators reveals an agenda that goes beyond creating meaningful celebrations and experiences. It arises from the assumption that worship is *our* creation, that *we* make and unmake liturgy, hence that liturgy must be constantly changing as we refashion and control it. Whether we criticize that approach as Pelagian, secularist, or deconstructionist is largely irrelevant. It is enough to recognize that it is contrary to the mind of the Fathers of the Second Vatican Council, set out in *Sacrosanctum Concilium*.

## Responding to the Problems

The problems associated with the ceremonial of our rite underline the need to offer more precise guidance to celebrants, deacons, M.C.'s, and servers. This is what motivated me to write *Ceremonies of the Modern Roman Rite*. This manual was able to draw on the greater precision of the 1984 *Ceremonial of Bishops* and marry this authoritative source to the details of the *General Instruction*. The wisdom of the best liturgists and rubricians of the past was respected, so as to offer more precise guidance in terms of the "continuity of our tradition". When I showed the manuscript of *Ceremonies* to a Roman expert, I was warmly encouraged because the manual anticipated the official revision of the *General Instruction* that has since been carried out along these lines. As a significant step toward a better order, this revision prepared for the third typical edition of the *Roman Missal* (2000) should encourage all who are seeking some kind of a "reform of the reform".

While *Ceremonies* was welcomed by many laity, and is now in its fourth printing, it was largely ignored by the liberal liturgical establishment. This was no surprise. But the book provoked one paranoid critique sponsored by the dominant school of liturgy in the Midwest of the United States. This was probably meant to send out a warning signal about the resurgence of rubricians. With some absurd allegations, *Ceremonies* was attacked precisely because it marked the rejection of the sixties philosophy of "let it all happen naturally" as well as the assumption that all priests are creative liturgists. Perhaps the attack on *Ceremonies* also reflected anger that lay people now have access to official sources to help them challenge abuses, although that was not my motive for writing the manual.[5]

In the light of research for *Ceremonies* and its sequel volume *Ceremonies of the Liturgical Year*, I still believe the crisis in ceremonial is not so much a question of *what* but of *how* the reform was implemented. This does not mean that the problem can be solved simply by regretting that a

---

[5] The lay response to *Ceremonies* led to *Liturgical Question Box* (San Francisco: Ignatius Press, 1998).

more gradual process of change was not followed and then requiring more education along politically correct lines. This is precisely the tiresome response of liturgists with an ongoing, if concealed, agenda for more change in the direction of innovation. The situation is more complex, and dissatisfaction is more widespread, than to permit ideological solutions to problems caused by naïveté. Only practical solutions are viable, that is, clearer and better directives and a policy of enriching our rite through good reforms.

If we need to diminish the verbosity of the current rite in favor of emphasizing visible ritual actions, this involves not only making more space for silence but a new emphasis on ceremonial. Until the third edition of the *Roman Missal* appeared, a rite of approach to the altar was retained in the rite of Mass without a congregation, now known as Mass with only a server assisting. In public celebrations this rite would remedy the abrupt way the Mass begins. The Gospel processions should go somewhere and not merely be a group movement from the chair to the ambo by the shortest route. The General Intercessions would be improved were the deacon to take a place at the center of the sanctuary facing the altar to proclaim the intentions, as in the East. Surely the Sign of Peace should take place before the procession of gifts, and not before Communion. We also need a clear directive to assure priests that celebrating Mass facing the people is not compulsory, as many imagine. This should extend to avoiding the confrontational arrangement of some churches, whereby concelebrants, even servers and lectors, face the people for the whole celebration of Mass.

Moving to finer details, I would envisage more signs of the cross to be made both by the celebrant and the people. For example, to enhance the Eucharistic Prayer and take emphasis off a monologue, more gestures should be prescribed for the celebrant, including genuflections and inclinations of the body. Precise directions concerning the use of the voice would help eliminate the distracting ugliness associated with a loud monologue. Moreover, clear counsel even as to where the celebrant directs his eyes would greatly improve the quality of eucharistic celebration facing the people.

## The Liturgical Setting

The transition to an open form of liturgy and the move away from the tableau had radical effects on the planning or remodeling of sanctuaries and churches. This has been a matter of loss and gain. But ceremonial raises the need to review the whole liturgical setting for the liturgical action. We need to pay greater attention to the sacred space in the church building, especially the sanctuary and altar, and to insist on better quality for all the objects used in ceremonial.

Surprising and irritating mistakes have been made in planning or remodeling sanctuaries at the purely practical level of making ceremonial possible. In some churches there is not enough room at the ambo for candle bearers and thurifer at the Gospel. In others, the altar has been placed on the edge of a step. Not only is Mass "facing the people" enforced but the celebrant, concelebrants, and servers need to move around that altar with caution. Some new altars are such trivial objects that they may scarcely be said to be the great sign of Christ in our midst. Some ambos have "stone age" proportions that visually crush lectors and homilists. The location of the presidential chair in some sanctuaries implies that this is the main object, and the parish church becomes a throne room for the priest. The font has even replaced the altar in a few churches as the major visual focus of attention, as if the RCIA were the measure for all liturgical planning and not a major factor to be borne in mind.

In terms of architecture, design, and taste, surely the specter of triumphalism needs to be laid to rest. There are signs of hope, such as the welcome neo-classicism of Professor Stroik and the Notre Dame School of Architecture. May this trend also free us from the puritanical dreariness and errors of that dated document *Environment and Art in Christian Worship*. Its exaggerated authority had to be demythologized. It exemplified a misinterpretation of "noble simplicity" that emphasized simplicity and lost sight of nobility. While it has been replaced by a better document *Built on Living Stones* (2002), the destructive legacy of *Environment and Art in Christian Worship* is still with us. Its devotees cite it as they continue to "renovate" churches, although this havoc is being reversed by new projects of restoration.

Turning to the finer details of church furnishing and liturgical art, we may see signs of better taste with less minimalism and cheapness. But the official directives in fact caused some of the very problems in taste and quality they set out to eliminate. The directive concerning sacred vessels in the first edition of the *General Instruction* (nos. 290–95) was inadequate, and the correction made with the authority of Pope John Paul II is still widely ignored (*Inaestimabile donum*, no. 16, revised *General Instruction* no. 328). Carafes, dishes, jugs, and wine glasses are not sacred vessels. The quality and form of vestments are also a variable, in spite of the revised *General Instruction*, nos. 335–46.

## Some Conclusions

It is only too easy to continue to cite cases and enter into interesting details. But the priority at this stage is to set out certain general conclusions as a strategy to improve Catholic ceremonial and its setting.

I believe a "reform of the reform" of the ceremonial of the Roman rite requires:

— more precise rubrics to govern the ceremonial of the Roman rite for the celebrant, deacon, servers, lectors, and so on;

— clear and strong counsel on reverence and dignified movement for all involved in liturgical ministries, because good rubrics by themselves will not transform everything;

— some significant changes in the current rubrics, but always in the direction of enrichment and addition, not simplification;

— a clear distinction between the solemn and simple forms of eucharistic celebration, while allowing for a workable *Missa normativa*;

— tighter control over the planning and renovation of churches so that they offer a worthy and workable setting for the celebration of the liturgy;
— elimination of the ambiguity from "noble simplicity", to promote beauty, splendor, and excellence, not forgetting the great heritage offered by the Christian East.

The last proposal illuminates the best approach to the "reform of the reform". Our problem is not so much a false start as an aimless diversion from the journey. But the New Jerusalem above still shines forth. Its light beckons Christians always to move forward, and that light is the radiant glory of the heavenly worship of the triune God. This is what we should strive to reflect and anticipate whenever we celebrate the sacred liturgy of Christ our Priest here on earth.